CRISIS IN COLLEGE FINANCE?

CRISIS IN COLLEGE FINANCE?
Time for New Solutions

Roger A. Freeman

The Institute for Social Science Research
Washington, D.C.

THE INSTITUTE FOR SOCIAL SCIENCE RESEARCH was organized in 1956 to conduct and foster research, education, and publication in economics, law, public administration, and the social sciences generally. The trustees choose subjects for Institute studies, but the conclusions and opinions in each work are those of the author.

Foreword

Education has become, it is said, America's largest "growth industry." How to finance the growth of education, particularly at the college and university level, is now one of the more urgent public issues, and is inevitably enveloped in controversy, at times ill informed and ill tempered. In this book, Roger Freeman attempts to state thoughtfully and forthrightly the complex nature of that issue. Naturally, some of the things he says will stir argument. Never mind: it is too important a subject to be dealt with casually or through the formulations of simplistic dogmatism or on the basis of what all the experts now "know" and say.

Many of the not-to-be-questioned assumptions behind much of the expertise on education these days have to do with calculations of needs based upon projections of the "tidal wave of enrollment." Roger Freeman chooses to question some of these assumptions and the projections upon which they are based. Not that he doesn't know about the population explosion, but he suggests that there has right along been a good deal of over-statement as to just how many young people will actually go to college at a given time and just how much in the way of new facilities will be required. Back of this line of questioning lie two almost un-American queries: Just how many young Americans should attempt to get a collegiate education, anyway? And do American educational facilities have to be so costly as they often are? A third query has been asked so frequently in recent years that we have grown used to it, and a bit bored by it: Can't the operating efficiency of our institutions be drastically improved through year-round operations, larger classes, and fewer courses? Freeman doesn't press these points, but they are legitimate questions to raise.

However these various questions may be answered, Freeman agrees that more funds are required to meet our educational needs. He does not agree with the evidently prevailing opinion in the national educational community: that practically all of those increased funds must come in the form of direct, appropriated subventions from the federal government. He argues vigorously for a kind of "mixed economy" in the financing of higher education and lays considerable stress upon the continuing value of voluntary giving and tuition support. He sees the use of indirect federal help through tax credits to individual tuition payers and donors as an important means for maintaining the diversity and freedom of American higher education.

Roger Freeman, a senior staff member of the Hoover Institution on War, Revolution, and Peace, at Stanford University, is eminently qualified to write this study. He directed the research for the Education Committee of the President's Commission on Intergovernmental Relations, was a consultant to the White House Conference on Education, subsequently served on the White House staff, has been assistant to the Governor of the State of Washington, and has held various other governmental and nongovernmental positions. His books on financing the public schools attracted wide attention and favorable reviews, and the present volume rounds out his study of educational finance.

It will be interesting to see whether the hard-nosed approach of an avowedly conservative fiscal economist can provoke a real debate on how best to deal with the problems of financing higher education—and on how to define the problems. If Roger Freeman does this, his book will have performed a real service for all of us involved directly in higher education and for the American public in general.

LANDRUM R. BOLLING
President, Earlham College

Preface

That many parents have trouble financing their children's college education and that educational institutions themselves cannot raise enough money to do all they feel they should or must do is an old story. But a combination of factors turns the old story into a grave challenge as we enter the last third of the twentieth century: The number of young men and women seeking admission is soaring as never before as the first of the postwar generation reach college age and as a steadily increasing percentage of them aim to—and must—continue their formal schooling beyond the twelve grades. The scope and depth of knowledge available and required are growing at an explosive rate; the nation's future depends increasingly on having its citizenry more broadly educated, yet more thoroughly trained in science, technology, and other special fields. Most of the scholars who have studied the economics of higher education have expressed doubt that present institutional arrangements will meet the financial requirements over the next decade without major innovations in the operation of colleges and universities and in the methods of supporting them.

I strongly believe that changes are needed and that current plans are inadequate—which is why I wrote this book. I had intended to explore higher educational finance more than ten years ago, when I directed the research for the Education Committee of the U.S. Commission on Intergovernmental Relations. But our time ran out and we were barely able to complete a report on the elementary and secondary schools. I felt then that a more comprehensive treatment was needed than the presidential commission had been able to prepare during its short life. So I subsequently wrote two books on financing the public schools. At that time, during the 1950's, the schools presented the most urgent problem as the tidal wave of postwar babies was moving through the twelve grades. The first of that generation graduated from high school in 1964; now the primary and secondary schools can expect a long period of only modest attendance growth. But over the next five years colleges face a proportionately far steeper expansion than the schools did a dozen years ago.

For some years a number of institutions have been preparing for the later 1960's by changing to fuller and more effective utilization of faculty and plant resources. But the great majority of colleges have been reluctant to leave traditional methods and experiment with new ways of doing things. This is why I describe some of the means, in use or proposed, to employ manpower and buildings more efficiently and thus expand instructional capacity without a proportionate financial investment.

But even if all available resources are used, colleges and universities will still need huge increases in financial support which present sources will be hard put to supply. Moreover the impact of enrollment growth is quite uneven. Until a dozen years ago attendance was about equally divided between public and private institutions. But an ever-widening tuition gap—with a present ratio in the size of fees of one to four between public and private colleges—and our perverse tax policies have channelled about four-fifths of recent enrollment growth into state and municipal institutions. This places a disproportionate burden on those institutions and on the taxpayers while it leaves hundreds of private colleges and universities too weak to meet the requirements of the years ahead. If current policies are not changed and present trends continue, we face within two decades the demise of much or most private higher education—aside from a few affluent prestige institutions.

Many of those who have studied the economics of higher education have expressed hope or expectation that the national government will come to the help of the institutions and solve their major financial problems. Various justifications for federal action have been advanced, some more, some less controversial. One of the more persuasive arguments is that the national government by imposing an exorbitant tax burden makes it more difficult, and according to some impossible, for families to pay higher tuitions and for states to levy heavier taxes for education. But most of the proposals now under discussion provide neither the type nor the amount of assistance required to fill the gap between revenues and essential needs which according to several projections is growing. By far the largest share of the federal funds now comes in the form of research grants which are concentrated in a few big name universities. Helpful as those funds are to the benefited departments in those institutions, they render the competitive position of small colleges even more precarious and make, it has been said, "the rich richer and the poor poorer." They also tend to encourage a "flight from teaching." Other federal grants are earmarked for selected types of construction such as science or mathematics buildings or restricted to specified, minor or peripheral programs.

None of the various grant-in-aid plans now in effect, including the programs enacted in 1965, will provide the help needed most urgently: assistance to the medium-income or lower middle-income parents who are struggling to put their offspring through college (and the vast majority of students' families are in that category); operating funds to hire additional competent teaching faculty at higher salaries; and funds for general classroom buildings. Nor is there much prospect that Congress will enact any bill for general support of colleges and universities, i.e., funds which can be used according to the judgment of their governing boards and administrators. The church-state controversy and other issues make it extremely unlikely that a magic formula will be found which would enable the national government to grant such general support. Moreover, direct federal subvention could raise grave questions about freedom and independence in higher education in the years ahead. Therefore, other types of plans have been devised in recent years which would use indirect means through the tax system to assist students' families and institutions without running head on into the troublesome problems of federal control or church and state. Proposals of that type have been attracting growing attention and support and are discussed in some detail in the last chapter.

Observers of the higher educational scene tend to agree that no one plan, no panacea, will solve all of the grave problems that lie ahead. Several federal programs were enacted or expanded between 1963 and 1965 which aimed to aid specific aspects of higher education. But they all avoid meeting the colleges' most pressing need: greater operating funds. That is why I have tried in this volume to describe a combination of methods, in institutional policy as well as in public policy, which can maintain and strengthen one of the most important instruments to keep America great and help it retain its position as a leader in the free world: our colleges and universities.

I want to thank many friends in the field of higher education who provided me with information or helped me with advice while this book was being written, particularly those who critically reviewed the manuscript. The Hoover Institution generously granted me the time in which to do the work. Mr. Brian Fry, research associate at the Hoover Institution, prepared the index. To all of them I am deeply grateful.

Roger A. Freeman

Stanford,
August 1965

Contents

Tables and Tabulations

1 Needed: Another Seven to Eleven Billion Dollars

American colleges and universities are in trouble. Not that many of them are likely to become bankrupt or go out of business, though some of them probably will. But there is a clear danger that higher education may not be able to do the job which this nation expects it to do in the years ahead if it is to survive and maintain its leadership in the free world.

Our institutions of higher learning—to which I shall henceforth simply refer as I.H.L.—managed to more than double their student enrollment since the end of World War II, to multiply their research activities many times over, and to sharply expand their services to government, communities, industry and to the public in general. In the process, the role and stature of higher education have grown tremendously. Its position in the life of the nation and in the councils of government and business is beyond anything known to earlier generations.

This dramatic advance did not come easily. There never seemed to be enough manpower or facilities to do the things which were demanded of the institutions or which their own aspirations called for. Much had to be improvised, some ambitious plans deferred. As time went on, administrators, scholars, trustees, and alumni increasingly turned into money raisers. College presidents became accustomed to devoting much or most of their time not to academic pursuits or intramural problems but to lugging around a begging

1

cup or to camping in legislative halls to lobby for higher appropriations.

We have come a long way but the crest of the hill is not nearly in sight. With each passing year the mountain ahead looks higher, the slope steeper, and a much needed respite farther away. Over the past twenty years I.H.L. have added almost four million students to their rolls. In the next five years they will be called upon to accommodate another one and a half million or more. Will they be able to do it? Clearly, the nation must, in this competitive and hostile world, offer *all* of its youth, regardless of color or economic background, an opportunity to develop its God-given talents to the utmost. It cannot retrench from this commitment. Nor can it afford to relax its research effort without running the risk of falling behind other countries bent on scientific advance.

The questions to which we must find answers are: Will the present effort of institutions, of governments, of donors, of students and their families be adequate to reach the essential goals or will they fall short? Will all those qualified and willing to acquire a higher education find adequate opportunity in the years ahead? Will our traditional methods of raising money and running colleges suffice or must we seek new ways of operating and financing them? What must we do *now* to forestall disaster in years to come?

Why Higher Education Needs More Money

Somehow, money has always seemed to run short in higher education. But several trends converge in the 1960's which give the old story a particularly ominous note. The low birth rates of the depression-1930's and of the war years resulted in a college-age population (eighteen to twenty-one years) which remained virtually stable at about nine million. In proportion to the rest of the population it declined. But the picture is changing. The "tidal wave" of post-war babies which swept through the elementary and secondary system is now concluding its twelve-year cycle in the lower schools and reaching college age. It began to pound on the doors of academe in the fall of 1964. By 1970 we shall have five million more eighteen to twenty-one year-olds than we had in 1960, a fifty per cent growth in ten years. In 1980 we shall have another two and a half million. The educational aspirations of our young people have been on the upgrade and pushed college enrollment from twenty-four per cent of the eighteen to twenty-one year group in the fall of 1951 to thirty-eight per cent in 1960. A few years ago the Office of Education projected the "enrollment percentage" in 1969/70 at forty per cent; as of now, forty-six per cent may be a more likely figure, forty-eight per cent a possibility.

Some observers feel that too many young people with inadequate ability, desire or tenacity are being pressured into college by ambitious parents and that admission standards ought to be tightened. But there is also evidence that many youngsters with sufficient intellectual capacity fail to enroll. Viewing the strong and persistent trend there can be little doubt that an increasing percentage of our young people will continue their formal education beyond high school graduation. By all appearances enrollment in I.H.L. will, during the 1960's, jump from three and a half million to between six and seven million. That calls for a huge expansion in manpower and plant facilities.

But numbers tell only part of the story. Knowledge and the need for it are expanding at an unprecedented pace, demanding ever greater specialization and the addition of more departments and increasingly costly laboratories and equipment. The prime factor, however, in all scientific advance is the ingenuity and technical competence of those who man the institutions. We need scholars who are able to penetrate more deeply into the mysteries of nature and of the human mind and human action, and we need more of them than we are now getting. And, whether we like it or not, there is a relationship between the level of compensation and the caliber of men and women whom we can attract into academic life.

Academic salaries have long lagged behind the advance in the general income level and behind the earnings in independent professions or industry. Pay scales must be substantially elevated if I.H.L. are to do justice by their major tasks: to train the natural intelligence of our young people, to do the research necessary for our national well-being and security and for the maintenance of American leadership in the free world, and to give governments and the public the services they have a right to expect.

All of those who have studied the needs of higher education agree that the job ahead calls for far larger sums than we are now allocating. To be sure, there are many other difficult questions to be resolved and I shall discuss some of them later on. But many observers agree with the panel on education of the Rockefeller Brothers Fund Midcentury Project, which concluded in 1958:

> All of the problems of the schools lead us back sooner or later to one basic problem—financing. It is a problem with which we cannot afford to cope half-heartedly. Education has always been essential to the achievement of our political and moral objectives. It has emerged as the necessary ingredient in our technological advancement. And now events have underscored its value in terms of sheer survival.[1]

The Rockefeller panel suggested that educational funds at least be doubled within ten years. Actually, education has been doing better than that for some years and several reports have suggested a speed-up in the rate of growth. So the question is, how much is enough?

How Big an I.H.L. Budget for 1970?

To project a budget for some years ahead is not simply a matter of applying the expected rate of enrollment growth to the current budget. There is much demand—and some hope—for increased efficiency (or "productivity" as industry calls it) and for savings from structural and technological improvements. On the other hand there is the matter of salaries which, as I mentioned before, must be substantially raised. And salaries are, of course, the biggest item in the educational budget.

To estimate a future educational budget takes much detailed study and above all a balanced judgment of institutional operations and of the country's fiscal and economic prospects. Several committees and individual researchers in recent years have selected 1970 as a convenient target year to project higher educational finances.[2] Unfortunately, some of them excluded from their computations such items as for example organized research institutes or auxiliary enterprises (dormitories, dining halls, etc.) so that some

---

[1] *The Pursuit of Excellence,* Education and the Future of America, Panel Report V of the Special Studies Project, America at Midcentury Series, Rockefeller Brothers Fund, Inc. (Garden City, New York: Doubleday and Company, 1958), p. 33.

[2] Office of Education, *Financial Statistics of Higher Education, 1959–60,* 1964; same, *Preliminary Report of Financial Statistics of Institutions of Higher Educ., F. Y. 1964,* July 1965.

adjustments are needed to make their figures comparable. But let us first review the historical record.

EXPENDITURES OF I.H.L. IN SELECTED YEARS 1940 TO 1964
(in billions of dollars)

Academic year	1939/40	1949/50	1959/60	1963/64
Current operations & student aid	$ 0.5	$ 1.8	$ 4.7	$ 7.7
Auxiliary enterprises	.1	.5	.9	1.5
Capital outlays	.1	.4	1.3	1.3
Total Expenditures	$ 0.7	$ 2.7	$ 6.9	$10.5

Between 1950 and 1960 total expenditures grew 159 per cent, and when adjusted for the shrinking value of the dollar, 110 per cent. In the succeeding four years the pace accelerated.

President Eisenhower's Committee on Education Beyond the High School headed by Devereux Josephs concluded in 1957 that I.H.L. would need by 1970 $6.8 to $7.0 billion, not including auxiliary enterprises, student aid or organized research. Adding an estimate for those items and for price changes since 1957 we would arrive at a total of about $12 billion.[3] In 1959 two of our best-known public finance experts, Harvard economics professor Seymour E. Harris and Brookings Institution president Robert D. Calkins, arrived at a total of $9.8 billion for 1969/70, excepting capital outlays and auxiliary facilities. Adjusted, the total would run to between $13 and $14 billion.[4] Alvin C. Eurich, vice president of the Fund for the Advancement of Education, and one of the country's most knowledgeable men in higher education prepared a comparable estimate.[5]

A later projection of the Office of Education, prepared by Selma J. Mushkin and W. Robert Bokelman, placed budgetary needs far higher. It suggested that instructional costs will triple and capital outlays double between 1958 and 1971; the 1962 report of the

---

[3] The President's Committee on Education Beyond the High School, *Second Report to the President*, 1957, pp. 85 & 86.

[4] Seymour E. Harris, "Broad Issues in Financing" and Robert D. Calkins, "The Role of Government Support," in: *Financing Higher Education, 1960–70*, ed. Dexter M. Keezer (New York: McGraw-Hill, 1959). Harris estimated that twenty per cent inflation during the 1960's would boost I.H.L. budgets proportionately.

[5] Alvin C. Eurich, "Increasing Productivity in Higher Education" in: *Higher Education in the United States, The Economic Problems*, ed. Seymour E. Harris (Cambridge: Harvard University Press, 1960).

Department of Health, Education and Welfare placed operating costs of I.H.L. in 1970 at $15.5 billion and capital additions at $2.5 billion for a combined total of $18 billion.[6] In 1964 the Office of Education projected 1970 spending at only $13.8 billion.[7] But a sample survey whose results it released in August 1965 disclosed a 28 per cent growth in current income and expenditures between 1962 and 1964 which rate, if continued, would bring total spending of I.H.L. in 1970 to $18 billion or more. That may well be the most likely outcome, by present indications.

Several methods have been suggested for fuller and more effective use of the available manpower and facilities which could keep the rise in financial requirements to more moderate proportions. A number of institutions have introduced such methods and others are experimenting with them. But long-established practices change slowly in education and it is quite uncertain just how optimistic we can be in expecting a widespread or general adoption of cost-saving measures.

The various projections I quoted foresee a rise from an actual outlay of $6.8 billion in 1959/60 to a requirement between $12 and $18 billion in 1969/70. Trends during the 1950's and early 1960's suggest that expenditures of I.H.L. will multiply between two and two and a half times between 1960 and 1970 with a good chance for an increase of about 120 per cent. This means then that I.H.L. must find an additional $7 to $11 billion during the 1960's. Where are these vast amounts to come from?

How Can I.H.L. Raise an Additional $7 to $11 Billion?

The major sources of funds for I.H.L. are: state appropriations, student charges, gifts and endowment earnings, federal research grants and contracts. In 1963–64 I.H.L. derived their current income as follows:

---

[6] Selma J. Mushkin and W. Robert Bokelman, "Student Higher Education and Facilities of Colleges and Universities: Projections" in: *Economics of Higher Education,* ed. Selma J. Mushkin, Office of Education, 1962. U. S. Department of Health, Education and Welfare, *Annual Report, 1962,* p. 269.

[7] Kenneth A. Simon and Marie G. Fullam, *Projections of Educational Statistics to 1973–74,* Office of Education, Circular 754, 1964, Tables 21 and 23.

	All I.H.L.	Public	Private
State and local governments	25%	43%	2%
Student tuitions and fees	20	11	30
Auxiliary enterprises (mostly student room and board)	17	17	17
Endowment earnings and gifts	9	3	16
Federal research grants, contracts and services	18	14	25
Other federal funds	4	5	2
Other sources	7	7	8
	100%	100%	100%

Source: U.S. Office of Education, *Preliminary Report of Financial Statistics of Institutions of Higher Education, F. Y. 1964,* July 1965.

Can such established major sources of higher educational income as state appropriations, student fees, donations, research grants, be sufficiently expanded during the current decade to meet the requirements? Or should the federal government's share in the general support of I.H.L. which so far has been minor be substantially expanded?

So far, the traditional sources of higher educational support have certainly displayed a strong capacity for expansion and they continue to do so. Income of I.H.L. has on the average more than doubled every ten years and has been rising at a faster rate than the country's economic resources, particularly in recent years. Current and plant fund receipts climbed from .9 per cent of the national income in 1930 to 1.3 per cent in 1950 and may be estimated to equal 2 per cent of the national income at the present time. This is a greater share than the Soviet Union devotes to higher education. To be sure, such comparisons are tenuous, to say the least, because of statistical uncertainties and differences in educational structure. But appropriations for higher educational institutions have been showing less than spectacular increases in the U.S.S.R. budget in recent years and barely equal one per cent of the national income.

It is exactly the sharp increases for American education in recent years which have caused some observers to believe that state governments, students' families and donors may have exhausted their capacity and cannot keep raising their contribution at the past rate. Secretary of Health, Education, and Welfare Arthur S. Flemming published a report in January 1961, on the day before he left office, in which he suggested that the traditional sources of revenue "will certainly be inadequate to meet increasing needs in full," and that the facts "point strongly toward federal assistance as a necessity."[8]

The American Council on Education declared simultaneously: "All the major studies show that after traditional sources of income including student tuition and fees, have been stretched to the limit, there will still be a large gap that can be filled only by greater support from the federal government."[9] The chairman of President Kennedy's Task Force on Education, President Frederick L. Hovde of Purdue University, testified in March 1961 before the United States House of Representatives Education Committee: "I don't think that the taxing power and the ability of the states is sufficient to meet this kind of growth in the next ten years." He specified "that the highest priority need of colleges and universities, both public and private, is for general operational support and particularly for faculty salaries."[10]

Reviewing ten recent books on the subject, J. Kenneth Little, former United States Deputy Commissioner of Education, found that the authors showed a surprising amount of agreement on the need for strongly increased federal financial support of higher education.[11]

Will the Federal Government Supply the Needed Funds?

What plans have been developed to have the federal government contribute a significant share of the $7 to $11 billion by which the revenues of our I.H.L. are to be increased during the 1960's? It will come as a surprise to many that there are no such plans on

---

[8] *Ten-Year Objectives in Education, Higher Education Staffing and Physical Facilities, 1960–61 through 1969–70,* Dept. of Health, Education and Welfare, 1961 (proc.), p. 4.

[9] *A Proposed Program of Federal Action to Strengthen Higher Education,* American Council on Higher Education, January 1961, p. 1.

[10] *Aid to Higher Education,* Hearings before the Subcommittee on Education, Committee on Education and Labor, H.R., 87th Congress, 1st Session, 1961, pp. 166, 169.

[11] J. Kenneth Little, "Higher Education and the Federal Government," *Higher Education,* October, 1963.

record. No national group in higher education has requested federal support of academic salaries—which as President Hovde in his above-quoted statement declared should have the highest priority—or for a substantial share of their other operational costs. Nor has any President of the United States ever recommended sizeable grants-in-aid either for current operations or for general construction at I.H.L. President Eisenhower's Committee on Education beyond the High School and President Kennedy's Task Force on Education advocated federal grants-in-aid for the construction of higher educational facilities, but neither President translated those recommendations into legislative proposals. In 1961 and again in 1963, President Kennedy proposed loans to I.H.L. for the construction of academic buildings. But such loans are, according to the testimony of most witnesses from higher education, of little if any help to institutions, most of which can borrow at equally or more favorable terms from other sources. As a rule I.H.L. do not wish to finance their plant needs through bonds.

The failure to advance major programs of federal aid to higher education has been criticized, and President David D. Henry of the University of Illinois complained at the annual meeting of the American Council on Education in October 1962 that the concern of United States Presidents seemed to be mere lip service: "Presidents have made speeches on the general importance of higher education, but the administrative practices of their departments and the thrust of their own legislative recommendations have not reflected this approach or concern."[12]

The grant-in-aid programs for higher education which President Kennedy proposed in his 1963 Message on Education were of relatively small size. They aimed to assist teacher institutes, general university extension, student work-study programs, graduate schools, library construction and acquisitions, etc. and totaled about $250 million per annum. If enacted they would have provided no more than about two to three per cent of the prospective over-all budgets. To be sure: Congress approved, and President Johnson signed, in December 1963, the Higher Education Facilities Act which provides $290 million in grants for science,

---

[12] David D. Henry, "A Program of Action for Higher Education," *Higher Education and the Federal Government,* Programs and Problems, ed. Charles G. Dobbins (American Council on Education, 1963), p. 103.

engineering, and other specified types of college construction and
$120 million in loans for academic buildings per annum. But those
grants cannot be used for general classroom or administrative
buildings nor, of course, for operating purposes and are thus quite
limited in their application. They equal barely three per cent of
the higher education budget. Congress authorized a substantial
increase in the amount of construction grants in 1965 but retained
the restriction on the use of the funds.

How can we explain this obvious discrepancy between the size
of the budgetary requirements which, according to many students
of the problem, cannot be met from the traditional sources, and
the nature and magnitude of current and proposed federal programs? Are the proposals intended to be mere down payments
for far larger programs yet to be advanced? Are the plans deliberately kept small so as to arouse less opposition? Should we then
regard them as merely a "foot in the door?" Or are statements about
the inadequacy of state and local revenues, student fees and donations not to be taken at face value? Is it then assumed that the
sources which have traditionally supplied most of the educational
funds for I.H.L. *are* capable and willing to continue providing
them? Do differences of opinion within higher education cause the
President and Congress to go easy on aid programs? Or are there
other reasons for the apparent reluctance to advance a program
of massive assistance to I.H.L.?

Obstacles to Federal Aid

At the annnual meeting of the American Council on Education
in 1962, at which President David Henry of the University of
Illinois made the earlier-quoted critical remark about the inadequacy of presidential plans for aiding higher education, Clarence
Scheps, vice president and controller of Tulane University, advanced his own explanation:

> Perhaps the most fundamental reason why there has been no major
> federal aid to higher education is the basic and instinctive objec-
> tion felt deeply by many, including those in education, to the gen-
> eral proposition of federal support to higher education. There are a
> great many sincere individuals who are concerned over any pos-
> sibility of federal control over our schools and colleges.[13]

[13] Clarence Scheps, "Federal Programs of Loans and Grants for Capital Improvements" in: *Higher Education and the Federal Government,* p. 53.

Only ten years earlier the Committee on Financing Higher Education sponsored by the Association of American Universities had strongly objected to an expansion of federal activities in education for that very reason.

Many of the participants in the debate over federal aid do not realize that the American tradition of education as a state-local and private responsibility is more deeply rooted than appears on the surface. They fail to understand the widespread aversion to giving the national government a major role in the field. Over the past quarter-century, federal spending for domestic public services jumped from less than $5 billion to $45 billion and grants-in-aid to the states from less than $1 billion to over $10 billion. But efforts to enact a program of general federal support for the operation or construction of schools or colleges have so far failed and face a doubtful future. Experience with federal aid programs in welfare, urban renewal, highways or agriculture, as well as sheer logic have convinced many that large-scale federal support would sooner or later lead to federal control of the institutions and their programs. This may be the basic reason why no broad popular support for major federal educational programs has developed, as members of Congress well know from their incoming mail and as observers of the national scene have regretfully acknowledged.

There is of course nothing new about federal moneys being channeled into education—now between $2 and $5 billion annually, depending on definition—with a major share going to I.H.L. Some of our largest universities have disclosed that almost half their revenues come from the federal treasury. But in most instances the federal agencies are not *aiding* higher education; they are *using* it for their own purposes. Most of the amounts which the Department of Defense, Atomic Energy Commission, or National Aeronautics and Space Administration pay to I.H.L. are compensations for services. They can no more be called "federal aid" than similar and far larger sums flowing into private industry. Those contracts benefit grantor and grantee equally, as may be expected of freely negotiated and fair contracts. Federal grants to I.H.L. for their instructional programs now amount to but a few million dollars and are insignificant in their budgets.

Advocates of federal aid tend to be impatient with the "federal control" argument which they deem insubstantiated, artificial, and a mere sham to cloak the true motives of the opponents. They point at the urgent need to multiply federal *general purpose* funds for I.H.L. and press for prompt action. But their demand has run into another and no less formidable roadblock—the church and state controversy.

Out of more than 2,000 I.H.L. in the United States, over 1,300 are under private auspices and 800 of them are church-connected. If the federal government were to aid only public institutions, as President Truman's Commission on Higher Education recommended in 1947, it would further tip a balance which in recent years has become increasingly lopsided. Until 1950 student enrollment was about evenly divided between public and private I.H.L. The sharply growing discrepancy between public and private tuitions was probably the main reason for the subsequent change. Of the 2.1 million enrollment increase between fall 1948 and 1964, 78 per cent went to public and merely 22 per cent to private I.H.L. So the private enrollment share dropped to 35.7 per cent. If this trend continues, it will dip to 33 per cent or less in 1970 and to 20 per cent later on, as a projection by the Fund for the Advancement of Education suggested.[14]

This is not at all unlikely, considering the relative size of tuitions and salaries. If large-scale federal support were made available to public institutions exclusively, hundreds of private colleges would within a measurable time have to close or turn public and only a limited number of prestige institutions would be able to survive. Such an event, many hold, would be a calamity. A free choice among a large number of diverse colleges and universities and a reasonable balance between public and private institutions are widely regarded as sources of strength of higher education and as essential parts of the American tradition which ought to be preserved. Few would favor a quasi-monopoly of public higher education for all but a few students from well-to-do families. It is thus understandable that Congress has always been careful to treat public and private I.H.L. alike and to make benefits available to both on an equal and nondiscriminatory basis.

---

[14] Sidney G. Tickton, *Letter to a College President* (The Fund for the Advancement of Education, May 1963), Chart 4.

But to appropriate federal funds for church-connected institutions raises some weighty problems, constitutional and otherwise. Convictions on this point run deep on both sides of the controversy and allow little leeway for compromise. Some will not vote for grants-in-aid if they include private institutions and some if they exclude them. Some object to proposed restrictions on the use of federal funds because they are too tight and some because they are not tight enough.

Some of our best brains have tried to devise a formula that can satisfy if not all then at least a majority in both Houses of Congress sufficient to pass a bill. For some years a construction aid program was kicked back and forth between the House and the Senate by apparent disagreement over technical points and terminology which revealed basic underlying conflicts. When a tenuous compromise was reached in December 1963 on a small construction program, it was concluded with many misgivings. Use of the funds was severely restricted. The difficulty of arriving at an agreement between the two Houses suggests that the drive for an expansion in coverage faces an uphill battle. That is why President Johnson, in an apparently correct appraisal of the political situation, refrained in his 1965 Education Message from suggesting anything approaching federal aid for general classroom construction or current operations at I.H.L. No compromise appears possible nor magic formula in sight for federal assistance to faculty salaries although they are the most critical item in the higher educational budget.

The record of the long drawn-out battle for federal aid to education is an ironic comment on a statement about the speed and magnitude of federal action by the Problems and Policies Committee of the American Council on Education in February, 1958: "The truth seems to be that the federal government is the only agency which can act with sufficient speed and on a scale large enough to enable schools, colleges and universities to accomplish their tasks."[15]

Only after many years of battle and after several defeats was a small program of federal grants for selected types of construction at I.H.L. enacted late in 1963 Even with an enlargement in 1965

---

[15] *Congressional Record,* April 3, 1958 p. 6190.

there is hardly a chance that the federal government might supply a significant share of the $12 to $18 billion which our I.H.L. will, according to the cited projections, need by the end of this decade. Seymour E. Harris and Robert D. Calkins, whose projections I cited earlier, both of whom favor increased federal funds for higher education, projected only moderate increases by 1970. Harris showed federal operational support at $500 million, Calkins at $250 million, in addition to unspecified but obviously limited construction funds.

Does this sound too pessimistic? Then why has no President of the United States ever sent to Congress a program of federal grants-in-aid for the general operation or construction of our I.H.L.? Advisory committees which Presidents Franklin D. Roosevelt, Truman, Eisenhower and Kennedy appointed suggested such plans. But none of those Presidents saw fit to transmit them to the Congress. Surely nobody will assert that the past four Presidents—or their predecessors—lacked interest in higher education. Why have even small-scale and highly restricted proposals invariably run into trouble? Are we to believe that the members of Congress are prejudiced against education? Is it not more likely that basic ideological convictions run too deep to be easily compromised? If a hundred-year battle over federal aid to education has not been able to produce a program of general federal support, what reason do we have to believe that the philosophical conflicts will soon be resolved and the situation changed radically within the next few years?

A Case for Federal Aid?

All of this does not mean that the national government should not or cannot aid higher education. There is much support and, in fact, a good case for some type of federal action, and the platforms of both political parties subscribe to it. But it seems that an effective approach has not yet been used which can accomplish the objective while avoiding the obstacles which have defeated the drive for federal aid year after year.

Few will question that there is a strong national interest in education. Under a division of labor, such as was established by our federal system of government, each level of government has a vital interest in the activities and satisfactory performance at the other levels. The word "federal" itself implies an obligation of mutual aid when needed. There is little doubt but that the national government by imposing an exorbitant tax burden has made the financing of education more difficult. If states, communities, and institutions are unable to meet their educational responsibilities and the national government has the necessary means at its disposal, then it appears proper that it render assistance.

Some will of course question the proposition that the federal government has the necessary means at its disposal. The national treasury is experiencing a succession of vast budgetary deficits and is probably in no position to engage in large new commitments. But let us assume that through restraint upon other expenditures and with the help of increased revenues the budget is brought into closer balance—however hypothetical that case may be at this time. Could the national government aid higher education by indirect methods if, as it seems, the direct approach appears blocked by insurmountable obstacles? If it is the magnitude of the federal tax burden which restricts the capacity of states and individuals to pay for higher education, could not carefully designed tax remission remedy the situation?

Tax Relief—an Indirect Way of Aiding Higher Education

About ten years ago a new type of proposal was advanced by the Yale Alumni Board and later sponsored by the American Council on Education and numerous other educational organizations: income tax relief for students and their families. The plan aimed to enable institutions to levy higher tuitions and fees without placing the whole burden upon those paying them. Such an indirect method of helping I.H.L. would avoid the two major roadblocks: the argument over federal control and the church-state issue.

The first educational tax relief plan was introduced in the 83rd Congress in 1953, and every succeeding Congress saw a substantial increase in the number of such bills. Over 100 bills on educational tax benefits have been introduced in the 89th Congress. There is probably no single type of proposal pending in Congress on which so many bills have been submitted, in both Houses and by members of both political parties.

Despite this apparent popularity of educational tax relief plans in Congress, no such bill or amendment was ever reported out by a proper committee (House Ways and Means or Senate Finance) or received consideration on the floor of either House in the 1950's although innumerable speeches praising the idea were delivered in both Houses. By the end of the 1950's some of the organizations which used to pursue this type of legislation tired of their repeated failures and decided to devote their efforts to securing direct grants-in-aid.

Deficiencies of Educational Tax Relief Plans and Their Correction

How can we explain the apparent paradox of the consistent failure of a proposal which, judging by the number of bills and speeches, enjoys great popularity with members of Congress? The cause probably lies in technical deficiencies of the bills which, if enacted, might defeat the purpose. With but few exceptions educational tax relief bills can be divided into three types:

a) Deductions: The cost of tuitions, fees, and also possibly books, supplies, travel and added living expenses would be deductible from adjusted gross income up to a specified upper limit.

b) Exemptions: A student or his family would be entitled to one or several additional personal exemptions of $600.

c) Credits: A specified flat percentage—most frequently 30 per cent—of the sum of tuitions, fees, and also certain other expenses attributable to attendance at an I.H.L. would be offset against the *tax liability*, rather than deducted from the income base as under (a) above.

The first two methods (a) and (b) above have been criticized for giving the greatest benefit—up to 91 per cent of the expenses involved (by the tax rates in effect until 1963)—to persons in high tax and income brackets and only 20 per cent to those of moderate income. A flat credit of 30 per cent or some similar percentage would reduce the amount of benefits going to the wealthy but would not provide enough relief to students from low- or middle-income families. None of the three methods would enable institutions to boost their tuitions and fees without burdening the student and his family with most of the increase, unless they happen to be in a high tax bracket. In other words, these proposals would help the least where help is needed the most. They would add little strength to the finances of I.H.L.

A 100 Per Cent Tax Credit or a Sliding Tax Credit Schedule?

More recently it was proposed to permit a 100 per cent offset against the federal income tax liability for tuition and fees, and for donations, instead of deductions from the tax base. That would offer substantial help both to institutions and to families with college students. Ceilings would have to be placed on such credits to avoid an incentive for exorbitant tuition charges and to limit the resulting revenue loss. Such a plan would be an effective and fair vehicle for carrying the tax relief idea into practice. But it has so far found little support in Congress. A low ceiling such as for example $100 would offer only limited aid. But as the ceiling is raised it becomes increasingly difficult to maintain a balance between low-tuition (public) and high-tuition (private) institutions.

As a compromise between conflicting interests and ideas a sliding tax-credit plan was developed in 1963 which would grant a 100 per cent tax offset (or close to 100 per cent) up to a low maximum (say, $100) and a series of declining percentages up to a liberal maximum of about $1,500. Another version would grant a 75 per cent credit for the first $200 of tuitions, fees, books, supplies and equipment, 25 per cent of the next $300 and 10 per cent of the next $100.

The sliding tax-credit plan avoids the shortcomings of some of the other proposals and soon gained the support of leaders in both political parties. It was debated in the Senate in February 1964 and narrowly defeated. Most observers agreed that a clear majority of the Senate favored the plan but that strong pressure by the President and the Treasury Department caused several of its original sponsors to vote against it when it appeared that the proposal was about to be adopted. However, the closeness of the final vote—45 to 48—and the evident strong popularity which the plan enjoys among the broad public encouraged its other sponsors who announced that they intended to continue the fight to victory. The proposal was reintroduced in January 1965 with greatly broadened sponsorship.

Neither the tax-credit plan nor any other single measure offers a "solution" to the financial problem in higher education. But tax credits for educational expenses and donations can make a significant contribution toward helping higher education weather the tremendous increase which the institutions are facing in the second half of the 1960's, and assist many families to bear the heavy cost of sending their children to college.

To be sure, the cost of attending college has grown no faster than the general cost of living in the past twenty-five years and, in fact, it has risen proportionately less than average family income. That enrollment keeps climbing steeply is in itself proof that the colleges have not been pricing themselves out of the market. But that economic fact offers slim comfort to the moderate income family which is trying to put several children through college. More of our young people now enroll in higher education, which places a severe strain on parental budgets.

Institutions try to avoid boosting tuitions and fees in proportion to spiraling costs, and some have in recent years sought means of controlling expenditures more effectively by fuller use of the available physical and manpower resources. An increasing number of I.H.L. are changing to all-year operation which not only reduces the need for additional construction but also enables some faculty members to earn more and some students to complete their degree in fewer years. Some colleges are improving the utilization of their building space which has been traditionally poor on most campuses. The trend toward community colleges helps to keep down the outlays of students—who can then continue to live at home—as well as to reduce institutional needs for construction and operations.

A reversal of the long-range trend toward course proliferation and lower faculty-student ratios, the use of television and teaching machines, cooperation between neighboring colleges, independent study and other methods of placing greater responsibility upon the student, have a great potential for keeping costs from rising too fast. Some I.H.L. have adopted such methods, some are experimenting, and others are merely thinking about them as a distant possibility. Only the force of necessity is likely to cause the majority of educational institutions to adopt new methods which mean radical changes from cherished and long-established traditions. But support of the essential activities in higher education in the years ahead is unlikely to be adequate without a combination of these and similar courses of action which will be discussed in greater detail in the succeeding chapters.

2 A Tidal Wave of Students

To plan for the financing of higher education would be much easier if enrollment increased each year at a steady rate. Unfortunately, the two major factors which determine enrollment do not move at a regular and uniform pace. The birthrate will soar for some years, then decline, then start climbing again. The ratio of young people who decide to study for a professional career may slowly creep upward, then spurt, then again slow down to a more gradual rise. Sometimes these trends run parallel and at other times they diverge. The results are erratic. So, to predict the number of students who will have to be accommodated on academic campuses throughout the nation requires much detailed study and analysis, and estimates do not always prove accurate, as we have learned from past experience. At this time I.H.L. are going through a period of spectacular growth which will continue for several more years and then flatten out to a more moderate rate. But we need to know, as precisely as possible, for how many students I.H.L. will have to plan, in terms of physical plant, manpower, and finances.

The Postwar Babies and the Tidal Wave

The first warning signals were hoisted in 1954 when the American Association of College Registrars and Admissions Officers prepared a booklet, *The Impending Tidal Wave of Students,* and the

American Council on Education sounded, *A Call for Action to Meet the Impending Increase in College and University Enrollment.* The number of births which had fallen to 2.3 million annually during the depression of the 1930's and remained below 3 million during most of World War II jumped to 3.8 million in 1947, receded slightly for a few years, and then advanced after the Korean conflict to a high of 4.2 million in 1957. Since then it has been declining slightly and the birth rate (per 1000 population) actually slid from 25.3 in 1957 to 20.3 in the twelve months that ended in June 1965, the lowest rate since 1941. It will come as a surprise to many who have heard about our population explosion that the United States is now experiencing the lowest birthrate in its history—save for the years of the Great Depression.

Demographers have long been predicting that the unusually high birthrates of the immediate postwar periods would not long persist and that the birth curve would again follow its secular pattern of a gradual decline. This suggests that the dramatic growth of the college-age group in the 1960's will be succeeded by little expansion during the 1970's and beyond. All members of the age group that will be attending college prior to 1978 were born in 1959 or earlier and were counted in the 1960 Census. The death rate at that age is low—barely one per thousand each year—and is just about offset by net immigration. The 1960 Census found 14.1 million children nine to twelve years old and we may expect that approximately just as many eighteen to twenty-one year-olds will be around in 1969. Most of our students in the academic year 1969/70 will come from their ranks.

Growth in the size of the college-age population will be no more uniform in the next few years than it has been in the past. Between 1950 and 1958 the population aged eighteen to twenty-one remained perfectly stable at 9.0 million. In the succeeding five years it increased an average of 427,000 annually. From 1963 to 1964 it grew 163,000. At that point the "tidal wave" hit: increases in the four succeeding years will average 735,000 annually. Then there will be no increase at all from 1968 to 1970. In the first half of the 1970's growth in the college-age group will average 348,000 a year, in the second half (1976 to 1980) only 155,000. There may be a decline between 1980 and 1985. Growth rates of the college-age group are projected to decline steadily:[1]

1965 to 1970	18.3% increase
1970 to 1975	12.2% increase
1975 to 1980	4.8% increase
1980 to 1985	3.0% decline

In other words, then, sixty per cent of the five million plus growth in college-age population between 1950 and 1970 will take place in the four years 1965 through 1968, which obviously will be critical. The question is: how many of these young people will seek a college education?

The Enrollment Ratio

Most college students are between eighteen and twenty-four years old, though one-quarter million were under eighteen in 1962 and three-quarter million twenty-five years or over.[2] The "normal" age for undergraduate students is eighteen to twenty-one years and it has become customary to express *all* degree-credit enrollment as a percentage of the population aged eighteen to twenty-one. For reasons of comparability, I shall follow that practice.

The "enrollment ratio" climbed from 4 per cent in 1900 to 18 per cent in 1940, to 25.5 per cent in 1950, to 37.5 per cent in 1960, and stood at 40.4 per cent in the fall of 1963. Its rate of increase appears to be slowing down. If we divide the past twelve years into three four-year periods we find the following *annual* increases in the enrollment ratio:[3]

1.80 percentage points between 1951 and 1955
1.38 percentage points between 1955 and 1959
0.95 percentage points between 1959 and 1963

What may be significant: During seven years when the college-age population remained stable (1951 to 1958), the enrollment

---

[1] Bureau of the Census, *Current Population Reports*, Series P-25, No. 286. Figures for 1985 are a mean of the two central of four projections.

[2] The median age of high school graduates is 18.1 years, of college graduates 22.9 years.

[3] *Digest of Educational Statistics*, 1964 Edition, Office of Education, 1964, Table 52.

ratio rose an annual average of 1.71 per cent. In the succeeding five years when the college-age population expanded 24 per cent, the ratio grew only .88 per cent per annum. This suggests the possibility of an inverse relationship between the rate of growth in the college-age population and the enrollment ratio. If so, we may expect the annual increase in the ratio to remain at or below one per cent during the balance of the 1960's.

The enrollment ratio is influenced by many factors, some of them interacting, such as admission standards of colleges in relation to high school curricula, tuition, scholarship and loan policies, economic growth, the professional job market, scientific progress, international developments, and above all, by the attitudes and aspirations of our young people, their parents, and the public at large.

Are Too Few Going to College—or Too Many?

Offhand probably most of us feel that the more of our young men and women attend college, the better off they and the nation will be. Our system of government calls for a citizenry that is well informed on a wide array of national and international issues and is able to exercise sound judgment. Moreover, in our rapidly advancing technological age, the knowledge needed to fill responsible jobs is steadily widening and increasingly goes far beyond the content of a high school curriculum. The controlling questions are, how large a percentage of our young people have the *capacity* to assimilate an academic education and how many have a sufficiently strong *desire* to continue their formal training for four or more years beyond the high school diploma.

In the fall of 1962, half of that year's high school graduating class—fifty-five per cent of the boys and forty-three per cent of the girls—were in college. Some believe that "we must be approaching our ceiling of capability."[4] But others have suggested that all American youngsters ought to continue to college: "The goal of universal education beyond the high school is not more utopian than the goal

[4] Wallace R. Brode, "Approaching Ceilings in the Supply of Scientific Manpower," *Science,* January 24, 1964.

of full citizenship for all Americans, for the first is becoming prerequisite to the second."[5]

As it is, about forty per cent of our young people now enroll in college immediately after high school or within a few years. This is four to five times as high a proportion as attend I.H.L. in most European countries, which appear to meet their requirements for professional manpower no worse than we do. Of course, such comparisons have only a limited validity because our first two years in college are in subject content and level, if not in the age of the students, more nearly the equivalent of the upper years in a European secondary school. It might be more appropriate to compare attendance in European universities with our graduate schools. The crucial question is whether those of our young people who are qualified for college have an opportunity to attend.

Who Should Go to College?

President Truman's Commission on Higher Education in 1947 reported that half the people had sufficient mental ability to attend college for two years, and at least one-third for four years. The proportion actually attending has risen since 1947 but still is below those goals. Several sample studies have shown that a substantial segment of our young people, sometimes estimated from one-fourth to one-third, have sufficient intelligence to qualify for college but do not attend. This, we are told, is a waste of a natural resource which the nation can ill afford. But I wonder whether those studies do not rather prove that an I. Q. test is not an adequate yardstick by which to judge qualification for higher education. The test does not measure willingness to work hard, genuine thirst for knowledge and intellectual exercise, or ambition to advance in the world or seek a professional career. Much less does going through an I. Q. test with a minimum "passing" grade prove the determination or strength of character to forego immediate gratification of desire for such things as financial independence, car ownership, or marriage. Impatience to get married is a greater factor in college nonattendance than is widely assumed: A Census Bureau study in October

---

[5] *Universal Opportunity for Education Beyond High School*, Educational Policies Commission of the National Education Association and the American Association of School Administrators, 1964, p. 36.

1962 found that five per cent of all college students eighteen to twenty-one are married but forty per cent of the young men and women in that age group who are *not* in school are married. Many of them might be attending college if they had not preferred marriage over a higher education.

It is significant that in the fall of 1963 the number of young men in college twenty and twenty-one years of age was only 62,000 lower than at age eighteen and nineteen, while the drop between those ages in college women was 230,000.[6] We may assume that many of the girls dropped out either because they could not combine marriage and study or because they had already found in their lower-class years what they had come to college for. A broad sample-study of freshman women in 1963 which inquired what the respondent wanted to be fifteen years later, found that 59 per cent hoped to be housewives without a career and only 41 per cent wished a career whether they were married or had children or not.

Another finding of the same survey of 13,000 entering freshmen by the Educational Testing Service sheds light on motivation for college attendance. When asked to express their philosophy of higher education, slighter more than half the respondents (men and women) opted for extracurricular activities—for the fun and social experiences of college, one-fourth for the vocational promise, and only one-fifth for the academic or intellectual aspects.[7] A 1963 study for the Office of Education by Edith S. Greer found that among students scoring in the top 25 per cent in I. Q. tests, only 60 per cent won grades that put them in the upper one-third of their classes. Of those "academically able" students, 12 per cent ranked in the lowest third and the remaining 28 per cent in the middle one-third of the class.

The Rockefeller Brothers Fund panel concluded in 1958: "We must not assume that native capacity is the sole ingredient in superior performance. Excellence . . . is a product of ability and motivation and character. And the more one observes high performance in the dust and heat of the daily life, the more one is likely

---

[6] Bureau of the Census, *Current Population Reports*, Series P-20, No. 129, Tables 2 & 5.

[7] Remarks by Henry Chauncey, President of the Educational Testing Service at the annual meeting of the College Entrance Examination Board, October 28, 1964.

to be impressed with the contribution made by the latter of the two ingredients."[8] John Stalnaker, president of the National Merit Scholarship program, expressed the same thought in a more pithy way: "Even the best steam locomotive gets nowhere unless there is a fire under the boiler."[9] Lack of motivation and personal preference are the main reasons for which young people of otherwise sufficient intelligence do not continue their education beyond high school. A college degree does not necessarily rate top priority in everybody's sense of values. Some would rather be electricians in New York and earn $198.40 for a thirty-five hour work week than make less on a white collar job.

We must of course see to it that the doors of opportunity are left wide open for all. No young man or woman should be prevented from getting a higher education merely by inability to pay the required fees and other expenses. But beyond arrangements for those *financially* less able, college attendance is and must remain a matter of self-selection among those who possess the required mental and spiritual qualifications.

Some believe that present admission standards are too high and keep too many would-be students out. Senator Wayne Morse told his Senate colleagues that, "we are doing great psychological damage to a lot of young men and women in this country by denying them admission to college because of the fact that they are *C* high school students."[10] He described the mail he received from "distraught parents with children who have graduated from high school with a *C* average. They cannot gain admission to college," and added: "The *C* student, when all is said and done, is the backbone of American education. The *C* student, the average student, is the backbone of American educational citizenry. We must stop denying the *C* student an opportunity to attend college."[11] Is it really true that the *C* student is "the *backbone* of American education," the structural element that keeps it up and gives it strength? Is a college education the birthright of every young person regard-

---

[8] *The Pursuit of Excellence,* Education and the Future of America, Panel Report V of the Special Studies Project, Rockefeller Brothers Fund, Inc. (Garden City, New York: Doubleday and Co., 1958), p. 17.

[9] Quoted in *Newsweek,* November 9, 1959.

[10] *Congressional Record,* March 12, 1958, p. 3666.

[11] *Congressional Record,* October 11, 1963, p. 18427.

less of his talent—or lack thereof? Can we make everybody fit for college by making college fit everybody? Are we going to get fewer sheep just by handing out more sheepskins?

Most observers will probably agree with a statement by John W. Gardner, president of the Carnegie Corporation for the Advancement of Teaching: "Not everyone has the right to be a college graduate, any more than everyone has the right to run a four-minute mile."[12] The "four-cylinder students in an eight cylinder society"[13] pose a problem to themselves and to others. The late Secretary of Labor James P. Mitchell reported a few years ago:

> College officials across the country have told me their classes are crowded with young men and women who do not want to be or should not be there. Pushed by parents who want their children to be college graduates, many of these reluctant scholars yawn their way through school. Frequently all they get from their four years is a white-collar career, doing work for which they are not at all fitted.[14]

Many similar observations could be quoted, including James Bryant Conant's conclusion that "to my mind too many people are going to college, not too few."[15]

The steady and substantial increase in the ratio of young people attending college certainly does not suggest that the barriers have been raised unreasonably high. That admission standards might be too low could be concluded from the high failure rate—25 to 30 per cent—in the freshman classes. It was interesting to note in the 1960 Census that there are more persons in the population with one to three years of college than with four. Some may have profited from a partial college education. But in many cases we may wonder just how sound the investment in time and money was for the institution or for the individual.

The pressure of numbers and sentiment in professional circles

---

12 John W. Gardner, "Can We Be Equal and Excellent Too?," *The Reader's Digest,* October 1961.

13 The term was coined by Dean James H. Robertson of the University of Michigan, "Why So Many Flunk Out," *The New York Times Magazine,* May 5, 1963.

14 James P. Mitchell, "Help Wanted: Skilled Blue-Collar Workers," *The Reader's Digest,* July 1958.

15 Quoted in *The Washington Post and Times Herald,* April 2, 1958.

now probably favors higher standards in colleges and universities and this suggests no relaxation in admission requirements. But "any attempt to increase selectivity runs full face into the democratic dogma," complained Laird Bell, Chairman of the National Merit Scholarship Corporation in a widely-read article criticizing lenient admission policies.[16] Those who oppose selectivity in higher education as being contrary to democratic dogma appear to be confused about the nature and principles of democracy. But the plaint and arguments of marginal and submarginal students and their parents will undoubtedly continue and call for an easing of standards of admission.

Dividends of Higher Education

There are many reasons why young people want to go to college or are pressured into going by their parents. Paramount among these reasons is the expectation that a degree will give them higher earning power and greater job security. The 1960 Census showed the average annual income of men twenty-five years and over with four years of high school at $5,437, of men with four or more years of college at $7,646. Some would credit the entire difference to education and even go as far as to promise young people that they can increase their earning power by more than $2,000 a year—and according to some by close to $180,000 over a lifetime—by continuing their formal education for four years beyond high school. In some cases this is probably true and may even be an understatement. But do the facts prove a causal relationship?

A recent study of the health records of nearly half a million men over forty showed the death rate of those who regularly engaged in no physical exercise to be almost twice as high as of those who engaged in moderate to heavy exercise. Some observers jumped to the conclusion that this proved, once and for all, that exercise is life-prolonging. But does it? Is it not more likely that men in good health enjoy exercise—and live longer, while weak, ailing, or frail men shun exertion—and die sooner?

The line of reasoning that regards the income differential as a result of additional years of schooling neglects the many other

---

[16] Laird Bell, "Admit and Flunk," *The Atlantic,* October, 1962.

factors which have a bearing on a man's income. To earn a college degree and to succeed in life economically call for similar personal characteristics. A person with high intelligence, ambition, judgment, a flair for study, eagerness to work hard, willingness to forego present pleasure for future gain, is much more likely to earn a degree than another who rates low in some or all of these traits. Also his chances are far better for advancing to higher positions and making more money—not so much because of his degree but because of his ability, attitude, and effort. Family background also has a significant bearing on whether a man attends college and winds up in the higher income brackets. Just how much of the income difference between college graduates and high school graduates should be attributed to education—or to the sheepskin—and how much to other factors, has long been argued. Few will question that more education will, on the average or in most cases, help to earn a higher income later on.

Income differentials between professional and manual workers have tended to narrow in the long run but this trend seems to have been halted, or possibly even reversed, during the 1950's. Far more analytical study will have to be undertaken in this field until we can say with any degree of certainty just how much four years of college education are likely to contribute to a person's earning power. The 1960 Census suggested that anything less than four years—i. e., one to three years of college—increases income very little. So it could be the degree that makes the real difference. Or it could be the ability to stick with a plan and carry it through to completion—whether in college or in life—that does. At this time there still are more hypotheses in this field than reliable conclusions to be drawn save one: a college degree is a good investment. But even that is at least partially based on faith.

The Job Market for College Graduates

A college degree, it has been said, is the best employment insurance. Few graduates remain jobless for very long even in these days of high and persistent unemployment. Unemployment rates are inversely correlated with years of school completed as a recent report by the Bureau of Labor Statistics shows:

UNEMPLOYMENT RATES FOR MEN 18 YEARS AND OVER BY
YEARS OF SCHOOL COMPLETED, MARCH 1962

College, 4 or more years	1.4%
College, 1 to 3 years	4.0
High School, 4 years	4.8
High School, 1 to 3 years	7.8
Elementary school, 8 years	7.5
Elementary school, 5 to 7 years	8.5
Elementary school, less than 5 years	10.4%

Source: Bureau of Labor Statistics, *Special Labor Force Report*, No. 30, 1962.

One out of thirteen men with but an elementary school education was out of a job, one in twenty-one with a high school education, but only one in seventy-one among those with four or more
years of college. Of course, the difference is not wholly attributable
to education. It appears significant that in the case of unemployment—just as in regard to the level of earnings—attending college
(or high school) for less than the full four years seems to bestow
little advantage. Maybe the element of failure is more important
than whatever additional education was acquired. Somebody with
the capacity to acquire a college degree is better able to land and
keep a job than a man whose mental endowment did not carry
him much beyond elementary or secondary school. Moreover, a
college man can "come down" when jobs at his own level are scarce.
There is little leeway for coming down at the lower levels, particularly where wage rates are set by law or union contract. Men with
little education and low or no skills are condemned to long-term or
perpetual unemployment by the establishment of wage levels
which exceed the value of their product or output potential.

With the proportion of jobs which require high professional or
technical skill steadily increasing, it appears reasonable to assume
that a college education will take on added importance in the years
ahead. The Department of Labor projected the number of professional and technical jobs to expand 43 per cent between 1960 and
1970, the aggregate of all other jobs only 18 per cent. But this will
actually mean a narrowing of the differential from the 1950's when
professional and technical jobs increased 66 per cent, all other jobs
a mere 7 per cent. In its 1965 *Manpower Report* (p. 54) the Labor
Department projected manpower requirements in the professional

and technical occupations to rise at a somewhat slower rate in the next ten years, to 1975, than in the recent past.

EMPLOYED CIVILIAN LABOR FORCE 1950, 1960 AND 1970 *(Projected)*

	1950	1960	1970	Increase in per cent 1950 to 1960	1960 to 1970
		m i l l i o n s			
All workers	59.7	66.7	80.5	12%	21%
Professional, technical and kindred workers	4.5	7.5	10.7	66%	43%
All other workers	55.2	59.2	69.8	7%	18%

Source: *Statistical Abstract of the United States,* 1963, pp. 219, 231. *Manpower Report of the President and a Report on Manpower Requirements, Resources, Utilization and Training* by the U.S. Department of Labor, 1963, p. 100.

Of course, not all professional and technical jobs call for a college degree, but more and more of them do. Also, many college graduates will become "managers, officials and proprietors," whose number is projected to expand 22 per cent between 1960 and 1970. The combined growth in the two occupational top categories— professional and technical, and managers, officials, etc.—during the 1960's was estimated by the Department of Labor at 32 per cent. The simultaneous increase in the number of college graduates was projected by the Bureau of the Census at 46 per cent.

While the number of professional and technical jobs will not grow as fast in the 1960's as in the 1950's, as the table above indicates, the college-age group and the number of new degrees will show a more rapid increase:

Population aged 18 to 21:[17] increase 1950 to 1960		+ 6%
1960 to 1970		+50%
Degrees conferred by I.H.L. (all levels)		
5 years centered at 1949/50	2,100,000	
5 years centered at 1959/60	2,391,000	
Increase 1950 to 1960:		+14%
degrees conferred in 1959/60	478,000	
degrees projected for 1969/70	899,000	
Increase 1960 to 1970:[18]		+88%

[17] Computed from: Bureau of the Census, *Current Population Report,* Series P-25, No. 265.

[18] Office of Education, *Earned Degrees Conferred 1959–60,* 1962, p. 3. *Earned Degrees by Field of Study and Level Projected to 1975* by Marie G. Fullam and Frances E. Ryan, Office of Education Bulletin 1964 No. 31, Table 1.

If these projections come true, the job market for college graduates might not improve during the 1960's, and it could deteriorate.

Let us consider the relative changes over the past twenty years. Between 1940 and 1960 the population of the United States expanded 48 million (an increase of 36 per cent); but the number of persons twenty to twenty-four years old—which is the age of most of those graduating from college—*declined* by almost 800,000 (minus 7 per cent). Their share in the total population fell from 9 per cent to 6 per cent. This was offset by rapid growth in the percentage of college attendance. The service needs of the additional 48 million persons in the population, as well as advances in technology and science, and deficiencies remaining from the war, demanded a sharp increase in professional and technical manpower, and the market easily absorbed the moderate growth in new degrees during the 1950's. But between 1960 and 1970 these relative changes will be reversed: the population of the United States will grow 15 per cent, the twenty to twenty-four-year age group 54 per cent, and the number of new degrees, as projected by the Office of Education, 88 per cent.

This could mean that the earnings differential between college graduates and others may revert to its long-range tendency to narrow and that incentives for college attendance may diminish. Warnings that the supply of college graduates may be growing faster than the demand are not new. Seymour Harris so suggested in 1948 and 1949 in his books, *How Shall We Pay for Education?* and *The Market for College Graduates.* In a paper for the National Manpower Council's Arden House Conference in November 1959, he predicted that it will not be easy to find openings for an average of half a million college graduates in the next ten years in management and the professions. This might not lead to widespread unemployment among college graduates but to a gradual drifting down in their average earnings relative to nongraduates, continuing the long-range trend of a declining earnings differential.

A study of population, enrollment, and employment trends led Robert J. Havighurst,[19] Professor of Education at the University of

---

[19] Robert J. Havighurst, *American Education in the 1960's* (Columbus: Ohio State University Press, 1960), pp. 25, 27, 37. Same author, "The Impact of Population Change and Working Force Change on American Education," *The Educational Record*, October, 1960.

Chicago, to the conclusion that the supply of college graduates will begin to exceed the demand at some point during the 1960's, and that degree holders might then find jobs harder to locate. A recent congressional report under the auspices of Representative Edith Green (Oregon), however, expressed opposite views.[20] Developments in the professional job market will inevitably affect enrollment and a tightening that might take place in the later 1960's would have its impact on the decision of some high school graduates to continue their formal education.

The Rate of Enrollment Growth—Increasing or Declining?

A sudden growth in the college-age population will take place in the second half of the 1960's as I showed earlier. But the rise in the enrollment ratio has been slowing down and the rate of enrollment growth in colleges, as well as in the lower schools, will be smaller in the next ten years than it was in the preceding ten. The numerical increase however is likely to be greater, at least in I.H.L.

FALL ENROLLMENT INCREASE 1953 TO 1963 *(actual)* AND
1963 TO 1973 *(projected)*
All (public and private) Educational Institutions

	Enrollment			Increase	
	1953	1963 — (000) —	1973	1953 to 1963	1963 to 1973
All levels	34,536	51,411	61,951	49%	21%
Elementary and high	32,300	46,917	54,000	45	15
KG to 8 (elem.)	25,500	34,754	38,000	36	9
9 to 12 (high)	6,800	12,163	16,000	79	32
College and profes- sional schools	2,236	4,495	7,951	101%	77%

Source: *Projections of Educational Statistics to 1973–74,* Kenneth A. Simon and Marie G. Fullam, Office of Education, Circular 754, 1964, Tables 1 to 4.

Enrollment at I.H.L. doubled over the past ten years and will expand another 77 per cent in the next ten. But much of the future growth will be concentrated in the next four years when the annual

---

[20] *The Federal Government and Education,* Committee on Education and Labor, 88th Congress, 1st S., 1963, pp. 131–39.

rate of increase will be close to 5 per cent, after which it will drop to about 4.5 per cent. In other words, the next four years—1965 to 1968—will be the most critical period in the enrollment explosion before us. The strain on over-all resources—manpower, construction, and finances—will be greatly eased by the fact that the period of soaring enrollments in the elementary and secondary schools is over. Expansion in those schools will fall from 45 per cent in the past ten years to a mere 15 per cent in the next ten, as the table above shows. The lower schools should not experience much difficulty financing a pupil growth of 1.5 per cent annually in an economy which is expected to expand close to 4 per cent or more. In fact, the quantitative pressures on education as a whole should be far easier in the next decade when the number of students will increase at less than half the rate of the past decade, and, in contrast to that decade, at a substantially lower rate than national income or product.

Projections of educational enrollment beyond the early 1970's become somewhat less certain. But those that have been prepared suggest a continued decline in the rate of enrollment increase. Attendance at I.H.L. expanded 45 per cent and 39 per cent respectively in the past two five-year periods (1953 to 1958 and 1958 to 1963) and is projected to grow another 42 per cent in the next five years (1963 to 1968). During the subsequent five-year period, the growth may slow to 24 per cent.[21] The Office of Education projected enrollment at I.H.L. to grow between 14 and 24 per cent in the first half of the 1970's while the Bureau of the Census' estimate was 15 to 19 per cent. Expansion in the second half of the 1970's was placed between 5 and 8 per cent by the Census Bureau.[22] These estimates suggest that once we get over the big hump in the next four years we shall face a much easier situation for as long as we can see ahead.

Other observers sense a trend in public policy which aims to make college attendance as universal as high school attendance is

[21] *Projections of Educational Statistics to 1973–74,* Table 4.
[22] Louis H. Conger, Jr., "College and University Enrollment: Projections," in *Economics of Higher Education,* ed. Selma J. Mushkin, Office of Education, 1962, Table 9. "Illustrative Projections to 1980 of School and College Enrollment in the United States," Bureau of the Census, *Current Population Reports,* Series P-25 No. 232, Table 1.

today. This could well be accomplished through low admissions standards combined with greatly liberalized governmental appropriations, purely nominal or no tuitions, and enrollment incentives, particularly if unemployment among young persons remains high, as appears likely.

Summary: The Outlook for Enrollment to 1970 and Beyond

The freshman class which was almost stable at slightly over a million between fall 1961 and fall 1963 will jump to almost 1.5 million when the colleges open in the fall of 1965. The wave will advance to the higher classes in succeeding years and be followed by more gradual increases from the end of the 1960's on. How big a total enrollment can we expect in 1970 and the years after? Let us first review the record of the past dozen years.

DEGREE-CREDIT ENROLLMENT AT I.H.L.
1951 TO 1964 (FALL)

Year	Opening Enrollment	Enrollment Ratio: Per Cent of Population 18 to 21
1951	2,102,000	24.0%
1953	2,231,000	26.4
1955	2,653,000	31.2
1957	3,037,000	34.3
1958	3,226,000	36.0
1959	3,365,000	36.6
1960	3,583,000	37.5
1961	3,861,000	37.7
1962	4,175,000	38.9
1963	4,495,000	40.4
1964	4,950,000	43.8%

Source: *Digest of Educational Statistics*, Office of Education, 1964, Table 52. *Opening (Fall) Enrollment in Higher Education, 1964,* Office of Education, 1964, Table 6. Bureau of the Census, *Current Population Reports*, Series P-25, No. 293, Table 1.

The table above shows a gradual inching up of the "enrollment ratio" to 1963 and a sudden jump in fall 1964. That jump is partly due to a statistical freak: World War II ended in mid 1945, demobilization of the Armed Forces followed, and the sharp rise in the number of births started in July and August 1946. The first wave of postwar babies entered school in 1952, graduated from high school in 1964 and enrolled in college in the same year. Most of them did not turn 18 until the *second half* of 1964 and thus were not included in the estimate of the population 18 to 21 years old as of July 1, 1964, on which the "enrollment ratio" is based. So there were several hundred thousand young people counted as students but not as "college-age population."

But there could be more to the sudden rise in 1964. Graduate enrollment is growing proportionately faster than first-time (i. e., freshman) enrollment and the holding power of colleges may be gaining. Also, more students seem to resume their studies part-time or full-time, after ventures into the job market. We cannot now adequately evaluate the enrollment jump, particularly since there appears to be a substantial discrepancy between reports of the Office of Education and of the Bureau of the Census. The two offices placed higher educational enrollment at virtually identical levels in the fall of 1962 (about 4,207,000). But in the fall of 1964 the Office of Education reported it 345,000 higher than the Bureau of the Census. In other words, the two-year increase equalled 18.6 per cent according to the Office of Education; only 10.3 per cent according to the Bureau of the Census.[23]

Presently available data do not enable us to resolve that discrepancy. But if the higher enrollment report proves true, then the Office of Education may have to raise its projections materially. In fact, some observers already predict that the "enrollment ratio" will climb to 60 per cent by 1980 and that enrollment may then total 10 to 11 million or more, instead of the 8 to 9 million which Census Bureau estimates have led us to expect.[24] Would such a development actually mean more higher education? Or, would it amount to a stretch-out of the high school program and a watering down of colleges?

If we base our estimates on trends up to 1963, the fall 1969 probability range for degree-credit enrollment appears as follows, based on a college-age population of 14,100,000:

---

[23] Bureau of the Census, *Current Population Reports*, P-20, No. 133. Office of Education, *Opening (Fall) Enrollment in Higher Education, 1964*, Table 2.

[24] The Carnegie Foundation for the Advancement of Teaching, *Fifty-Ninth Annual Report*, 1964, p. 11. Wilbert E. Moore, "Forecasting the Future: The United States in 1980," *The Educational Record*, Fall 1964, p. 343.

Percentage of college-age population	Number of students
44%	6,204,000
46%	6,486,000
48%	6,768,000
50%	7,050,000

The Office of Education has projected fall 1969 enrollment in I.H.L. at 6,674,000, a more recent report for the Council of State Governments placed it about 10 per cent higher.[25] Governmental and institutional policies will of course have a major bearing on the final result. Current trends suggest that enrollment may be in the neighborhood of 6.5 million, with a possible deviation of 250,000 in either direction. This would mean an increase of 91 per cent over fall 1959—the highest rate of growth during any decade in the twentieth century. In the first half of the 1970's college enrollments will expand at a moderate rate and may add another million students or more to the rolls. During the second half of the decade the rate of enrollment growth is likely to slow down further unless admission, appropriation, tuition, and scholarship policies combine to bring about a more rapid upswing.

The share of private I.H.L. will, by all appearances, continue to shrink. Private I.H.L. enrolled 50 per cent of all *first-time* students in fall 1947, 40 per cent in 1955, and 34 per cent in 1964. The reason for this shift from private to public education is easy to see. The difference in tuition and fees between public and private I.H.L. jumped from an average of $205 in 1947 to $562 in 1962. In 1947 tuition and fees in private I.H.L. were 164 per cent higher than in public; according to the latest reports they are 306 per cent higher (i. e., about four times as high).

The structure of American higher education is rapidly changing. Only a few years ago—as recently as 1950—the student body was evenly divided between public and private I.H.L. But four out of every five students *added* since then chose a public institution. Tuition differentials continue to widen and there is no sign

---

[25] *Projections of Educational Statistics to 1973–74*, Table 4. *Public Spending for Higher Education, 1970*, by Selma J. Mushkin and Eugene P. McLoone, The Council of State Governments, Chicago, 1965, Table 8–1.

that the tuition policies of the institutions or governmental support policies are about to change. We may then expect that the enrollment share of public I.H.L. which climbed from 50 per cent in 1949–50 to 59 per cent in 1959–60 and to 64 per cent in 1964–65 may be at 70 per cent by 1969–70 and reach 80 per cent by 1980 or sooner. Thus within slightly over a quarter century the historic balance in higher education will have been converted to one of predominant public education and the situation will then not differ significantly from that existing in the elementary-secondary school field: only a small minority will obtain its education at institutions other than those under direct governmental control. Increasingly only students who come from well-to-do families or have a substantial scholarship will be able to afford a private college.

3 Roofs Over Their Heads

If the nation's campuses are to accommodate nearly twice as many students in 1970 as in 1960, I.H.L. will have to construct new buildings at a record pace throughout the decade. The United States Commissioner of Education, Francis Keppel, described the situation in moving terms to a congressional committee:

> Our institutions of higher learning are in dire straits. On hundreds of campuses, students are jammed into obsolete and overcrowded classrooms. The colleges are facing a situation for which there is no precedent in history. They must try to meet a staggering increase of enrollments while handicapped by shortages or creeping obsolescence of buildings. There are simply not enough classrooms, laboratories, or libraries for the rising flood of applicants.[1]

To find the means with which to finance the needed huge construction job calls for careful advance planning. So, several national studies were undertaken in recent years to ascertain the magnitude of the aggregate requirements throughout the country, and many states and individual institutions have studied their own needs and possible ways of meeting them.

Surveys of Facility Needs

The American Council on Education, which had issued an early warning of the impending flood of students (see beginning of

---

[1] *Education Legislation—1963,* Hearings before the Subcommittee on Education of the Committee on Labor and Public Welfare, U.S. Senate, 88th Congress, 1st S., 1963, vol. V, p. 2358.

preceding chapter), prepared a report in 1958 which estimated plant expansion and replacement requirements for all purposes— instructional, research, administrative, residential, etc.—at $12 to $15 billion between 1958 and 1970, for an annual average of $1.0 to $1.2 billion.[2] In 1960, the Office of Education released the results of a comprehensive *College and University Facilities Survey*,[3] which placed the cost of new construction for increased enrollment between 1956 and 1970, and for replacement, rehabilitation, and depreciation from 1958 to 1970, at $1.2 billion annually. That called for a sharp increase in the pace of building because plant expenditures totalled only $686 million in 1956. Annual outlays have since doubled—but so have need estimates. A Fact Sheet attached to the President's 1963 Message on Education said: "To provide for additional students, replace obsolete structures, and modernize usable buildings, institutions of higher education should invest an average of $2.3 billion annually. Expenditures currently fall short of this by $1 billion."

A substantial boost in the earlier estimate was foreshadowed in an article by Ernest V. Hollis, Director of the College and University Administration Branch in the Office of Education, in January 1960, in which he referred to the just-completed *College and University Facilities Survey* as "an austere $16 billion proposal for providing the bare minimum of facilities for higher education. There is ample justification, however, for investing $33 billion in the improvement and expansion of college plants between now and 1970." Mr. Hollis then went on to explain how much more could be done with the larger amount, mentioning that in 1959 only $750 million had been spent on plant by I.H.L., and concluded that "in my judgment, the economy can afford to invest at least four times as much in the seedbed that will determine its future."[4]

The College and University Facilities Survey was no sooner published than the Office of Education embarked upon a new study whose results were presented to congressional committees by

---

[2] John D. Long and J. B. Black, Jr., *Needed Expansion of Facilities for Higher Education—1958–70,* American Council on Education, 1958.

[3] Part 2, by W. Robert Bokelman and John B. Rork, Office of Education, 1960.

[4] Ernest V. Hollis, "Facilities for Higher Education," *Higher Education,* January 1960.

Secretary of H. E. W. Abraham Ribicoff in March and August 1961 in support of the President's recommendations for construction loans to I.H.L.[5] The report computed total plant requirements during the 1960's at $18.9 billion for an annual average of $1.9 billion. It estimated that funds totaling $16.4 billion might become available from established sources and that the cumulative deficiency would total $2.5 billion by 1970.

A year later the same author prepared three sets of projections of plant needs between 1961 and 1970.[6] He showed the medium projection at an unchanged $18.8 billion, the high and low projections at $16.3 and $22.9 billion, respectively. The President based his 1963 message on the high projection whose annual average exceeds actual expenditures in 1960 by $1 billion, suggesting a deficiency of possibly up to $10 billion during the 1960's. And during congressional hearings in 1963, the Office of Education reported facility needs in higher education at an average of $2.5 billion annually for the balance of the 1960's.[7]

It is small wonder that the observer finds this plethora of plant-need estimates confusing and is reminded of the sequence of conflicting public school classroom-shortage reports during the 1950's which became known on Capitol Hill as "the numbers game." It may be well to recite that experience before we try to explore the discrepancies in college plant-need estimates.

The Classroom Shortage in the Public Schools

The Office of Education placed the deficiency in 1950 at 250,000 classrooms. In October 1954 the Commissioner of Education testified that it had risen to 370,000 and the chairman of the Senate Committee on Labor and Public Welfare stated on January 27, 1955, that "each day the shortage of classrooms grows more severe" and predicted that "within three years our shortage of classrooms

---

[5] *Ten-Year Objectives in Education,* Higher Education Staffing and Physical Facilities 1960–61 through 1969–70, proc. Department of H. E. W., 1961. *Aid to Higher Education,* Hearings before the Subcommittee on Education of the Committee on Education and Labor, H.R., 87th Congress, 1st S., 1961, p. 17. *Aid to Higher Education,* Hearings before the Subcommittee on Education of the Committee on Labor and Public Welfare, U. S. Senate, 87th Congress, 1st S., 1961, p. 42.

[6] *Economics of Higher Education,* ed. Selma J. Mushkin, Office of Education, 1962, p. 193.

[7] *Education Legislation—1963,* p. 2414.

throughout the nation will have climbed to 600,000."[8] Two months later the Secretary of H. E. W. testified that the estimates had been reviewed and that "we find that the estimated classroom deficit by the year 1959/60 would be 176,000 classrooms rather than 407,000."[9] When the school year 1959/60 came around, the Office of Education reported the shortage at 135,264 and has since lowered its estimate to 124,300 in the fall of 1963. It also proved that the fears in 1955 that school construction would be unable to keep up with the enrollment increase had been groundless: the number of *pupils per classroom* dropped from 29.4 in the fall of 1955 to 26.8 in the fall of 1964.[10] Of the 600,000 new classrooms which the President indicated in his education messages of February 20, 1961, and February 6, 1962, to be needed during the 1960's, 280,000 were completed in the first four years, which corresponds to a *decennial* construction rate of 700,000.

The history of the school classroom shortage did little to enhance general confidence in surveys of that type. Some observers feel that it should not be overly difficult to compute educational plant requirements objectively and reliably. They believe that we might simply multiply the expected number of additional students with actual average plant cost per student. But they underrate the extent of judgment involved.

How Much Plant Do the Colleges Need?

The survey which the Office of Education published in 1960 estimated the cost per student of instructional and general facilities at $2,500, of housing at $4,700. That was based on a space allowance of 125 square feet per student for instructional purposes and 235 square feet for housing, and a cost per square foot of $20. The resulting aggregate bill averaged $1.2 billion annually. The memorandum which the Secretary of H. E. W. presented at Congressional hearings in 1961 estimated the cost per student of instructional facilities at $4,800, of housing for single students at $7,110 and

---

[8] *Emergency Federal Aid for School Construction,* Hearings before the Committee on Labor and Public Welfare, U.S. Senate, 84th Congress, 1st S., 1955, p. 1.

[9] *Federal Aid to States for School Construction,* Hearings before the Committee on Education and Labor, H.R., 84th Congress, 1st S., p. 282.

[10] *Enrollment, Teachers, and School Housing, Fall 1962,* Office of Education, Circ. No. 703, 1962; Office of Education *Release,* January 7, 1965.

for married students at $17,160. That was based on a space allowance of 160 square feet per full-time student for instructional purposes, 237 square feet for housing of single students and 572 for housing of married students, and a cost per square foot of construction, including land and equipment, of $30. The resulting aggregate bill averaged $1.9 billion annually. Subsequent estimates run from $2.3 billion per year on up. It is apparent that there is a great deal of discretion in these estimates and projections. The 1961 study, the most recent one for which details have been disclosed, shows the following components of need:[11]

Instructional	Billion	
Additional students	$8.4	
Graduate & professional schools	3.1	
Replacements	1.0	
Rehabilitation	0.4	$12.9
Residential		6.0
Total facility needs between 1960 & 1970		$18.9 billion.

The book value of the total I.H.L. plant at the end of the academic year 1960 was $13.6 billion, which includes most items at book value and some at a lower or no value. The current worth in 1960 could well have been in the neighborhood of $20 billion. The proposition of the 1961 study then seems to be to double I.H.L. plant investment during the 1960's. At first glance this may seem reasonable because enrollment will almost double. But to build within ten years a volume of physical facilities to equal the total plant investment in all American I.H.L. since their founding may justify more basic considerations than the use of a multiplication table. The assumption that an increase in student enrollment of several million necessarily calls for a proportionate increase in plant space and investment has been increasingly challenged in recent years.

Some factors, such as the growing role of graduate and professional schools and of research in the natural sciences, suggest that the bill might climb even faster than proportionally. But some of

[11] *Aid to Higher Education* (1961), p. 48.

the traditional practices have come under closer scrutiny which has led many observers to conclude that outlays for physical plant ought to rise substantially less. Some of the points they make are:

Present space utilization in many or most I.H.L. is exceedingly wasteful. Fuller space use could save billions of dollars.

A growing number of I.H.L. are changing to all-year use of their facilities, by the four-quarter or trimester plan which can expand the student capacity of their present plant by one-fourth to one-third.

I.H.L. are expanding particularly in metropolitan areas where most of the students' homes are. The growth of the "asphalt campus" may make it unnecessary to build so much student housing.

Community colleges are increasingly taking the place of four-year institutions for the first two years of study. They are less expensive to build and usually require few residential facilities.

Various methods, such as TV courses, self-study, programmed instruction, larger classes, part-time study through evening classes and correspondence, can save much plant space.

Several of these potential savings are discussed in the balance of this chapter. Other innovations will be covered in the chapter on faculty needs.

Space Utilization in Higher Education

Recent discussions of the utilization of available facilities in I.H.L. suggest that there is much room for improvement. The Fund for the Advancement of Education[12] reported:

> Particularly in the use of space—classrooms, laboratories, and libraries—most colleges and universities persist in traditional and inefficient practices that waste their resources and result in un-needed construction. Studies showing excessive waste of existing space were reported in the first manual on space utilization prepared with Fund support by the American Association of Collegiate Regis-trars and Admissions Officers in 1955 and, again, in a brochure published in 1962 by the Educational Facilities Laboratories. Some institutions are now demonstrating that it is possible to have well-filled classrooms and laboratories throughout the day and in late afternoons, evenings, and Saturdays, and to use classrooms and laboratories during the summer without loss in quality of the educa-tional program.

---

[12] *A Report for 1961–62*, p. 29.

The space utilization manual referred to, reported that I.H.L. used their classrooms and laboratories an average of 44 per cent of the possible periods in a 44-period week, and that student stations were used only 25 per cent of available time. The manual's senior author, John Dale Russell of New York University, the country's leading authority in such studies, told the Committee on Higher Education in New York State in 1960, that "if classrooms were used to the greatest extent possible during the day and evening and all through the year, *present classrooms could handle four times the present number of students.*"[13]

The mentioned study for the Educational Facilities Laboratories, by the College of Education at Michigan State University, found:

> Considered from almost any point of view, utilization of classroom and laboratory space in the colleges covered by this study is low. Classrooms are used about 18 times a week, or about 40 per cent of the time they could be used; laboratories about 11 times a week, or 25 per cent of the time. As for student stations, in general classrooms they are used about 9 times a week, and in labs about 7 times. This is 22 and 15 per cent of possible utilization on the basis of a 44-hour week. No matter which way it is juggled, this leaves a lot of empty classrooms and vacant seats. Worse to say, there is little reason to suspect that other colleges of this type or any other type do much better.[14]

A report under the auspices of the American Council on Education stated:

> Without stopping to enumerate the studies made from Florida to California and throughout the United States regarding the utilization of existing space in our colleges and universities, it is generally agreed that we use no more than 50 per cent of our rooms and 25 per cent of our student stations on a forty-five hour week. This may be a luxury we can no longer afford and one which we can hardly justify.[15]

Alvin C. Eurich, vice-president of the Fund for the Advancement

[13] *The Year-Round Campus Catches On,* by Sidney Tickton, The Fund for the Advancement of Education, 1963, p. 6.
[14] *To Build or Not to Build,* Educational Facilities Laboratories, N. Y., 1962, p. 35.
[15] Ronald B. Thompson, "Educational Alternatives," in *Vital Issues in Education,* American Council on Education, p. 117.

of Education, told of an experience during the time when he was
vice-president of Stanford University:

> At Stanford University, when we made a study of the utilization of
> space in 1941–42 in order to plan for the post-war rise in enrollment,
> we found that our classrooms were used primarily in the morning
> up to noon, our laboratories were used in the afternoons but never
> in the mornings. We concluded from this study that we could
> double the enrollment, and do all the teaching in the existing space.
> In the post-war years we found that with more than twice our pre-
> war number of students, practically no new classrooms or labora-
> tories had to be built for teaching purposes. More careful scheduling,
> so that both laboratories and classrooms were used throughout the
> entire day, solved the problem.[16]

Numerous similar examples could be cited. When a public junior
college for 4,500 students was to be constructed in St. Louis in
1964, the space requirements were fed into a computer which
produced a schedule to keep the instructional areas in use for
80% of the college's 45-hour week. As a result, 100,000 square feet
were cut off the original plans with total savings estimated at $3
million. Of course, better space utilization is a job that requires
constant attention lest wasteful practices gradually become preva-
lent again.

The Educational Facilities Laboratories described ten ways of
improving space utilization:[17]

More even distribution of classes by days and hours;

Extending the school week to at least 44 hours;

Extending the school year;

Divide curriculum units more evenly or staggered;

Divorce the credit system from clock hours;

Reserve laboratory use for those students who need it;

Keep classrooms more flexible so that they can serve different
subjects and purposes;

Control diversity of course offerings (particularly of small
classes);

---

16 Alvin C. Eurich, "Increasing Productivity in Higher Education," in: *Higher
Education in the United States, The Economic Problems,* ed. Seymour E. Harris
(Cambridge: Harvard University Press, 1960), p. 186.

17 *To Build or Not to Build,* pp. 34–38.

Restrict departmental space assignments which lead to pro-
    prietary attitudes;
Don't let space assignments turn into status symbols.

John T. Wilson, deputy director of the National Science Foundation, commented in 1963:

> Various estimates show billion-dollar construction needs on the one
> hand, yet other studies show intolerably low space utilization in
> practically all colleges and universities, defined either in terms of
> academic- or of calendar-year usage. On balance, there are very
> strong arguments for attempting to strengthen and broaden exist-
> ing physical facility programs rather than attempting to obtain new
> general physical facility support legislation.[18]

Space Utilization Analysis, a group of New York management con-
sultants who have done work for several universities, government,
and industry, placed the 1957–70 facility requirements of I.H.L.
at $12.7 billion under current utilization practices, but estimated
that with better space programming in new buildings the amount
could be cut to $7.2 billion, with such practices in all (new and old)
buildings to $4.3 billion.[19]

Year-Round Use of Academic Facilities

Year-round operation of I.H.L. would sharply reduce the need
for additional educational facilities. President Grayson Kirk of
Columbia University said at the dedication of the new N.E.A.
Building in Washington:

> Some of our institutions with physical plants involving an invest-
> ment in each case of scores of millions of dollars remain largely idle
> for several months each year. We should ask ourselves if it would
> not be better to operate these great institutions on a plan which
> would divide the academic year into three parts, one which would,
> in effect, replace the present six-weeks summer school with a full-
> fledged summer semester.

Since the institution would be able to serve the needs of one-third
more students in a given period of years than it now can, an

[18] John T. Wilson, "Higher Education and the Washington Scene: 1963," *The Educational Record*, April 1963.

[19] *Space Programming and Physical Plant Investment in American Colleges and
Universities 1957–1970*, Space Utilization Analysis, Inc., New York, 1958.

approach of this kind to the problem of student numbers might enable us to meet our expanding student needs without such a huge expenditure for additional plant construction.[20] In a recent interview President Kirk was quoted as saying that "within 20 years, every college and university in the United States will either be on a year-round schedule or will make such an acceleration of the college years possible for those students who want it."[21]

Chancellor Edward H. Litchfield of the University of Pittsburgh, which has been operating a tri-semester plan since 1959, wrote: "Educators and legislators have greeted it as a means of getting more efficient use of existing educational plants, which cost the same to maintain whether they are operated eight, nine, or eleven months of the year. The plan, if adopted nationwide, could reduce the $10 billion needed in the next decade for new facilities to about $6 billion."[22] Dean Elmer Easton, of Rutgers University Engineering College, pointed out in a booklet, *Year-Around Operation of Colleges,* that a tri-semester schedule would provide up to 56 per cent more degrees per year, make up to 30 per cent more use of instructional facilities, and increase faculty salaries approximately 30 per cent. This could lead to far greater savings than the present partial use for summer school.

Former U. S. Commissioner of Education, Earl J. McGrath (now executive officer of the Institute of Higher Education at Columbia University Teachers College) has for several years been crusading for year-round college operation. He wrote in a recent article:[23]

> If the three-term plan advocated here were put into effect, present institutions could take one-third more students than they can now. Consider this arithmetic: In the fall of 1962, our colleges accepted 1,037,000 entrants. In the academic year 1965–66, according to present estimates, they will be asked to accept 1,507,000. Where

---

20 Grayson Kirk, "Looking Ahead in Education," *Vital Speeches*, March 1, 1959.

21 *Our Colleges: The Crisis in Change,* pamphlet by Terry Ferrer, education editor of the *New York Herald Tribune,* 1965.

22 Edward H. Litchfield, "The Trimester System," in a symposium, "Colleges Can Operate *All* Year," in *Saturday Review,* December 15, 1962.

23 Earl J. McGrath, "Plea for the Year-Round College," *The New York Times Magazine,* April 28, 1963. For other literature on college space utilization, see: E. Eugene Higgins and Linda L. Wright, *Space Utilization Bibliography,* College and University Physical Facilities Series, Office of Education, Division of Higher Education, OE 51004-12A, January 1964.

will they find room for the extra half-million? The best answer
would be a three-year course to increase our college capacity by
one-third.

College and university plants now commonly stand idle for from a
few weeks to more than three months in each twelve. Yet while
classrooms, dormitories, libraries, laboratories, and other facilities
are unused for these long periods, presidents clamor for billions of
dollars for new buildings. Robert Bokelman of the United States
Office of Education estimates that between 1961 and 1975 the
average annual requirement for capital expenditures will be between $1.5 and $2.2 billion. Each additional full-time student will
impose a building burden of about $6,150.

To the degree that institutions can make fuller use of existing facilities by keeping them in steady use, these figures can be correspond-
ingly reduced. The three-term plan will save taxpayers and donors
millions of dollars that would otherwise be needed for new facilities
under the conventional academic year.

Mr. McGrath sees many other advantages in an all-year plan. He
wrote:

A properly designed three-term academic year can provide a 20 to
30 per cent increase in faculty incomes and still leave adequate time
for scholarly activities and recreation. . . .

The average student could complete the requirements for the degree
in something less than three calendar years rather than four. . . . The
economic advantages to the student would be great since he would
pay less for his education while in progress and enter gainful employment a year earlier.

Subsequently Mr. McGrath said: "Five years ago there weren't
more than half a dozen U. S. colleges and universities on a year-
round basis; today there are at least 70 and a good many more are
preparing to join them."[24]

A recent booklet by the Fund for the Advancement of Education recited the experiences of 40 institutions which have established formal plans for operating their campuses on a year-round
basis. All permit the student who desires to do so to earn his B.A.
degree in three rather than in the usual four calendar years . . .
without requiring him to carry more than a 'normal' full-time course
load."[25] It suggested the plan as an alternative to constructing

[24] Mitchell Gordon, "Academic Overtime," *The Wall Street Journal,* August 5, 1963.
[25] Sidney Tickton, *The Year-Round Campus . . .* , p. 6.

facilities which were listed as "required" in some of the recent
facility-need surveys. All of those estimates were based on the traditional four-year undergraduate study on a two-semester or three-
quarter basis.

Beloit College worked out another plan to educate 1,800 students with a plant that accommodates only 1,200. It will use a
year-round program whereby students will be "on campus" part
of the time and engaged in "off-campus activity" part of the time.
By staggering the off-campus terms, the college plans to have only
1,200 students on campus at any one time.

President Mason W. Gross of Rutgers University testified at a
congressional hearing in 1963:

> Beginning this academic year the University of Kansas is starting
> classes at 7:30 and running them through the noon hour on into the
> evening, thus giving continuous use of the facilities. Clemson Col-
> lege, in South Carolina, and the State University of Iowa are extend-
> ing their summer sessions from 9 to 12 weeks, thus putting their
> operations on virtually a year-round basis. Wayne State University,
> in Detroit, has gone on the quarter system as has North Carolina
> Agricultural and Technical College. Florida State University uses
> the tri-semester plan for year-round operation as do three other
> state universities in Florida.[26]

The University of California and the California state college
system are planning to change to a full, all-year operation during
the second half of the 1960's. And late in 1963 the Southern
Regional Education Board published a study, *The Year-Round
Calendar in Operation* by W. Hugh Stickler and Milton W.
Carothers, which analyzed the case for the full all-year use of the
campus and pointed at the major institutional economies resulting
from it.[27]

How can more I.H.L. be persuaded to adopt a trimester or four-
quarter or similar plan reasonably soon? Mr. McGrath, in his mentioned article, wrote that "it is as hard to change an educational
practice as to move a graveyard." Many academic institutions—and

---

[26] *National Education Improvement Act,* Hearings before the Committee on Education and Labor, H.R., 88th Congress, 1st S., 1963, p. 539.

[27] For further discussion see: *The University Calendar,* American Association of
Collegiate Registrars and Admission Officers, American Council on Education,
Washington, 1961 (proc.).

most others—can be motivated to change from long-established practices and habits only by force of necessity. If requested funds were made available in full, most I.H.L.'s would keep building new facilities without major improvement in space utilization practices or going over to all-year operation.

How Much Student Housing Is Needed?

According to the 1961 estimate of the Office of Education, about one-third of all capital outlays in the 1960's would go toward student housing. Residential facilities have been accounting for a growing share of plant expenditures, rising from 28 per cent of all new construction in 1951/52 to 32 per cent in 1955/56 and to 37 per cent in 1958/59, the last year for which this information has been published.[28] Residential construction has been growing *relative* to other building because college administrators regard it as "self-financing" and are not reluctant to borrow for it from H.H.F.A. or otherwise. They generally shun debt financing for academic facilities.

To call student housing self-financing is correct in terms of college accounting practices, but somewhat misleading. Students pay fees to their institution for instruction and for room and board. They usually pay full cost for the two last-named services, but only a fraction of the cost of instruction. Maybe the institutions assume that the students recognize the value of room and board and the tangible return they get for their money and thus are ready to pay a fair price but are less certain about the value of or return on education. In public I.H.L. the cost of room (not counting board) averages more than required tuition and fees. If financial ability places a limit on the size of charges, then it is obvious that higher rates for one service mean less capacity left to pay for the others. The need to pay full fare for room and board depresses the students' ability to pay tuitions and fees. I intend to discuss this in more detail in Chapter 6.

In any case, it is clear that room and board is a major (and often *the* major) cost of college attendance to students and that construction and operation of residential facilities consume very sub-

---

[28] W. Robert Bokelman and Leslie F. Robins, *Progress in the Construction of Higher Education Facilities*, Office of Education, 1962, Table 12.

stantial college recources. We may well ask whether it is necessary to have so many students live on campus. When colleges were founded in sparsely settled areas, far from the centers of habitation, the institutions had to provide accommodations for students. Also, some colleges wanted to exercise control over their students' conduct. Today, if certain recent reports can be trusted, dormitory living in some institutions seems to have effects quite different from those originally intended. Moreover, cities and towns have grown around or close to the colleges, and most of the institutions are now in urban surroundings or within easy commuting distance. College expansion is now largely taking place in metropolitan areas, and the rapid growth of the "asphalt campus" should restrict the number of students for whom more residential facilities must be provided. Since it costs much more to house a student than to provide him with classroom space, the resulting savings could be very substantial.

Over the past ten years, first-time enrollment at four-year institutions expanded 82 per cent, at two-year colleges 130 per cent. About one-third of all I.H.L. are now two-year colleges, and they accommodate more than one-fourth of the freshman class. Community colleges are taking care of a steadily growing proportion of the student population for the first two years of their post high-school education and, according to some state plans, should eventually accommodate most of them. Junior colleges are less expensive to build and operate, are located within commuting distance of most families, and usually require few, if any, residential facilities.

Summary:
At What Rate Should I.H.L. Be Building New Facilities

Several surveys have been prepared in recent years of present and prospective facility requirements in higher education. Their estimates of the needed annual capital outlay range from $1.2 to $2.5 billion, depending on their comprehensiveness, concepts, and assumptions. All of these surveys assume that the present practices of space utilization in higher education will continue without major changes. They do not consider methods for fuller space utilization, all-year campus use, or other innovations by which, according to some estimates, savings up to one-third and more could be achieved. Several dozen colleges and universities have adopted space-saving methods, and others are planning to join them. But the great majority of I.H.L. give no indication of wanting to abandon cherished practices and traditions.

In education, as in most other fields, change-over to a system of greater efficiency and productivity engenders only mild enthusiasm among those most directly affected. Only the pressure of necessity can force widespread adoption. The extent to which such pressure will be brought to bear within the next five to ten years—or substituted for by the supply of enlarged funds—remains to be seen. The measure of more intensive plant utilization will determine the magnitude of plant needs in higher education. For the balance of the 1960's annual requirements may be about $2 billion—considerably less if space-saving techniques are widely adopted.

Capital outlays of I.H.L. equalled $1.3 billion in 1960 and were estimated at $1.8 billion in 1963/64.[29] They still are somewhat below the need estimates in some of the recent studies. To raise the building volume to the required level may not be easy. But it seems reasonable to assume, in the light of apparent trends, that this will be done through a combination of current-revenue financing and borrowing.

Views differ on the present plant situation. The 1962 State of the Union Message proclaimed that "nearly half [of the able high school graduates] lack either the funds or the facilities to attend college." The Commissioner of Education presented a similar plea at congressional hearings in 1963, which I cited earlier in this chapter. On the other hand, stories of a college shortage have been called myths by several well-informed observers who reported numerous vacancies at hundreds of colleges.

To cite just a few examples: Gene Hawes, author of *The New American Guide to Colleges*, wrote an article "The College Shortage is a Myth!";[30] the Student Admissions Center in New York estimated college freshman vacancies for the academic year 1963/64 at 100,000;[31] Benjamin Fine and Sidney Eisenberg reported in their national column on education that 795 accredited

[29] *Digest of Educational Statistics*, 1964 ed., Table 110.
[30] *This Week Magazine*, November 4, 1962.
[31] *Education Summary*, July 12, 1963; *The New York Times*, December 8, 1963.

colleges had unused room for students and conclude: "When viewed nationwide, a deficiency of college facilities does not exist,"[32] and college surveys by such magazines as *Better Homes and Gardens* (June 1963) and *Changing Times* (May 1965) confirmed the findings that sizable vacancies exist in numerous I.H.L. throughout the country. Many students, to be sure, are unable to gain admission to the college of their choice. But this may not necessarily be due to lack of space. One reason for the many vacancies at some colleges and crowding at others is the level of tuition rates, now so high in some of the private colleges that they have trouble attracting a sufficient number of applicants. On the other hand, certain state and city colleges with low entrance requirements and low tuition charges will always have more applicants than they have space for.

[32] *Washington Evening Star,* August 18, 1963; *San Francisco Examiner,* Oct. 6, 1963.

4 Scholars to Teach Them

When schools were opening for the fall term of 1963, the *New York Times* reported: "While buildings may be going up on schedule, college deans are getting increasingly uneasy about the prospect of staffing them with able professors."[1] That described the situation succinctly. Physical facilities are being built at a record pace and their rate of construction can, if necessary, be stepped up. New classrooms can be erected within a year or two, with makeshift arrangement serving in the interim. I.H.L. are only a minor factor in the construction market and expansion plans would not be hampered by the capacity of the building industry. If overcrowding becomes serious and funds are raised or borrowed, under the pressure of the emergency, actual building can be started and completed without too much time lost, provided that plans have been prepared in advance.

But it takes more than a few years to produce a sharply enlarged faculty of high caliber. An interim or makeshift faculty won't do. The supply of scholars is far more limited than that of bricks, cement, steel, or construction labor, and the institutions must compete with government and industry for the available talent. To do so successfully will call for higher teaching salaries than I.H.L. have been used to paying. The American Council on Education

---

[1] Fred M. Hechinger, "Class of 1967: Deceptive Calm on College Scene Obscures Tough Problems Ahead," *The New York Times*, September 2, 1963.

proposed in 1961 that the number of faculty members and their salaries be doubled in the current decade.[2] To double both numbers and compensation calls for a quadrupling of funds, which raises a weighty question: Will it be *possible* to quadruple within ten years the biggest item in the educational budget, academic salaries? But some ask: Is it *necessary* to increase simultaneously both the number and salaries of the teaching staff by 100 per cent?

Must Faculty Be Expanded in Proportion to Enrollment?

The size of the student body is projected to grow about ninety per cent during the 1960's (see Chapter 2). Does this mean, as the American Council on Education seems to suggest, that I.H.L. have to expand their teaching staffs at least in proportion to the students? Must the present faculty-student ratio be maintained? The faculty-student ratio is a somewhat elusive concept for which there is no uniform definition. Available statistical data are not sufficiently refined to permit the computation of accurate faculty-student ratios for historical or international comparisons. We have no reliable information on the division of faculty time between instruction, research, and other nonteaching activities. Many student-related functions such as counseling have been shifted to nonacademic personnel. Still, the record shows that between 1930 and 1952 the number of students slightly more than doubled but the faculty tripled. The trend then reversed and the faculty-student ratio declined slightly between 1952 and 1964. It has currently been estimated at an average of 13 to 1, ranging from 6 to 1 in some institutions to over 20 to 1 in others. These computations are crude, but there is little doubt that the faculty-student ratio is lower here than in most European universities.

In the field of elementary-secondary education, steadily declining faculty-student ratios have long been vigorously and successfully pursued by teacher organizations. In the public schools, class sizes have been substantially and consistently reduced, even in periods of sharp enrollment growth, and they are still falling. But organizations active in higher education generally have not advanced the thesis that, on an over-all basis, the number of

---

[2] *A Proposed Program of Federal Action to Strengthen Higher Education,* American Council on Education, January 1961, p. 1.

students per faculty member ought to be reduced. Quite the contrary: many scholars who have studied the subject in recent years concluded that the effectiveness of teaching does not depend on a low faculty-student ratio and that the quality of education could be improved by certain innovations which would tend to increase the ratio.

The President's 1963 Manpower Report suggested that the number of full-time college and university teachers should be increased by 80 per cent during the 1960's—simultaneous with an enrollment growth of about 90 per cent—and the Office of Education recently projected the instructional staff of I.H.L. to expand only 70 per cent during the 1960's, which would mean a rise in the student-faculty ratio from 1:11.9 to 1:14.5.[3]

Some would go much farther. Alvin C. Eurich, vice-president of the Fund for the Advancement of Education, proposed under the heading of better utilization of human resources: "Establish a student-faculty ratio of about 20:1, which would be considerably above the 13:1 ratio now existing at colleges and universities. This could be gradually achieved as the student body expands, by grouping students according to what they do to learn, rather than what the teacher does. . . . This would lead to large economies and, in many cases, better education."[4]

To extend the use of the faculty is important, not only for reasons of economy, but also because there simply are not enough competent scholars available. Many teaching jobs in colleges go begging. Some observers expressed concern that I.H.L. may be lowering their hiring standards when the National Education Association reported that the percentage of faculty members in I.H.L. having a doctor's degree equalled 40.5 per cent in a 1953–54 sample survey, but was as low as 27.2 per cent among newly hired college teachers in 1964–65.[5]

More recent studies under the auspices of the American Council

[3] *Manpower Report of the President, and Report on Manpower Requirements, Resources, Utilization, and Training* by the U.S. Department of Labor, March 1963, p. 101; *Projections of Educational Statistics to 1973–74*, Tables 6 and 18.

[4] Alvin C. Eurich, "Increasing Productivity in Higher Education," in *Higher Education in the United States, The Economic Problems*, ed. Seymour E. Harris (Cambridge: Harvard University Press, 1960), p. 186.

[5] *Teacher Supply and Demand in Universities, Colleges, and Junior Colleges, 1963–64 and 1964–65*, by Ray C. Maul, National Education Association, 1965, Table 2.

on Education, however, "suggest that over the last decade the percentage of teaching faculty holding the doctorate has actually risen in the four-year colleges and universities from approximately 44% to 51%."[5a] In certain fields such as physical and health education, journalism, industrial and vocational art, fine arts, home economics, languages, business, and commerce, it is customary to hire competent (if possible, outstanding) practitioners with special knowledge or talent regardless of their academic credits. So the percentage of doctor's degrees is low in those fields which, in turn, drags down the over-all average. Also, it has become a widely accepted practice to engage in full-time college teaching while completing requirements for the doctor's degree. In state and private universities and land-grant colleges the percentage of doctors among new staff members has actually risen in recent years. It continued to drop in state colleges and private liberal arts colleges.

The annual output of doctors shows a healthy upward trend. The Office of Education, in 1959, projected the number of doctor's degrees earned to grow from 9,700 in 1959–60 to 18,100 in 1969–70.[6] Four years later the National Academy of Sciences predicted that, if present trends continue, the nation's universities will produce 24,000 doctorates a year by 1969, compared with fewer than 12,000 in 1962.[7] Even so, it probably will not be easy to fill all available teaching positions in I.H.L. with highly qualified scholars. Greater efficiency in the use of the faculty will become increasingly important. A consensus seems to be developing that the faculty-student ratio should be permitted to rise in the years ahead. Numerous methods have been suggested to accomplish this.

Needed: More Effective Use of Teachers

The past few years have seen many experiments and much research and experimentation, aimed at finding methods for making fuller and more effective use of the manpower resources in higher education. The Fund for the Advancement of Education, a

---

[5a] Allan M. Cartter, "Economics of the University," *American Economic Review,* May, 1965.

[6] Louis H. Conger, Jr. and Marie G. Fulton, *Projection of Earned Degrees to 1969–70,* Office of Education, September 1959.

[7] Lindsey R. Harmon and Herbert Soldz, *Doctorate Production in U.S. Universities 1920–1962,* National Research Council, National Academy of Sciences, Washington, 1963.

subsidiary of the Ford Foundation, took the initiative in the early 1950's and has since sponsored or supported many projects to increase the productivity of the college teacher.

In an imaginative article, written as if he were looking back from the year 2000, Alvin C. Eurich, the Fund's vice-president, who probably has visited and studied more campuses in recent years than anybody else, described the innovations which he hopes will be generally adopted in higher education before the close of the twentieth century. Some of the major changes reported as taking hold in the mid-1960's are: instructional television, curriculum simplification, programmed learning, clusters of institutions sharing facilities, programs, and faculty, and many others: "Through such relatively simple reforms as year-round operation, control over proliferating courses, and better use of independent study, many colleges found they could enroll up to one-third more students without any significant increase in costs."[8]

In a report, *Better Utilization of College Teaching Resources,* the Fund for the Advancement of Education surveyed projects it sponsored in twenty-seven colleges and universities and suggested four "handles" to increase efficiency: place greater responsibility on students for their education, rearrange course structures, discover new resources both in teaching and in performance of duties ordinarily expected of the teacher, increase the institutional reach of I.H.L. The report described several manpower-saving techniques which merit the attention and consideration of I.H.L. everywhere. More recently twenty-one educational experts authored a volume *Higher Education: Some Newer Developments*[9] which describes experiences with methods of more efficient use of resources in numerous colleges and advances numerous suggestions for further improvement.

Class Size

That smaller classes mean better education than large classes is widely believed but has never been proven. No fewer than 265

[8] Alvin C. Eurich, "Higher Education in the 21st Century," *The Atlantic Monthly,* June 1963.

[9] Ed. Samuel Baskin (New York: McGraw-Hill, 1965). A summary by Terry Ferrer appeared in an article series in the *New York Herald Tribune* early in 1965 and was also published as a pamphlet *Our Colleges: The Crisis in Change.*

studies of class size have been counted between 1900 and 1958.[10] Their conclusions are predominantly on the side of large classes. The *Encyclopedia of Educational Research* surveyed class size studies and summarized: "On the whole, the statistical findings definitely favor large classes at every level of instruction except the kindergarten . . . the general trend of evidence places the burden of proof squarely upon the proponents of small classes."[11]

President Eric Walker of Pennsylvania State University reported mathematics classes of seventy—limited only by room size—which proved effective in terms of student performance and "clearly show that we cannot simply assume that a low teacher-student ratio is, in itself, the mark of superior instruction." He called belief in small classes a "prejudice."[12] After a recent series of experiments in the teaching of economics, investigators reported that "the overwhelming weight of the findings is to the effect that large classes from 40 to 250 are as effective as small classes of less than 40, where effectiveness is defined as student achievement on objective-type examinations."[13]

Philip H. Coombs, who served as Assistant Secretary of State for Educational and Cultural Affairs and is now Director of the International Institute for Educational Planning in Paris, concluded:

> Much of the problem arises from the fact that the quality of education is too largely judged by input factors and too little by output and performance. In the folklore of education, quality is judged especially by the smallness of the student-teacher ratio. But if, in order to keep the ratio low, available funds must be devoted to hiring the statistically correct number of teachers at salaries too low to attract real competence, "all that is accomplished," in the words of the late President Charles Johnson of Fisk University, "is to enable the teacher to communicate his mediocrity in an intimate environment." The student-teacher ratio, taken by itself, is a poor

10 Howard E. Bosley, "Class Sizes and Faculty-Student Ratios in American Colleges," *The Educational Record*, April 1962.

11 *Encyclopedia of Educational Research*, rev. ed., 1950, pp. 214, 215.

12 Eric A. Walker, "Quality and Quantity," *The Educational Record*, April 1959. Same author, "A Second Look at American Education," *School and Society*, January 30, 1960.

13 Wallace B. Nelson, "An Experiment with Class Size in the Teaching of Elementary Economics," *The Educational Record*, October 1959.

indicator of quality. The mere physical proximity of teacher and students, regardless of the size of the group or the frequency of its meetings, does not guarantee learning.[14]

Lewis B. Mayhew, professor of education at Stanford University, put it plainly: "The blunt fact is that class size apparently has very little relationship to student achievement."[15]

Despite the absence of proof that students learn more in small classes, class sizes have been coming down, particularly in elementary-secondary schools[16] but also in some I.H.L.[17] Some feel that a student-teacher ratio of 10:1 in higher education is "somewhere near the ideal," probably on the theory that this would ease the task of the professors. But no evidence has been advanced of a relationship between an easing of the work load—no matter how measured—and improved education. In an overview of a Conference on the Measurement of Faculty Work Load, John W. Hicks, assistant to the president of Purdue University, concluded: "To the best knowledge of the author, no objective study has ever been made of the relationships between quality of faculty performance and faculty work load."[18] But the "normal" teaching load for faculties has been drastically reduced over the past twenty years.

Television and Teaching Machines

The tremendous potential of instructional television has barely begun to be exploited. An outstanding course on TV, once on tape, such as the famous White physics course, can be taught to many thousands at a fraction of the cost of live instruction. In 1961, about 250 I.H.L. were offering credit courses on TV to about 250,000 students. In addition, some 300 institutions were offering credit for courses taught on "Continental Classroom," a nationwide program

---

[14] Philip H. Coombs, "An Economist's Overview of Higher Education," in *Financing Higher Education, 1960–70*, ed. Dexter M. Keezer (New York: McGraw-Hill, 1959), pp. 24–25.

[15] Lewis B. Mayhew, "Curricular Reform and Faculty Well-Being," *The Educational Record*, January 1963.

[16] Roger A. Freeman, *School Needs in the Decade Ahead* (Washington: The Institute for Social Science Research, 1958), pp. 78ff.

[17] Bosley, *loc. cit.*

[18] John W. Hicks, "Faculty Work Load—An Overview," in *Faculty Work Load*, A Conference Report, ed. Kevin Bunnell, American Council on Education, 1960, p. 4.

broadcast five days a week. In Chicago, an entire junior college curriculum is on TV. The student watches his courses on his own set and goes down to the college to take his exams when the series is over. There are now 2,700 students taking credit for these TV courses.

Some believe that the possibilities of programmed instruction are at least as great as those of TV, if not greater. One of the principal inventors of the teaching machine, Harvard psychology professor B. F. Skinner, wrote that "exploratory research . . . indicates that what is now taught by teacher, lecture, or film can be taught in half the time and with half the effort by a machine."

Widespread experience has shown that students can learn as well by TV or programmed instruction as by traditional methods or better.[19] But opposition to TV and teaching machines has developed. They have been called "mechanical scabs" and "tax rate gimmicks." "Organized teachers," the *Education Digest* reported, "are expected to fight the introduction of the gadgets in the classrooms with the same fervor that eighteenth century workers fought the automatic loom."[20] One major report on educational television explained: "Some of the resistance to large-scale credit instruction by television is prompted by the fear of some college and university administrators that such course work may well reduce the amount of resident tuition that will be available. Why should the student pay high tuition when he can get the same thing so much less expensively?"[21]

Ernest R. Hilgard, a psychiatrist at the Stanford Medical School, concluded that "universities, Stanford not excepted, view technical

---

[19] A vast literature has developed in recent years on educational TV and programmed instruction. The Fund for the Advancement of Education has contributed several publications. Among others: Charles A. Siepman, *TV and Our School Crisis* (New York: Dodd, Mead and Co., 1958); Edward B. Fry, *Teaching Machines and Programmed Instruction* (New York: McGraw-Hill, 1963); *Teaching Machines and Programmed Learning, a Survey of the Industry,* Office of Education, 1962; Jerome P. Lysaught and Clarence M. Williams, *A Guide to Programmed Instruction* (New York: Wiley, 1963).

[20] *Education Digest,* November 1952, p. 52. For the two cited remarks: *The Reporter,* May 30, 1957, p. 11, and "Teaching Machines Hit as Tax Rate Gimmick," *Los Angeles Times,* August 14, 1960.

[21] "A Survey of Informed Opinion on Television's Future Place in Education," by Lester Asheim in *Educational Television: The Next Ten Years,* The Institute for Communications Research, Stanford University, 1962, p. 25.

learning aids with alarm,"[22] and Richard G. Axt, associate director of the Western Interstate Commission for Higher Education, facetiously referred to a rumor that "the American Association of University Professors has established a new committee which has as its purpose a study of the feasibility of the detection and, if necessary, the destruction of hostile flying objects"—referring to the DC-7's which, flying 23,000 feet above central Indiana, broadcast televised instruction in thirteen subjects to about 500,000 students in schools and colleges in a six-state area of the Midwest.[23] The chances are that, just as in the case of other technological progress, resistance will delay but cannot prevent the growing use of manpower-saving machines.

Curriculum Reform

In its report, *Nature and Needs of Higher Education,* in 1952, the Commission on Financing Higher Education criticized the proliferation of curricula: "The greatest extravagance in almost every type of institution from the smallest to the largest lies in the curriculum." One of the Commission's members, Henry M. Wriston, former president of Brown University and now chairman of the American Assembly, a few years later proposed "a great reduction in the number of courses offered. Enormous sums of money and many instructors are now being wasted by extravagant curriculums. When we are short of money and teachers—as we are—such waste is intolerable."[24]

Seymour Harris documented the vast expansion which has occurred in the number of courses and called the proliferation "a scandal from the viewpoint of both economics and education."[25] Lewis B. Mayhew of Stanford University suggested that "the larger the number of courses offered by institutions of higher education, the less favored financially have been the professors who teach them," and concluded,

---

[22] Ernest R. Hilgard, "Teaching Machines and Creativity," *Stanford Today,* Autumn 1963.

[23] Richard G. Axt, "Assumptions Underlying Present Ways of Measuring Faculty Work Load," in *Faculty Work Load,* p. 12.

[24] "How Colleges Can Handle the Throngs," *Life,* October 6, 1958.

[25] Seymour E. Harris, *Higher Education: Resources and Finance* (New York: McGraw-Hill, 1962), pp. 522 ff. Same author, "Broad Issues in Financing," in *Financing Higher Education, 1960–70.*

that faculty salaries are intimately bound to the number of courses a liberal arts college offers. If the number of courses can be reduced with an attendant increase in the average class size, it is possible, over a period of years, to reduce the number of faculty members needed and to raise faculty salaries. Or if enrollment is increasing, it is similarly possible to retain a faculty at its present size and, as enrollments increase, to increase salaries rather markedly. Although some faculty members have accepted the principles of these analyses, they have typically not willingly put them into practice. Indeed, when the matter of curriculum reduction is mentioned, a variety of objections is raised why the number of courses should not be decreased.

Professor Mayhew found that "virtually every student of college curricula for the past several decades has inveighed against the proliferation of courses" and advanced "principles for curriculum reform."[26]

Inadequate admission standards force I.H.L. to operate many unnecessary courses. A study by the Office of Education disclosed that in a sample of 855 institutions, one-fourth of the entering freshmen taking mathematics in the fall of 1960 were enrolled in pre-college level courses in that subject.[27] Much valuable college faculty and space is devoted to teaching students what they should have learned in high school.

Cooperative arrangements between several colleges in the same general vicinity help keep the number of courses under better control and extend the use of the faculty and other resources. A few examples of such groups are: Bryn Mawr and Haverford in Pennsylvania; Smith, Mt. Holyoke, Amherst, and the University of Massachusetts in the Connecticut Valley; the six New England State Universities; ten colleges organized as Associated Colleges of the Midwest (Beloit, Coe, Grinnell, Lawrence, Carleton, Knox, Monmouth, St. Olaf, Ripon, Cornell [Iowa]). Even more ambitious is a plan under the auspices of the Western Interstate Commission for Higher Education which covers thirteen states. Five universities in the District of Columbia agreed early in 1964 to pool their facilities for graduate students.

---

[26] Mayhew, *loc. cit.*

[27] Clarence B. Lindquist, "Entering Levels and College Courses in Freshman Mathematics," *School Life*, April 1963.

Independent Study

In his book *The Education of American Teachers*,[28] James B. Conant critically refers to the fact that "American colleges and universities of all types seem to be almost totally committed to the shibboleth of the 'course' involving a certain amount of time in a certain room":

> But it is high time to challenge the assumption that education takes place only when the student is physically present in the classroom. *Opportunities for examining out should be offered much more widely than they are*, especially in the area of general education. The use of examinations in place of course work would create greater flexibility for the student in arranging his course of study, especially in the first two years, and would encourage the fruitful use of free time in the summer or during recess. It would also encourage initiative, and free the student, to some degree, from the role of school-boy. Finally, the option of meeting requirements by examination, rather than by course-taking, places the emphasis where it should be: on the subject itself rather than on the arbitrarily defined segment of it.

Several Office of Education reports and a new symposium volume vividly describe the practice of independent study, trying to encourage and promote it. They stress the advantages to the student and praise the potential savings in personnel time from taking credit by examination in certain courses in lieu of class attendance.[29] One report, *Quest for Quality*, concluded:

> Students, it seems, are able to learn as well with much less class time than has customarily been required of them. The evidence indicates that there should be a closer examination of the "class hour formulae" and increased attention to the development of the student's initiative and responsibility for what he studies. . . .
> Rather than representing mutually contradictory goals, the search for economy and the search for quality may go hand in hand as institutions of higher education go about the serious business of providing improved programs for increasing enrollments.

Chancellor Franklin D. Murphy of the University of California at Los Angeles was quoted: "The day of spoon-feeding in higher

---

28 New York, McGraw-Hill, 1963, pp. 78–79

29 Office of Education, *Independent Study. Quest for Quality, The Credit System*, 1960–61. *Independent Study: Bold New Venture*, ed. David W. Beggs and Edward G. Buffie (Indiana University Press, 1965).

education is past. We must encourage independent study, put the student more on his own responsibility and treat him like an adult as European universities do."[30] More than half the students in Soviet universities pursue their education through part-time courses in the evening or through correspondence courses. In contrast, only 135,000 students are enrolled for college credit by mail in the United States, despite the advantages it offers.

Faculty-Student Ratio and Salary Level

Beardsley Ruml and Donald Morrison (both since deceased) proposed in their book, *Memo to a College Trustee*, prepared for the Fund for the Advancement of Education, to trim the curriculum of excess content and to double the number of students per faculty member to about twenty. This would enable I.H.L. to double salaries without additional funds. The authors concluded that "new money is not needed in anything like the amounts presently estimated. Many of the necessary funds are already at the disposal of the college or can be made so, but they are being dissipated through wastes in curriculum, wastes in method of instruction, wastes in administration, and in the property and plant" (pp. 9–10).

American Education—Stretched Over Too Many Years?

Some fundamental questions have been raised regarding the structure of American education. We have stretched the process of formal schooling to more years than any other country in the world with unsatisfactory results at both ends of the ability scale. American secondary schools, a wonderment and a mystery to the rest of the world, have not yet found a satisfactory way toward an education which challenges the academically talented, educates the great majority "in the middle" for its civic and occupational tasks, and trains those of low intelligence in the simple type of work which they have the capacity to perform. It may well be that greater differentiation at the secondary level, between academic and vocational high schools, and a general tightening up of the process are better answers than a further stretching out.

---

[30] Ben Hibbs, "California Builds Big for Education," *Reader's Digest*, July 1963, p. 171.

In a book, *The Production and Distribution of Knowledge in the United States* (1962), Fritz Machlup,[31] Professor of Economics at Princeton University, proposed to shorten education from first grade through college from the present sixteen to twelve or thirteen years.

> A system of accelerated schooling is at the same time more effective and less costly. This is one of the rare instances where we really can "get more for less." The proposed acceleration of the school program can permit an acceleration of the economic growth of the nation that could not be attained in any other way. For we would not only save several million man-years annually now wasted in semi-idleness at school, but also several million man-years wasted in the unemployment of those unemployable because of inadequate schooling.

This parallels the proposals of Admiral Hyman G. Rickover in his recent book *American Education: A National Failure* (New York: Dutton, 1963).

Academic Salaries

In a report for the Fund for the Advancement of Education in 1955, Beardsley Ruml and Sidney Tickton demonstrated that university professors had lost, salarywise, over the preceding half century compared with public school teachers and industrial workers. This illustrates the long-range trend in the American economy of narrowing income differentials and of relative greater increases for persons in the low wage brackets than for those in higher brackets. The authors discussed means of correcting the deterioration in the economic position of professors and predicted:

> The situation will be met not with more money only, but with increased efficiency, new ideas on teaching methods, drastic reorganization of the curriculum, and finally a belief in education as a value for its own sake and not as an excuse for a variety of adolescent activities that were formerly carried on without academic sponsorship.[32]

---

[31] Professor Machlup is a past president of the American Association of University Professors and president-elect of the American Economic Association.

[32] Beardsley Ruml and Sidney G. Tickton, *Teaching Salaries Then and Now*, The Fund for the Advancement of Education, New York, 1955, p. 25.

When the report was brought up to date six years later, it disclosed the reaction of the teaching profession to the proposals in the first edition:

> Increased productivity is a fighting concept in education quarters when school teachers hear that it means more students per teacher—even if it means no more hours in class and is accompanied by a substantial raise in pay. . . .
>
> But educators can't deny that in industry, increasing productivity has been the one approach (besides tight unionization) that has pushed up the "real" income of skilled workers across the country during the past generation (net after changes in cost and income taxes). In the swift-moving decade of the 1960's it may provide the leverage on teaching salaries that has long been lacking.[33]

In his widely used textbook *The Finance of Higher Education,*[34] John Dale Russel of New York University remarked that "to some extent the problem of low faculty salaries is a result of the constant pressure within instructional departments for additions to the faculty." He demonstrated that a college could double its faculty salaries by doubling the student-faculty ratio.

The most significant fact in regard to academic salaries in recent years is the reversal of the long-range trend of a *relative* decline: professors are now improving their economic position vis-á-vis most other groups each year—while the student-faculty ratio is rising. The Ford Foundation's College Grant Program played an important role in priming the pump. From its earlier studies the Foundation concluded: "It was equally clear that the principal impediment to college teaching as a career was chronically low financial reward. Higher education could win a larger share of the nation's best talent only by adjusting its salaries to a more competitive position in the nation's professional market place."[35] The Foundation's decision in 1955 to distribute $260 million among all 630 private, accredited four-year colleges and universities for salary increases stimulated action throughout the country. In the succeeding eight years college salaries increased more than twice as fast

---

[33] Sidney G. Tickton, *Teaching Salaries Then and Now: A Second Look*, The Fund for the Advancement of Education, 1961, p. 10.

[34] University of Chicago Press, rev. ed., 1954, p. 164.

[35] *The Pay of Professors*, A Report on the Ford Foundation Grants for College-Teacher Salaries, Ford Foundation, 1962, p. 3.

as the average annual earnings of the employees of all private industries or personal income per household. The higher academic ranks, i. e., full professors, gained on the lower ranks (see following table).

MEDIAN SALARIES FOR NINE MONTHS OF FULL-TIME
TEACHING IN I.H.L.
1955/56 AND 1963/64
and other comparative earnings

	1955/56		1963/64	Increase in Per Cent (Constant Dollars)
	Current $	1963/64 $		
All ranks combined	$5,243	$5,993	$ 8,163	36.2%
Professors	7,076	8,088	11,312	39.9
Associate Professors	5,731	6,551	8,969	36.9
Assistant Professors	4,921	5,625	7,539	34.0
Instructors	4,087	4,671	6,114	30.9
Public school teachers	4,156	4,750	6,203	30.6
Average earnings of full-time employees*				
Private industries	3,876	4,430	5,181	17.0
Government	3,710	4,241	5,229	23.3
Average money income per family	4,421	5,074	6,249	23.2
Total personal income per household				
Families and unattached individuals	5,640	6,360	7,510	18.1%

* Calendar years 1955 and 1963 respectively.
Source: National Education Association, *Salaries Paid and Salary Practices in Universities, Colleges, and Junior Colleges, 1955–56*, p. 188; same report: *1963–64*, p. 11. National Education Association, *Estimates of School Statistics, 1964–65*, p. 18. *Survey of Current Business*, April 1964, July 1964. Department of Commerce, *U.S. Income and Output*, 1957, p. 213. Bureau of the Census, *Current Population Reports*, Series P-60, No. 43.

On a decennial basis, college teachers' salaries have been climbing at a rate of 47 per cent in dollars of *constant* purchasing power, which compares very favorably with the simultaneous growth of wages in private industries of 22 per cent and in government of 30 per cent. Even public school teachers' salaries were improving only at the decennial rate of 40 per cent. Full-time college teachers in continuing service did even better: their salaries have been rising at an annual average of 6.5 per cent for the past nine years, which corresponds to a decennial rate of 87 per cent and, when expressed in *constant* dollars, of 63 per cent. In the academic year 1963/64, 40 per cent of the full professors were paid more than $12,000 for nine months of service, and over 10 per cent $16,000 or more.[36]

A salary comparison tells only part of the story. The availability of research grants, authors' royalties, speaking and writing honorariums, and other types of professional income has been growing in recent years. More and more scholars, particularly in the natural and the social sciences or in such fields as engineering, business, law, or medicine, have been spending their summers and other spare time in remunerative pursuits and boosting their income to very respectable levels.

In a widely read article, Spencer Klaw described "The Affluent Professors" who devote an increasing share of their time and efforts to nonteaching tasks. He found that "at the big universities that set the style of academic life in America the professor never had it so good."[37] Irving Kristol vented "Disquieting Thoughts about Academic Affluence": the movement of academicians to business, government, trade unions, and news media has been reversed because those organizations often can no longer afford to match the going academic wage.[38] A survey by *The Wall Street Journal* found late in 1964 that "at college after college an increasing percentage of graduates is shunning business careers in favor of such fields as teaching, scientific research, law and public service."[39]

While the professors' newly gained affluence tends to be concentrated among the upper strata in big-name institutions and is not typical of junior ranks, many small colleges, or certain subject fields, enough of the manna is filtering down and being distributed to make an academic career financially more attractive, particularly for men of above-average capacity and initiative. The massive

---

[36] National Education Association, *Salaries Paid and Salary Practices in Universities, Colleges and Junior Colleges, 1963–64,* 1964, pp. 15, 27; Ray C. Maul, "University and College Salaries, 1963–64," *The Educational Record,* Winter 1964.

[37] *The Reporter,* June 23, 1960.

[38] *The Educational Record,* Winter 1964.

[39] "Scorning Business," November 10, 1964.

growth of research grants and outside work in general, such as consultation or other professional practice, tends to reduce the teaching hours of faculty members and to restrict student access to some of the best-known professors. But it has helped to keep on the campus many eminent scholars who otherwise might have shifted entirely to extramural pursuits. It is likely to draw more promising and ambitious young men into academic life.

Summary: Faculty Productivity and Salary Levels

If teaching staffs were to be added at the same rate as student enrollment, they would have to be expanded by ninety-one per cent during the 1960's. If, however, many or most I.H.L. were to introduce some or many of the methods for making more effective use of the available manpower and physical resources, the increase in the size of the faculty could be held to much more moderate proportions. The resulting savings could then be applied to salaries, just as in industry greater productivity accrues to the benefit of the workers.

The American Council on Education has suggested doubling faculty salaries in the current decade. Nobody expects this actually to happen. Over the past nine years, a period of substantial improvement in the economic situation of academicians, the decennial rate of salary improvement for continuing faculty members ran at sixty-three per cent in *constant* dollars. That rate could be maintained, or might even be boosted, depending on the magnitude of the available funds and the number of staff members among whom they are to be split.

If the faculty were to expand 91 per cent, a 50 per cent salary boost would call for a tripling of the funds. This is unlikely to be achieved. Historical trends suggest that the income of I.H.L. might multiply between two and two and a half times during the 1960's. A 140 per cent growth appears quite possible. If staffs meanwhile were to expand 70 per cent, as the Office of Education projected, they could receive a 41 per cent salary increase. If staff numbers expanded only 60 per cent, their pay might go up 50 per cent. In the first case a full professor's average nine months' salary would rise from $9,109 in 1960 to $12,844 (1960 $) in 1970; in the latter case it would go to $13,664. While the major decisions on operating methods in I.H.L. are made by boards of trustees and legislatures, faculty views toward the adoption of innovations have much influence on those decisions. Seymour Harris concluded that "the faculty are co-managers, not really employees. They, more than the administration, are responsible for the wastes and the reluctance to adopt improved techniques in higher education."[40] He added:

> Faculty pay would be much higher if faculties were more disposed to economize without seriously affecting the educational product. What can be accomplished is suggested by President Hutchins' experience in the Great Depression at Chicago. The faculty dropped 450 courses when the president announced that the one objective was to maintain faculty pay. This the faculty achieved by a drastic reduction in the college offering.[41]

In conclusion then: Faculty attitudes and action toward greater productivity will have a major bearing on the size of future salary increases and on their personal economic well-being.

---

[40] Seymour Harris, *Higher Education: Resources and Finance,* p. xi.
[41] *Higher Education in the United States, The Economic Problems,* p. 18.

5 Facing the Bill by 1970 and After

The purpose of the many computations, projections, and considerations of enrollment and of requirements for faculty and plant is to find an answer to the overriding and often-asked question: How much money will the colleges and universities need in a given year in the future, say, for example, 1970? What should be the target toward which we should aim our plans to finance higher education?

It is, of course, always possible to set a high goal, an ideal, and leave it up to the future to live up to it. But if a projection is to serve as a working plan to help in the making of decisions, then it should not differ too drastically from the eventual results. Therefore it must be drawn in realistic terms, in terms not only of the possible but of the probable, after weighing the forces that impinge on it and are likely to affect the outcome. Above all, the researcher should avoid, if he can, coloring his estimates or predictions with his wishes. He should be able to look back at his figures many years later without having to offer too many explanations or alibis.

The only appropriate answer to the question of how much the I.H.L. will need in 1970—or in some other year—is: That depends. It depends on the questioner's views on how a college ought to operate. Supposing he believes that I.H.L. should forthwith change over to an all-year schedule, full space utilization, mass lectures,

TV courses on tape, independent study controlled by periodic examinations, curriculum simplification, limited number of seminars—mostly at senior year and graduate levels—higher standards of admission and minimum grades, etc. If I.H.L. did all that conscientiously and efficiently, they could handle a large enrollment with only a moderate increase in financial support.

If, on the other hand, our questioner feels that faculty-student ratios should be maintained or even lowered to permit intensified personal contact, that, for example, the number as well as the salaries of the faculty ought to be doubled between 1960 and 1970, then it is clear that funds will need to be quadrupled or, if certain other items rise less than proportionally, at least more than tripled. If it is his judgment that the teaching staff should grow in proportion to enrollment and that salaries ought to be boosted by one half, income will have to triple. But if he suspects that the staff should expand at only half the rate of the students, and that a salary boost of close to forty per cent in the 1960's will do the job, budgets only need to double. There is, of course, an infinite variety of possibilities in between these examples.

The conclusion is that the magnitude of the financial need of I.H.L. is more a matter of policy than of mathematical, noncontroversial computation. If the bodies which have power over major policy, such as state legislatures or some boards of trustees, also raise the required funds—or at least set the level of taxes, appropriations, and fees which control the size of the funds—then they can weigh operating and fiscal considerations against each other. They can say what the institution ought to do and provide money accordingly. If their authority over sources and size of appropriations is limited—as is true of boards of public I.H.L.—then they must cut the garment to fit the cloth. They cannot, as a rule, spend more money than they are being given; they will rarely spend less.

On the whole, the support of higher education has increased much more than most of those who prepared projections some ten to fifteen years ago dared hope. But progress tends to make us more conscious of whatever shortcomings remain and to enhance our optimism for the future. So, many—when asked how much money I.H.L. ought to get—will simply reply: More. Maybe 50 per cent more, or maybe 100 per cent, of whatever they get at any particular time. That could be as good an answer as any but it probably satisfies no one. It will appear agnostic or heretical to some, cynical to others. Most questioners will insist on a more specific and quantified answer on as rational a basis as possible and with a respectable statistical underpinning. Such answers can be developed, and I propose to do so, but we should keep in mind that, no matter how much we try otherwise (and we should certainly try as hard as we can), some of the ingredients that go into the mix are value judgments based on our philosophy rather than mere arithmetic.

Cost Savings in the 1960's?

Enrollment is, of course, the base from which budget computations usually start. It is not entirely devoid of policy issues, such as the level of admission standards and tuitions, but is likely to be more certain than most other factors. The question at this point is not whether major changes in prevailing practices *should* be made but whether they *will* be made and, if so, when. Will I.H.L. continue to follow traditional operating procedures well into the 1970's? Or will many, particularly the big institutions, adopt a significant number of plans for making fuller and more effective use of available physical and manpower resources? Will these plans, when widely adopted, live up to their promises? Or will some or many turn into disappointments? Whether they work or not will, to some extent, depend on the spirit in which they are accepted and the enthusiasm with which they are carried out.

Some observers believe that the squeeze between growing numbers and limited resources will soon force the hand of many I.H.L. which, if given the necessary funds, would carry on in the traditional manner. But, on the whole, the educational establishment has tended to resist change and introduced major innovations only with great reluctance, under heavy pressure, and with much delay. It has been said that if the Edsel division had been a department in a university, it would still be there. We are now halfway through the 1960's and with the years passing rapidly there is a serious question just how optimistic we can be about savings that are likely to be achieved by 1970, even under the best of circumstances. Some of the plans, such as the year-round campus, may save large construction outlays in the long run but will, at the start, substantially boost operating expenses.

So, on the whole, it may be safer to assume that past cost trends will continue for the next few years with but moderate improvement, and that much of any additional savings from procedural innovations will be applied to boosts in faculty salaries, or come only in a more distant period. This suggests that we revert to the traditional practice of projecting past trends into the future, with such adjustments as we find necessary. At this point it may be well to trace past expenditure trends and see what they forebode.

Expenditure Trends

In the academic year 1959/60 expenditures of all I.H.L. totaled $6.9 billion, two-thirds of which was allocated to instructional, research, and general purposes:

	Million	Per Cent
Instructional and general expenditures	$3,511	50.5%
Organized research	1,024	14.7
Auxiliary enterprises	918	13.2
Student aid	174	2.5
Additions to plant	1,319	19.0
	$6,947	100.0%

The following table shows that the trend of expenditures has not only been upward but that the *rate of increase* has been growing. Part of this is due to the spectacular expansion of organized research in the past two decades, but instructional outlays have also been pointing in the same direction. Costs on a per student or per credit hour basis would be very helpful in refining our analysis, but the scarcity of the available statistical data makes such computations hazardous. It is, however, obvious that per student costs have been climbing rapidly.

EDUCATIONAL AND GENERAL EXPENDITURES OF I.H.L., 1930–64

	Actual $	1959–60 $	Decennial Rate of Increase (Constant $) Per Cent	Per Cent of National Income
	(Million)			
1929–30	$ 379	$ 657		0.46%
1939–40	526	1,104	68	0.68
1949–50	1,718	2,107	91	0.75
1959–60	4,536	4,536	115	1.11
1961–62	5,798	5,660	203	1.31
1963–64	7,421	7,072	201	1.50%

Includes research expenditures. Source: U.S. Office of Education, *Financial Statistics of Institutions of Higher Education 1959–60*, 1964 Table 2; same, *Preliminary Report of Financial Statistics of Institutions of Higher Education, Fiscal Year 1964*, July 1965, Table 2.

It may be well at this point to review the record of expenditures for all education—higher and lower, public and private—in the United States. The share of the national income allocated to education has shown a consistent long-range upward trend as far back as our statistics go. In a research report a few years ago[1] I estimated total educational outlays:

> In 1890 at 1.4 per cent of the national income
>
> 1902 at 1.7 per cent of the national income
>
> 1913 at 2.2 per cent of the national income

In the past twelve years, between the school years 1951/52 and 1963/64, expenditures at all levels of education, public and private, tripled, rising from $11 billion to $34 billion. As a percentage of the national income, they jumped from 4.05 to 7.04 per cent, a far more spectacular increase than any student of education or public finance, writing in the early 1950's, thought possible. There is no sign—nor likelihood—that the trend of allocating a growing share of the national income to education is about to be halted or reversed.

---

[1] *School Needs in the Decade Ahead* (Washington: The Institute for Social Science Research, 1958), p. 5.

The Office of Education showed totals for selected years since 1929 as follows:

TOTAL EXPENDITURES FOR EDUCATION IN THE UNITED STATES
Selected Years, 1929–63

School Year Beginning in:	Amount (Billion)	Per Cent of National Income
1929	$ 3.2	3.68%
1939	3.2	4.40
1949	8.8	4.04
1951	11.3	4.05
1953	13.9	4.57
1955	16.8	5.09
1957	21.1	5.76
1959	24.7	6.17
1961	29.4	6.88
1963	33.7	7.04%

Source: *Digest of Educational Statistics,* 1963 ed., Office of Education, Table 98; 1964 ed., Table 112.

Higher education has a just claim and a good chance to receive in the years ahead a greater share of the enlarged educational funds. In the decade of the 1950's the biggest enrollment and financial expansion took place at the elementary and secondary level. But during the balance of the 1960's enrollment growth in the lower schools will be much smaller, and the sharpest gains will occur in I.H.L. (see Chapter 2). It is thus reasonable to expect that the financial requirements of the common schools will increase at a somewhat slower rate, which ought to give higher education more leeway. I.H.L. have been gaining relatively at the state level for some years. The ratio betwen state expenditures for higher education and for local schools declined *from 1 to 2.36* in 1954 to 1 to 1.61 in 1964. This trend is likely to grow stronger.

Expenditures in 1969–70

We saw earlier that current educational and general expenditures of I.H.L. increased 115 per cent between 1950 and 1960 (*constant* dollars). In the 1960's they will at least double, and the chances are that they will go up between 130 and 150 per cent, conceivably even as much as 170 per cent. This means that they will, in 1970, certainly exceed $9 billion (1960 $), and more likely run between $10.5 and $12.5 billion. The total outlays of I.H.L., including construction, may then equal $14 to $18 billion (1960 $). Higher education will claim a substantially bigger slice of the national income. In the 1950's educational and general expenditures of I.H.L. grew 0.36 percentage points of national income; the total of all expenditures, including capital, 0.51 percentage points. In the current decade, educational and general expenditures of I.H.L. may grow from 1.1 per cent of the national income in 1960 to between 1.7 per cent and 2.0 per cent in 1970; all higher educational costs might rise from 1.7 per cent of national income in 1960 to between 2.5 per cent and 3.0 per cent in 1970.

During the 1950's total educational outlays jumped 2.1 percentage points of the national income with three-fourths of this going to the lower schools. In the 1960's it should be possible to channel a major share of whatever increase education gets to the I.H.L. Total expenditures—and income—of I.H.L. are likely to rise by $7 to $11 billion or more during the 1960's. Much of the additional funds will come in more or less automatically. Expanding enrollment will add to tuition and fee receipts and be considered in setting the size of state appropriations. Organized research grows as sponsors request it and supply the necessary wherewithal. Earnings of endowment funds will go up. But in the aggregate these additions will at best account for half the needed increase and probably for less. A major part will have to come from higher tuitions and fees, larger donations, and heavier taxes—or bigger deficits. Governments could, of course, also make greater funds available to higher education by cutting down on other types of expenditures. But this does not quite jibe with the plans of the spokesmen for those "other" types of expenditures and cannot be counted on. More likely, greater funds for I.H.L. will mean higher tuitions and fees and heavier taxes than would otherwise prevail at one or several levels of government.

In 1960 about one-half of all expenditures was allocated to instructional and general purposes and the other half divided into three almost equal parts: organized research, auxiliary enterprises and student aid, and capital outlays. By 1970 the share of instructional expenditures may slightly increase to almost sixty per cent of the total, the share of capital outlays is likely to decline, and the relative standing of the other items may not change significantly. Organized research should be wholly supported from funds provided by governmental or private sources for those purposes and constitute no—or at least no material—drain on general institutional income. Nor should the operation of auxiliary enterprises require a sizable subsidy.

Capital outlays present a different and more complicated picture. Their amount may be expected to rise substantially from the 1960 level and could reach a total of $2 billion or more by 1970. Between one-fourth and one-third of all construction will be for residential purposes and continue to be financed by borrowing—H.H.F.A. or other—to the extent to which it exceeds the funds donated or appropriated for student housing by outside sources.[2]

A good case could be made for financing nonresidential construction, i. e., for academic and general buildings, through borrowing. Most of the enrollment increase will take place in the next four years after which it will flatten out and be followed by a period of slow growth. Since the new buildings will serve for several decades, there seems to be no valid reason why their cost should not be stretched out over a longer time than the few years of peak enrollment growth. State and local governments and industrial enterprises raise funds for regular—and most certainly for extraordinarily heavy—plant expansion by bond financing. The fact is, however, that few I.H.L. resort to debt financing for academic buildings. Private institutions have never done so, save under very unusual circumstances. No private college or university has sold building bonds, except for student housing, in many a year. They prefer to rely on donations as their major source for plant expansion funds.

Public I.H.L. usually require authorization from their state legislature (or even from the voters in some cases) for the issuance of bonds but do not often show eagerness to seek it. Only ten to fifteen per cent of general plant funds of public I.H.L. comes from institutional securities while about three-fourths is derived from state appropriations and tax levies. It is the state government more often than the university which issues building bonds for higher

---

[2] A pay-as-you-go leasing plan for college dormitories has been developed by C.I.T. Educational Buildings, Inc., a subsidiary of C.I.T. Financial Corp.

education. Only public junior colleges, which in many states are organized in districts similar to school districts, sell bonds for construction purposes whenever needed and approved by the voters.

It is not that I.H.L. could not sell their bonds in the market. Most of them could, if they wanted to, finance a very large expansion through long-term securities. But boards of trustees are opposed to debt financing for academic buildings because repayment and interest would cut into future general revenues and restrict funds available for faculty salaries and other operational costs. So, if plants are not expanded, or not expanded fast enough, then it is not for inability to raise the required funds but because of reluctance to use future general income for that purpose. This suggests that institutions generally have found it easier to get money for permanent buildings, whether from private donors or from state legislatures, than for salaries and other current purposes. Also, that the real problem is not so much to get sufficient resources for necessary plant expansion as for salaries and operations. In the final analysis the financial problems of I.H.L. boil down to securing general and unrestricted income, which is the hardest to get from any source.

Will it be possible to boost taxes, tuitions, and donations sufficiently to bring the income of I.H.L. to the stated goals? State and local governments have been raising their taxes at a rapid pace since the end of World War II, largely for the benefit of education, and may well continue to do so. They have increased their share of institutional support. The national government has never contributed significant amounts for the instructional purposes of I.H.L. Most federal funds have gone for services and research contracts or been otherwise earmarked. The construction program enacted in 1963 is the first truly general aid but is also restricted. The outlook for sizable operational grants from the federal government is dim. Institutional income from tuitions and fees *relatively* declined in the 1950's—from thirty-eight per cent of all educational and general income to twenty-five per cent—because veterans' tuitions paid by the federal government have all but disappeared, and I.H.L. have not raised general tuition rates sufficiently to offset the loss. To what an extent they can or should be raised is one of the most controversial issues in higher education. Donations and endowment earnings showed an encouraging growth in the 1950's, which is likely to continue. But no spectacular developments can be expected.

Summary: I.H.L. Budgets in the 1970's

Enrollments will nearly double in the 1960's and continue to rise, at a slower rate, in the 1970's. So, staff and physical plant will have to be substantially enlarged; salaries will need to be lifted to higher levels if a sufficient number of competent teachers are to be attracted to a career on the nation's campuses.

Many institutions have in recent years adopted various methods of fuller and more effective use of plant and manpower which can result in major economies. The extent to which those methods will be used by our two thousand higher educational institutions and the efficiency with which they will be carried out have a major bearing on the magnitude of the prospective budgets.

Expenditures of I.H.L. may be expected to multiply between two and two-and-a-half times between 1960 and 1970 (in *constant* dollars) if the necessary funds can be raised. The record and present trends suggest that this can be done but will require a major effort by all supporters of higher education.

The most difficult problem is not the financing of the physical plant expansion—which, if necessary, could be substantially accelerated through borrowing—but the raising of adequate funds for salaries and general operations. How this can be done will be explored in greater detail in the remaining chapters.

Between 1970 and 1975 enrollment growth is projected to drop to an annual rate between 4 and 4.5 per cent and in the second half of the 1970's to about 2 per cent. Over the entire decade enrollment may expand by about one-third, following a 90 per cent growth in the preceding ten years.

While for some time enrollment has been increasing faster than the rate of growth of the national income, and will so continue for a few more years, it will expand more slowly than the national economy in the 1970's. This will measurably ease the problem of financing higher education, as soon as the institutions get over the major "hump" caused by the tidal wave of postwar babies. The next big push should not come until well into the 1980's when the postwar babies' children will be ready for college.

6 The Student Pays

Next to federal aid, tuitions are easily the most controversial subject in the field of college finance. The question is: Should the student and his family bear a greater share of the cost of his education than they now do, or a lesser share? That putting several children through college means a real struggle for most families and sometimes causes genuine hardship, few will deny. Many observers hold that tuitions already put an indefensibly tall barrier in the path of students from a middle- and low-income background, that they demand needlessly severe sacrifices and discourage many young people from continuing their formal education.

Others contend that the institutions and faculty are worse off than many of their "customers" and that in our affluent society with its steadily rising income level, the size of educational charges is, for most students, more a question of relative values than of capacity to pay. They point at rapidly expanding aid programs which assure each qualified high school graduate who genuinely aspires to a higher education an opportunity to enroll. They believe that loans, work-study programs, and scholarships could take care of students of limited means, even if the fees were substantially boosted, and that there is no justification for offering a college education at a fraction of its costs to all comers, whether able to pay full fare or not. They insist that tuitions ought to carry a greater share of the institutional expenses. Some authors, as for example

Milton Friedman and Herbert Solow, have suggested that fees should be so set as to pay for the full cost of instruction, allowing exceptions only for students unable to pay full fare during their years of college attendance.[1]

The Carnegie Foundation for the Advancement of Teaching wrote in its *52nd Annual Report, 1956–1957* (p. 19):

> By charging tuition fees that are a fraction of the true cost and meeting the balance in hidden subsidies, our institutions have given the public a wholly erroneous notion of the cost of higher education. Nothing is more certain than that their reticence on this score will have to end. Private institutions may eventually have to charge the full cost of education in tuition. They can then go even further than they have to date in providing various forms of scholarship aid for those students who need it. It has been suggested that public institutions also announce a fee corresponding to the true cost of education and then waive or reduce it for children of taxpayers.

How Much of the Cost Does the Student Pay?

The Carnegie Foundation was correct in saying that the public is not aware of the true cost of higher education and overrates the share which the students and their families bear. Most probably realize that the fees of state and municipal institutions do not cover all expenses but are surprised to learn that private I.H.L. also charge only part of the cost. Even in Ivy League colleges with top fees, students pay only for a fraction of the outlays, and President Robert F. Goheen recently reminded his alumni that "no Princeton undergraduate has ever paid more than half the true cost of his education while he was here."[2]

In the academic year 1961/62 tuitions and fees accounted for twenty-one per cent of all *current* revenues of I.H.L. If we exclude outlays for organized research and auxiliary enterprises, student charges equalled close to one-third of what may be called "instructional costs." The academic and general plant is almost always

---

[1] Milton Friedman, "The Role of Government in Education," in *Economics and the Public Interest,* ed. Robert A. Solo (Rutgers University Press, 1955), pp. 123 ff.; revised in Milton Friedman, *Capitalism and Freedom* (University of Chicago Press, 1962), pp. 85 ff. Herbert Solow, "Are Colleges Too Cheap?" *Fortune,* September 1957.

[2] Robert F. Goheen, "Federal Financing of Princeton University: A Report to the Alumni," *Princeton Alumni Weekly,* April 19, 1963.

supplied for "free" and does not enter into student costs. As so often, national averages are somewhat misleading because they hide the contrast between public and private I.H.L. In private I.H.L. student charges accounted for approximately one-half of the current instructional costs excluding buildings, organized research and auxiliary enterprises, with donors making up much of the remainder. In public I.H.L. students contributed through tuitions and fees about fifteen per cent of the current instructional costs, with the taxpayer footing most of the rest. In addition, residential students also pay close to or full costs of their room and board. That may include a share of the capital outlays for the housing and dining facilities besides the operational costs which equal about seventeen per cent of current expenditures of I.H.L.

Higher Tuitions vs. Lower Tuitions

The material benefits which the student is likely to derive from his degree are the argument most frequently used to defend or justify higher tuitions. If a college education yields the graduate a higher income for the rest of his life, why should he not at least pay a major share of the cost? Why should he pass it on to the taxpayers, a majority of whom do not enjoy the privilege of a college education?

Families whose head had completed four years of high school averaged a money income of $6,845 according to a sample survey of the Bureau of the Census in 1963.[3] If a family head completed four or more years of college, family income averaged $9,709. So the college man's family was $2,864 a year ahead of the high school man's family. Even more striking is the lifetime earnings differential which Herman P. Miller of the Bureau of the Census computed on the basis of 1960 Census returns. Miller estimated that a man with four years of high school will make $247,000, a man with four or more years of college $417,000, both working from age 18 to 64. That amounts to a truly impressive difference of $170,000 in lifetime earnings.[4]

---

[3] Bureau of the Census, *Current Population Reports*, Series P-60, No. 43, Table 7.
[4] *Equal Employment Opportunity*, Hearings before the Subcommittee on Employment and Manpower of the Committee on Labor and Public Welfare, U.S. Senate, 88th Congress, 1st S., 1963, p. 335.

Miller qualified his computations and urged caution before jumping to conclusions.[5] But many of those who used his figures— and used them liberally—did not read the fine print. Even some of our highest government officials have been quoting $170,000 as the value of a college degree or as the amount which a young man can add to his lifetime income by continuing through college instead of quitting after high school. This does seem to make a powerful argument for (a) attending college, and (b) making the student pay for it.

Criticism was not long in coming. Christian E. Burckel, editor and publisher of *The College Blue Book,* declared those claims to be "as misleading as cosmetic commercials on television which try to make you believe that a certain skin lotion will make you as beautiful as a movie star. If the actress was not blessed with the kind of features which the people admire, the cream would not help much."[6] That college graduates have a higher income does not prove that they owe all or most or even any of it to their college attendance. They could be making more money due to the same traits that caused them to earn a college degree in the first place: such as greater intelligence and drive, ambition, determination, stricter working habits. Also, college graduates tend to come from a higher socio-economic background and may have had their way eased by relatives or have inherited businesses or fortunes. The income figures shown above are total income (including property income), not just earnings, and much of the college man's income may be unrelated to his education. Nor do the computations consider certain other factors such as the postponement of the earning career, taxes (which diminish the differential substantially), capitalized interest ($3,000 to be earned in 1990 are worth far less in 1965).

Several economists have seriously questioned Miller's computations and expressed the view that the increase in income which can be attributed to college education is certainly far less and might

---

[5] Herman P. Miller, "Annual and Lifetime Income in Relation to Education: 1939– 1959," *The American Economic Review,* December 1960.

[6] Christian E. Burckel, "Don't Go to College," *Congressional Record,* October 25, 1962, p. A 7901.

be quite small or imaginary. James Morgan and Martin David attempted to isolate the effect of education from other income-related factors and then discounted the earnings differential to arrive at its value at age 15. Their conclusion: a bachelor's degree is worth only between $10,150 and $17,050 in lifetime earnings for white males.[7] H. S. Houthakker of Harvard University wrote:

> Indeed, we cannot even be sure that the apparent effect of education on income is not completely explicable in terms of intelligence and parents' income, so that the *specific* effect of education would be zero or even negative. The evidence which could settle this point is not available; offhand, I would hardly expect the extreme possibility just mentioned to be realized.[8]

Similar views were expressed by Edward F. Renshaw, University of Chicago; W. Lee Hansen, University of California; D. S. Bridgman, National Science Foundation; Fritz Machlup, Johns Hopkins University; and others.[9]

An average high school graduate is not likely to add to his lifetime income anywhere near the much-quoted fabulous sums by going to college for four years. Nor will lack of a degree keep a brilliant and highly motivated man from making his way in life. But the great majority of young men and women find it far easier to hunt for, land, and keep a well-paying job with a college degree in their pocket than without. They can, to a limited extent, substitute education for intelligence and other desirable traits (and vice versa). On the average, college graduates probably get a respectable return on their investment in time and money, which may be comparable to the return on other types of investment, as Gary S.

---

[7] James Morgan and Martin David, "Education and Income," *The Quarterly Journal of Economics*, August 1963.

[8] H. S. Houthakker, "Education and Income," *The Review of Economics and Statistics*, February 1959.

[9] Edward F. Renshaw, "Estimating Returns to Education," *The Review of Economics and Statistics*, August 1960. W. Lee Hansen, "Total and Private Rates of Return to Investment in Schooling," *The Journal of Political Economy*, April 1963. D. S. Bridgman, "Problems in Estimating the Monetary Value of a College Education," in *Higher Education in the United States, The Economic Problems*, ed. Seymour E. Harris (Harvard University Press, 1960), p. 180. Also, Fritz Machlup, *The Production and Distribution of Knowledge in the United States* (Princeton University Press, 1962), pp. 112 ff.

Becker of Columbia University found in a study for the National Bureau of Economic Research.[10]

If investment in a college education yields the individual tangible and intangible dividends in terms of money, status, security, cultural advance, then it does not appear unfair to demand that he bear a significant share of the cost involved if he is able to do so, either during his attendance or later. Since the benefits of higher education accrue both to the individual and to society, it seems appropriate that society foot part of the bill. Unfortunately, this principle is more easily announced than put into practice in an equitable manner. We cannot, at the present stage of our knowledge, compute with any degree of accuracy how the benefits of higher education are divided among their recipients. How then are we to split the costs?

If the individual is fairly compensated for his services during his professional earning career, in money and in status, then he probably gets the greater share of the benefits of his college education. Why, then, should government bear six-sevenths or seven-eighths of the cost of building and operating public colleges and universities? Does it not seem that such low tuitions are putting a heavier load on the taxpayer than his fair share?

However, the taxpayer is not the only one whom low tuitions force to carry a greater burden. The President's Committee on Education Beyond the High School concluded:

> through their inadequate salaries, are subsidizing the education of students, and in some cases the luxuries of their families, by an amount which is more than double the grand total of alumni gifts, corporate gifts, and endowment income of all colleges and universities combined. This is tantamount to the largest scholarship program in world history, but certainly not one calculated to advance education. Unless this condition is corrected forthwith, the quality
> The plain fact is that the college teachers of the United States,

[10] Gary S. Becker, "Underinvestment in Education?" *The American Economic Review*, May 1960. In a subsequent book, *Human Capital* (Columbia University Press, 1964), Becker estimated return on investment in college at 10–12 per cent p.a., which certainly is a respectable rate, but provided no final answer to the question of what that person's income would have been if he had invested his money and talents in other than a college education. But Morgan and David in their earlier mentioned study estimated "that investment in education pays a modest 4-6 per cent return."

of American higher education will decline. No student and no institution can hope to escape the consequences.[11]

The Ford Foundation levied the same charge: "In practice the student subsidy [i. e. low tuitions] has been paid for to a considerable extent by low faculty salaries."[12] Faculties themselves are divided on the question and keep the economics of tuitions a lively issue on many campuses.

The economic arguments over the proper size of tuitions hide a deep ideological chasm between those who favor a gradual shift of responsibility and decision-making from the individual to organized society, and those who view such trends and the decline in personal responsibility with grave concern for the future of the country and its citizenry. Much of the tuition debate has been carried on in highly emotional terms which give little hope of soon finding a rational solution that is acceptable to both parties. Their basic controversy is over the size of government and the role of the individual. The argument over tuitions is but one manifestation of this greater issue. Another manifestation is the conflict between public and private education.

Public vs. Private Higher Education

An extensive discussion of the tuition problem at a Ford Foundation sponsored conference of some of the leading experts found:

> Underlying many of the financial problems of colleges and universities, and the difficulty of arriving at a satisfactory tuition policy, is the competition—and the differences in position and viewpoint—between private and public institutions. The private colleges fear that the tax-supported low-tuition state institutions may eventually run them into bankruptcy; the public universities are anxious about the ability of private schools to draw the best students with attractive scholarship offerings, leaving to them the obligation of low quality "mass" education. Put in its strongest form, there is an element of war between the two groups.[13]

The tuition differential between public and private I.H.L. is

---

[11] The President's Committee on Education Beyond the High School, *Second Report to the President*, 1957, p. 6.
[12] *The Pay of Professors*, Ford Foundation, 1962, p. 7.
[13] *Higher Education in the United States, The Economic Problems*, ed. Seymour E. Harris, p. 37.

large and steadily growing and the resulting problem becomes more serious with every passing year.

MEDIAN CHARGES FOR FULL-TIME UNDERGRADUATES 1963–64

	Public	Private	Difference	Private as Percentage of Public
All institutions	$191	$ 734	$543	384%
Universities	268	1,200	932	448
Liberal arts colleges	185	807	622	436
Technological schools	250	1,151	901	460
Junior colleges	128	526	398	411%

Source: *Higher Education Basic Student Charges 1963–64*, by Louis A. D'Amico, Office of Education, Circ. 755, 1964.

The difference in tuition and fees between public and private I.H.L. averaged $543 in 1963-64; ten years earlier it had been only $292. In 1954 private I.H.L. charged three times as much as public I.H.L.; in 1964 they charged four times as much.

The high school graduate has a broad choice of I.H.L. in terms of fees. He can enter a public junior college and pay $128 or a public liberal arts college at $185. Or he may apply to a private university with a charge of $1,200. Of course, these are national averages and the range is actually far wider. Ten per cent of the public universities charge $179 or less, ten per cent of the public liberal arts colleges no more than $67. Several considerations enter into the selection of a college or university, of which size of fees is only one, though it is often decisive. Many families can, if they try hard, scrape up $1,000 in addition to all the other college expenses for each of their children for four years. But how many can do so without a real struggle?

It is of course always possible to charge more for a superior service. But can the private I.H.L. truly claim that they offer an education which is superior to that available at public I.H.L.? Can they justify charging four times as much? Some of our major private universities and colleges rank second to none in the world. But hundreds of liberal arts colleges may find it difficult to prove a claim of superiority over corresponding state institutions. Private colleges pay their faculty on the average 10% less than state colleges but charge their students 336% more, as the following table shows. The full professor at a private college gets $1,282 a year less than his colleague at a state college. An instructor at a private college averaged less than a public school teacher ($5,992) and an assistant professor little more. Faculty at church-connected colleges ranked lowest—with surprisingly little difference between the various denominations—at about $1,700 less than private independent colleges.[14]

MEAN 9–10 MONTH SALARIES OF FULL-TIME FACULTY MEMBERS IN
LIBERAL ARTS COLLEGES, 1963–64

	Public	Private	Difference
All ranks	$ 8,391	$7,549	11%
Professor	11,165	9,883	13
Associate professor	8,905	7,926	12
Assistant professor	7,539	6,815	11
Instructor	6,386	5,792	10
Tuitions and fees	$ 185	$ 807	336%

Source: *Digest of Educational Statistics*, 1964 edition, Office of Education, Table 69.

Such differences in the salary level must eventually affect the caliber of the faculty which private colleges are able to attract and keep. Who will then want to pay a college with an inferior faculty four times as high a tuition as he would have to pay a state college?

In a survey of American higher education, examiners for the O.E.C.D. (Organization of Economic Cooperation and Development) predicted a weakening of private institutions: "a vicious spiral of lowered capacity to compete for highly qualified and increasingly costly faculty; reduced standards of plant and facilities; and lowered standards of output both qualitatively and quantitatively."[15] It is small wonder that the weight of enrollment is rapidly shifting to public I.H.L. Over the past sixteen years (fall

[14] W. Robert Bokelman, Louis D'Amico, and Anna Jane Holbrook, "Faculty Salaries and Basic Student Charges at Private Institutions of Higher Education," *The Educational Record*, July 1963.
[15] *Higher Education and the Demand for Scientific Manpower in the United States*, O.E.C.D. Review of National Policies for Science and Education, O.E.C.D., Paris, November 1963, p. 26.

1948 to 1964) degree-credit enrollment at public I.H.L. grew 169 per cent, at private I.H.L. 46 per cent. The increase in first-time enrollment over the same period was divided: 79 per cent public, 21 per cent private. The enrollment share of private I.H.L. meanwhile dropped from 51 per cent to less than 36 per cent. By the end of this decade it might well be down to 30 per cent and some time later, if present trends continue, to 20 per cent or less.

It is not inconceivable that the rate of the shift will accelerate as the discrepancies become more obvious and widely known. True prestige institutions which are heavily endowed or able to elicit large donations, and can afford to raise tuitions because of their known excellence—or because attendance is a status symbol—may be able to maintain their position. But even they are becoming concerned. Chancellor Lawrence A. Kimpton of the University of Chicago once told a group of state university administrators, with amazing frankness: "To put it in the crassest terms possible—and I know this will offend many of the brotherhood—it is hard to market a product at a fair price when down the street someone is giving it away."[16]

The fact is that many private colleges now have difficulty filling their facilities up to capacity and wind up with vacancies. This explains the reports of large numbers of freshman spaces available in hundreds of colleges which appear in magazines and newspapers from time to time (see Chapter 3). Registrars sometimes find it difficult to maintain admission requirements and are tempted to relax the rules lest the college be left with too many vacancies and aggravated budgetary troubles. But several state universities reported in the fall of 1964 that they were unable to accept all qualified applicants.[17]

The shift from private to public higher education is a very expensive proposition for the taxpayers. They must continue to build facilities at a rapid pace and support a disproportionate enrollment growth at public I.H.L. with $1,000 a year or more for operational costs. Large public funds could be saved by a

[16] Lawrence A. Kimpton, "The Public and the Private University," *University of Chicago Magazine*, January 1960.

[17] "Now: Crisis for State Universities?" *U.S. News and World Report*, February 1, 1965.

slowing down of the private-to-public enrollment shift, which could be accomplished in one of two ways or a combination of both: (a) higher tuitions at public I.H.L. so as to reduce the cost differential; (b) a tangible recognition in an *indirect* way at one or several levels of government of the public service which private I.H.L. render. The Ford Foundation has presented a nonfinancial plea for private higher education:

> The case for the maintenance and strengthening of private colleges and universities rests largely on the value of pluralism in higher education. A diversity of concepts, ideals, and approaches contributes to the vitality of the entire system. Publicly supported institutions also embody great diversity. But private universities and colleges generally have greater flexibility and freedom to innovate—to set new goals and undertake new departures (which is not to say that private universities have a monopoly on creativity and excellence). Also, private institutions presently educate two million students, and it is unlikely as well as undesirable that this responsibility could be shifted to the public sector.[18]

A governor's committee on higher education in Kentucky reported some time ago: "It is recognized that, if the state enters into this picture and provides an institution of higher learning in the Louisville area, it would probably put the University of Louisville out of business."[19] That describes the situation in many other areas. If present trends continue, the demise of many private colleges is but a question of time.[20] Within two decades most higher education in the United States except some prestige institutions may be under public control, at a tremendous increase in cost to the taxpayers. Some observers may regard such an event as not merely inevitable but desirable. Others will deem it unfortunate.

Are I.H.L. Pricing Themselves Out of the Market?

Slow enrollment growth—if any—and vacant spaces at many private I.H.L. suggest that their tuitions and fees may have reached

---

[18] *Toward Greatness in Higher Education* (A First Report on the Ford Foundation Special Program in Education), Ford Foundation, pp. 4–5.

[19] *Report of the Findings and Recommendations of the Governor's Commission on the Study of Public Higher Education*, Frankfort, November 1, 1961, p. 5.

[20] See Paul Woodring, "Does the Small College Have a Future?" *Saturday Review*, January 17, 1965.

marginal levels. Public I.H.L., on the other hand, are reluctant to boost their charges for fear that by doing so they might jeopardize opportunities for many capable students of limited means. By this policy they also restrict their own institutional resources.

AVERAGE TUITIONS AND FEES AND TOTAL COSTS IN I.H.L.
1940, 1950, 1960 and Projections to 1980
in 1960–61 Dollars

Academic Year	Tuitions and Required Fees		Total Cost of Attending College	
	Public	Private	Public	Private
1940–41	$170	$ 559	$1,718	$2,236
1950–51	164	492	1,272	1,760
1960–61	179	676	1,400	2,090
Projected				
1970–71	353	1,115	1,840	2,780
1980–81	$760	$1,815	$2,400	$3,640
As a percentage of family personal income				
1940–41	4.1	13.5	41.5	54.0
1950–51	3.0	8.9	22.9	31.7
1960–61	2.6	11.0	20.4	30.4
Projected				
1970–71*	4.1	13.0	21.4	32.4
1980–81*	7.1	16.9	22.4	33.9

*Assumes a decennial increase in personal income per family of 25 per cent. Computed from: *The Federal Government and Education,* Committee on Education and Labor, H.R., 88th Congress, 1st S., 1963, p. 165. Basic data:

	Tuition and Required Fees		Total Cost of Attending College	
	Public	Private	Public	Private
	—actual (current) dollars—			
1940–41	$ 82	$270	$ 830	$1,080
1950–51	138	414	1,070	1,480
1960–61	179	676	1,400	2,090
Conversion of dollar value (CPI):				
1940–41	48.3	family personal income		$2,000
1950–51	84.0	" " "		4,670
1960–61	100.0	" " "		6,875

Seymour E. Harris, who has advanced the best documented and most persuasive case for higher tuitions in his comprehensive volume on the financing of higher education, based his plea not so much on considerations of equity, which as we have seen are controversial, as on the fact that neither public nor private I.H.L. will be able to obtain the funds they need without substantially raising their tuitions: "Essentially my position is that I.H.L. need large additional resources, and the additional funds required are not likely to be forthcoming from government and philanthropic sources. Hence it would be necessary to obtain relatively more from tuition."[21] Harris estimated that current income of I.H.L. should triple between 1958 and 1970 (the equivalent of a 150 per cent increase between 1960 and 1970), and that neither governments nor donors would multiply their contributions sufficiently. This realistic if disillusioning appraisal leaves institutions with a choice between higher fees and inadequate funds.

Tuitions have, of course, been rising right along. But when the amounts are adjusted for the shrinking value of the dollar or related to the rising level of income, they present a different picture. The Office of Education prepared a table which combines the historical record of tuitions and costs of college attendance with projections into the future. The table on page 94 shows data for the decennial years from 1940 to 1980, converted into constant (1960–61) dollars and as a percentage of average family personal income.

These facts emerge from the table on page 94 in regard to fee changes between the academic years ending in 1941 and 1961: *Public I.H.L.:* Tuitions and fees did not rise when adjusted for the value of the dollar, and the total cost of attending college actually declined. As a percentage of the average family personal income, fees were reduced by one-third, total attendance costs by one-half. *Private I.H.L.:* Tuitions and fees slightly increased when expressed in constant dollars but declined in relation to family income. Total college attendance costs shrank slightly in constant dollars, dropped more than forty per cent in proportion to family income.

In other words, then, college costs when expressed in meaningful terms, have declined over the past two decades. The charge that higher education is pricing itself out of the market is hard to sustain in view of the fact that the enrollment ratio of the college age group has climbed from eighteen per cent in 1940 to over forty

---

21 *Higher Education in the United States, The Economic Problems,* p. 9.

per cent in 1964 (see Chapter 2). Rather, I.H.L. have widened their market by charging users a declining share of the cost, with the result that more than twice as large a percentage of the college-age population now can afford to avail itself of the opportunity to attend college, and in fact does so. This is all to the good. It is not entirely a new experience that the sale of a product can be multiplied by offering it at a fraction of its cost. But neither is it novel nor surprising that inadequacies and scarcities develop in a product, and trouble descends upon its maker, if the price is set substantially below the cost of producing it.

Still, there is something to the charge that some of the private I.H.L. are pricing themselves out of the market. Not that they have boosted their charges disproportionately to costs or to the family income level, which expresses the purchasing power of their market. But their "competitors" offer comparable services at a small fraction of the production cost. No business can long survive against such odds.

The above-cited projection by the Office of Education suggests a substantial narrowing of the fee differentials between public and private I.H.L. from 1:4 at the present time to 1:3.2 in 1970–71 and to 1:2.4 in 1980–81. This would be accomplished by doubling fees at public I.H.L. in the 1960's and doubling them again in the 1970's (in *constant* dollars), while raising tuitions at private I.H.L. at a slower rate. Prospects that this estimate will materialize do not now seem bright. Tuitions are climbing more slowly than projected. A 26 per cent increase in tuitions at public I.H.L. had been projected for the 1959–64 period. The actual rise equalled only 16 per cent. At private I.H.L. a 36 per cent tuition boost had been projected but only a 26 per cent increase materialized. The ratio between public and private tuitions at universities grew from 1:3.5 to 1:4.5.[22] Whether developments in the long run will follow more closely the expectations of the Office of Education depends largely on the policies which state and federal governments and the institutions will pursue. Also, of course, on the rate at which incomes will grow in years to come.

---

[22] Office of Education, *Planning and Management Data 1958–59*, Circular No. 549, Table 23; *Basic Student Charges 1963–64*, Circular No. 755, Table 4.

Capacity to Pay for College

Over the past twenty years the economic capacity of American families increased more rapidly than the cost of attending college. Average personal income per household unit (families and unattached individuals) climbed from $2,209 in 1941 to $7,510 in 1963, an increase of 240 per cent in current dollars and, when adjusted for higher prices, of 63 per cent. It is significant that income also became more widely dispersed and the percentage of families in the lower income groups declined sharply.

Households by Real Income Level (1963 Dollars, Before Taxes)

Year	Under $4,000	$4,000 to $7,999	$8,000 and over
1929	68%	23%	9%
1947	44	40	16
1963	29%	38%	33%

The years 1940 or 1941 are not shown in the table from which these data were taken; the two closest years are 1949 and 1947. Source: *Survey of Current Business*, April 1964.

Little information is available on the average income or the income distribution of the families of college students. But we can safely assume that the percentage in the low-income groups is far lower than the figure which appears in the table above. A survey of the California State Scholarship Commission in 1964 yielded these results:

INCOME DISTRIBUTION OF COLLEGE STUDENTS' PARENTS IN CALIFORNIA, 1964

	State colleges	Private colleges	Denomina-tional colleges	Univer-sity of Calif.	Private univer-sities
Under $4,000	4%	3%	5%	5%	2%
$4,000–7,999	27	18	23	19	12
$8,000–13,999	48	40	45	38	33
$14,000 and over	21%	38%	27%	39%	53%

Source: Edward Sanders and Hans Palmer, *The Financial Barrier to College Attendance in California,* a Report for the California State Scholarship Commission, November 4, 1964.

The personal income of all families (not including unattached individuals) in 1963 may be estimated to average $8,400. Families of college students probably averaged more than $10,000. Some of the reasons for the higher economic level of students' families are: Fathers of college students tend to be in their peak earning years. A sample survey of the Bureau of the Census in March 1964 showed that men between the ages of 35 and 54 earned on the average almost twice the total earned by men above or below those ages.[23] College attendance is strongly correlated with a professional or managerial occupation of the father, which, as a rule, means a higher income. The farm population, which has a low average income, is less than proportionately represented in college enrollment. Some well-to-do families are determined to send their children to college, whether they are talented or not, and by a diligent search often manage to find a college willing to take them. Genetic influences are undoubtedly also present but their relative importance must be left to speculation.

As personal income grew the basic necessities of life claimed a declining share. For example, expenditures for food, clothing, housing, and household operations dropped from seventy-one per cent of all personal consumption in 1940 to sixty-two per cent in 1963. While outlays for food, clothing, housing, and household operations doubled, the balance of all disposable income (i. e., the share not consumed by the mentioned four requirements) tripled (all in *constant* dollars). Thus the "discretionary" income grew sharply and a family's capacity to finance its children's higher education grew proportionately faster than income itself. No major category of personal expenditures expanded as much as education. All consumption slightly more than doubled between 1940 and 1963 (in *constant* dollars) but private spending for higher education more than quadrupled. This was due not to a relative rise in fees but largely to enrollment growth.

The incidence of car ownership and use well illustrates the growing affluence of the student body. On the 1961 opening day of Los Angeles State College which enrolls 14,000 students, 7,000 students tried to park there.[24] When the new College Heights

---

23 Bureau of the Census, *Current Population Reports*, Series P-60, No. 43, Table 20.
24 *Los Angeles Times*, September 19, 1961.

Campus of the (junior) College of San Mateo opened in 1963, 3,100 student cars parked there—of a total student population of 5,600.[25] Neither of those colleges charges tuition because education is free at California state institutions. Which suggests the question: If one half or more of the students can afford to own and drive a car, why can't they afford to pay a fair share of the cost of their education? The Legislative Analyst of the California Legislature has repeatedly suggested the imposition of $100 tuition in state colleges and the University of California but struck no responsive chord—even though the California Coordinating Council for Higher Education recently concluded "that tuition free education . . . has failed to maximize college attendance by those from the lower economic levels and that it has benefited primarily those from the upper economic levels which have the highest representation in the public colleges."[26]

What sense of relative values do we establish among our young people when a student spends on his car far more than he is charged for his education? President John Cranford Adams of Hofstra College complained: "The car becomes his way of life. It is his horse, his club, his dream, his motive for working—and his need to work. It is his peer culture, and this experimental program of ours is designed to fight it."[27] Student cars in themselves have become a major headache for college administrators but few dare take drastic action. Stiff parking fees could kill two birds with one stone but when Fordham University, located in New York City, tried to collect the fees, 2,000 students staged a demonstration and sitdown strike.[28]

The automobile has become the foremost status symbol on the campus and many would rather give up college than driving although students with cars usually have lower grades. There are

---

[25] *Palo Alto Times*, September 30, 1963.

[26] *An Evaluation of the Tuition Free Principle in California Public Higher Education*, A Staff Report to the Committee on Finance, California Coordinating Council for Higher Education, March 5, 1965 p. 62.

[27] John Cranford Adams, "The Hofstra Experiment for Commuters," in *Higher Education in the United States, The Economic Problems*, p. 137.

[28] "Fordham Students Fight Parking Fees," *The New York Times*, October 22, 1963. The Office of Education has prepared a bibliography of campus parking which lists no fewer than thirty-seven publications dealing with the subject: *College and University Physical Facilities Series* OE 51004-10, August 1962.

of course many students who have no car and find financing a college education difficult. But why should the institutions enable half or more of their students to enjoy a car, by charging them only a token amount for their education? One redeeming note: Emory University reported having financed forty-three scholarships of $500 each with $21,000 in parking fines.[29]

Some public I.H.L. are now upping fees. The State University of New York, where more than half the students used to pay no tuition, raised its charges for in-state undergraduates to $400 in 1963–64. The impact is being mitigated by the operation of a "Scholar Incentive Program" of grants to students from low-income families. But the municipal colleges in New York City still are tuition free which creates an inequitable and difficult situation. In raising tuitions it is essential to assure students who are unable to pay the fees an alternative way of financing them, through earning money, borrowing it, through scholarships or in some other manner.

How to Pay for College

On the average, sixty per cent of a student's college expenses are paid by his parents, one-fourth comes from his own earnings, and the remainder is from scholarships and other sources. Some young people do not have enough income—personally or through their parents—to pay college expenses from current earnings during their four years of attendance. This can be helped by extending the number of years over which the costs are borne. Some borrow and pay later. Other parents start saving long before the children reach college age. In fact, half of the families with sons or daughters in college support them with money set aside in prior years.[30] So the interest works *for* them rather than *against* them, as it would if they borrowed the money. Also they *know* that the money will be ready and won't have to worry. But some cannot save either

---

[29] *Education Summary*, May 12, 1963, p. 5. Bills have been introduced proposing "deferred" tuitions, payable after the student has completed his education and is engaged in a gainful occupation. That idea has a great deal of merit but has received little consideration.

[30] John B. Lansing, Thomas Lorrimer, and Chikashi Morigushi, *How People Pay for College,* Survey Research Center, Institute for Social Research, University of Michigan, 1960, p. 40.

because they earn so little or because they cannot resist the spending urge. Cases are known of families with very low income who saved enough for college expenses by pinching pennies and accumulating them over ten or twenty years. But many others lack the will power and sense of purpose to do likewise. They have several other avenues open to them.

How to Save on College Costs

Students of limited means should above all try to keep college expenses as low as possible. Many have demonstrated that this can be done by an appropriate choice of the college and living arrangements. Tuition and fees account for only a fraction of all expenses of college students. The Office of Education placed their share at 13.5 per cent in public and at 33 per cent in private I.H.L. in 1952–53.[31] Recent data from the Education and Labor Committee of the House of Representatives show almost identical results.[32] But these are average amounts, and students with *below* average funds may be expected to spend less for less essential purposes.

The cost of on-campus living is the biggest item in the expense budget of many college students. Room and board accounted for seventy-six per cent of all required charges at public I.H.L. in 1963–64: tuition and fees averaged $191, room and board $599.[33] Even in private I.H.L. almost half the fees go for room and board. The most effective way of reducing the cost of attending college to a minimum is to continue to live at home and commute to college, as residents of urban areas usually can. That reduces the out-of-pocket expenses to carfare, books, supplies, tuition and fees. Even if tuition and fees at public I.H.L. were doubled they would still not be of significant size in the annual budget of most families with a son or daughter in college. Tuition and fees of public liberal arts colleges averaged $185 in 1963–64, and in one-fourth of them $114 or less.

By living with their parents, students can not only save themselves two major items of expense, room and board, they also make

---

[31] Ernest V. Hollis and Associates, *Costs of Attending College,* Office of Education, 1957, p. 40.

[32] *The Federal Government and Education,* p. 165.

[33] *Higher Education Basic Student Charges 1963–64,* Tables 2, 4, 7, 8.

it unnecessary for the institutions to build so many dormitories and dining halls. In fact, the majority of students now lives off campus. In most universities on the European continent, on-campus living is unknown because there is no such thing as a campus, and a student's living arrangements are his own business and no concern of the university. Some feel that the "asphalt campus" has important advantages over the residential campus,[34] a view which many others do not share. But there is no gainsaying the money-saving aspects for the student who has to watch his pennies.

For the first two years of study one cannot beat the economies offered by public junior colleges. Their tuition and fees in 1963–64 averaged $128, and one-fourth charged an average of $35. A student to whom such amounts loom large can always get a scholarship if his other qualifications measure up. Community colleges have been the subject of many studies and now boast a sizable literature.[35] Most of the new colleges built in recent years are of the two-year type and located in metropolitan areas. Their popularity is still growing and some authors feel that the junior college may eventually replace the lower division of the traditional four-year institution which will then concentrate on what now are the upper division and the graduate schools. This would bring the cost of the first two years of college within the reach of all but a tiny number of students and reduce the need for outside aid.

Work-Study

Generations of students have worked their way through college and many still do. In numbers of students and amounts, earnings from work total more than all other aid programs combined. Between one-third and one-half of the male students, and a somewhat smaller proportion of the girls, work during the academic

---

[34] David Boroff, "The Case for 'The Asphalt Campus,'" *The New York Times,* April 21, 1963.

[35] D. G. Morrison and S. V. Martorana, *The Two-Year Community College, An Annotated List of Studies and Surveys,* Office of Education, 1958, Bull. No. 14. Same authors and Ken August Brunner, *The Two-Year Community College, An Annotated List of Unpublished Studies and Surveys, 1957–61,* Office of Education, 1963, Bull. No. 28. An informative booklet was published by the Prudential Insurance Company of America, in 1963: *Facing Facts About the Two-Year College.* See also "Junior Colleges—Students' Hope for the Future," *U.S. News & World Report,* May 17, 1965.

year, typically about fifteen hours a week. At least as many work during summer vacations. On-campus jobs are more plentiful at big institutions though labor unions sometimes keep a peeled eye on the kind of work a student may do. Some types of work, particularly in the food service, are quite unpopular because they tend to lower a student's status among his colleagues, and such jobs are going begging in several major universities which found it necessary to turn to high-schoolers and others to get the more menial chores done. Opportunities for outside jobs are more diversified and more easily available in the larger cities where sometimes three-fourths of the student body is gainfully employed. It is of course most helpful to have an alert and effective student employment office hunt for suitable openings and serve as a clearing house. Part-time students usually spend the balance of their time working at a job and they account for a growing segment of the enrollment. Their number tripled over the past ten years and they now account for thirty-one per cent of all degree-credit students.

A few years ago it was reported that a male student who worked averaged around $600 in earnings during the academic year and a similar amount during summer vacations. Today the figures would probably be somewhat higher. Two studies during the 1950's showed about one-fourth of the students' income as coming from their own earnings.[36] Since not all students work, we may assume that for those who do, earnings average one-third or more of their total income. It takes, of course, firm determination and will power to forego more pleasurable pursuits and perform tedious or menial tasks. Such determination is often lacking in students with a low motivation to start with who are averse to burning the midnight oil.

Some colleges have established formal work-study plans such as sponsored by the National Commission for Cooperative Education. Under a typical plan, most frequently in enginering or business administration, two students alternate in holding down a full-time job in industry or a government agency on a semester or quarter basis. This may extend the time for earning a degree but gives each student half a regular salary and thus enables both to finance their education. In one-fourth of the families the student's parents engage in more work than they otherwise would, in order

[36] *Costs of Attending College*, p. 48. *How People Pay for College*, p. 21.

to finance his education. It is usually the mother who takes a job though the father also often does some "moonlighting."

Borrowing for College Expenses

One major source, which remained largely untapped until recently, is the future income of the students. Borrowing for college expenses was rarely resorted to, and when it was used, it was the parents twice as often as the students themselves who incurred the debt. Institutional loan funds went begging. If we regard education as an investment, then there is no reason why we should not spread its cost over more than the four years of undergraduate study plus the time of graduate work and shift the load to the years when the returns are coming in.

To borrow has become the most common way of paying for big expense items which exceed one's savings and current earnings. It is the customary method by which most persons going into business finance the necessary investment in merchandise and facilities. Why should this not also apply to education? Some would extend loans for as long as the benefits last—a lifetime. But terms of repayment within five to eleven years after graduation are more customary. The use of long-term credit also enables the student in this inflationary period to benefit from the gradual decline in the value of the dollar. And the longer the period, the greater the discount he gets.

Numerous types of "study now, pay later" plans, under commercial, nonprofit, or governmental auspices, have sprung up in recent years and are coming into wider use. "Low-tuition" supporters tend to criticize this as "mortgaging" a young person's future and one spokesman wrote that "the educable masses, seeking loans, will be indentured for many years." To start his earning career with a sizable debt is of course not an easy decision to make for a young man or woman. Particularly those with little confidence in their personal capacity and potential may hesitate to incur such debts and some may abandon college plans. Yet few of them display an equal reluctance to borrow for a car, appliance, or other consumption goods. Many assume family responsibilities long before they are able to support themselves, let alone a family. They blithely contract a mortgage with little if any down payment. Are we then to conclude that it is proper to incur debt for items of personal consumption or convenience but not for one's education?

Are we justified in asking the taxpayer to invest in the future of a person who is not willing to take a chance on it himself?

Attitudes seem to be changing and college loans are now starting to come into their own. It has been estimated that "between 1955 and 1962 personal loans for education negotiated in one year just by colleges [not including loans by banks or other outside sources] have increased almost 1,000 per cent, from $12,000,000 to $120,000,000."[37] It was the National Defense Education Act of 1958 which broke the ice and made borrowing for college expenses not only acceptable but popular in wide circles. Banks and other organizations now take a greater interest in student loan programs, state loan programs are multiplying, and there is no sign that we are anywhere near the saturation point either on need and demand for student loans or on the size of the available funds. An important new source was added late in 1964 when the Federal Home Loan Bank Board authorized the country's 2,000 federal savings and loan associations to make college loans.

Even girls who used to be even more reluctant than boys to go into debt for college purposes—probably because few planned on an uninterrupted earning career—now borrow freely, and under the N.D.E.A. program proportionately more often than boys. Many probably regard campus residence as a good investment which hopefully will return satisfactory dividends even without counting professional earnings.

Some students find it difficult to locate acceptable co-signers or to establish credit, and cannot obtain loans from nongovernmental sources at reasonable rates. To meet their needs, several state-wide programs came into being which guarantee commercial loans to students for educational purposes. A national plan, United Student Aid Funds, was created in 1960 with a $2 million grant from the William Volker Fund. Active in all states save Alaska and by cooperative agreements with nearly 700 I.H.L. and 5,500 banks, it now guarantees loans at a rate of more than $30 million a year.[38]

---

[37] Rexford G. Moon, "More Students are Studying Now, Paying Later," *Saturday Review*, June 15, 1963.

[38] Testimony of Allen D. Marshall, *Higher Education Act of 1965*, Hearings before the Subcommittee on Education, U.S. Senate, 89th Congress, 1st S., pp. 1008–29; See also: William B. Johnson, "How Guaranty Loans Expand Student Credit," *College and University Business*, April 1964.

A combination of earnings and loans should enable most students to bridge the gap between the financial requirements of college and the support they get from their parents. Some, however, also need outright grants in the form of scholarships or fellowships.

Scholarships and Fellowships

Nobody knows how many scholarships are available to students in the United States nor their total amount. Aside from the institutions themselves and federal, state, and municipal governments, there are thousands of business corporations, foundations, associations, and individuals sponsoring from one or a few scholarships to large and continuing programs. Colleges and universities are the largest source of scholarship funds. They awarded more than three times as many scholarships in 1964 as they had in 1950 while their total amount multiplied six times:

SCHOLARSHIPS AWARDED BY I.H.L. 1949–50, 1959–60, 1963–64

	Number	Value (Million)
1949–50	124,223	$27.0
1959–60	287,589	$98.2
1963–64	388,000	$163.0

Source: Elmer D. West, *Financial Aid to the Undergraduate,* American Council on Education, 1963, p. 8. Richard C. McKee, "College and University Financial Aid for Students," *H. E. W. Indicators,* July 1965.

A survey by the College Entrance Examination Board in 1963–64 reported that colleges which account for about half the national enrollment aided one-fifth of their undergraduates for an annual average of $520. One-half of the amount of $251 million was in scholarships, one-third in loans, one-sixth in pay for work, with several types of aid often awarded to a student as a "package."

The demand for scholarships—as for any kind of cash grant—of course always exceeds the supply. The point at question is whether the number or amount of available scholarships is adequate to meet genuine need or whether qualified young men and women are prevented from attending college by financial reasons and the nation suffers a talent loss.

The term "financial reasons" covers much ground. It seldom means inability to pay the required fees, which as a rule can be remedied by choosing an appropriate college and living arrangements or through earnings, loans, or existing scholarships, provided that the applicant's qualifications are adequate. "Financial reasons" for not enrolling in college more likely means that the young man prefers earning a regular wage and being independent to scrimping for another four years. He possibly might like to go to college if he could do it under circumstances which are no more inconvenient or stringent than if he were holding a full-time job. This is where he must make his choice between present or future gain. A scholarship, as we now understand it, can take care of necessary college expenses. It cannot replace a regular wage.

A young man who has to support others besides himself, who has taken on family responsibilities, deliberately or otherwise, without having an adequate economic base, as an increasing number of young men do, may often not be able to enroll or continue in college. Today's scholarships are usually not designed to support a family. Almost every fellowship for graduate students requires supplementation by earnings if several people are to live on it.

It has often been suggested to raise tuitions and earmark part of the new revenue for additional and enlarged scholarships. Such a combination of higher tuitions and expanded scholarships would protect the talented but impecunious student. It might make it harder for a young man or woman of mediocre intellectual endowment and limited means. So it comes down to the philosophical question, how much public subsidy such a student is entitled to in financing his college education. It is consideration for the marginal and not for the gifted student that defeats proposals for higher tuitions coupled with more scholarships.

Because in the keen competition for scholarships many applicants fall by the wayside, suggestions have been advanced in recent years for a major federal program of student aid, either in the form of scholarships or of tax relief for college expenses. They will be discussed in subsequent chapters.

Summary:
Can Tuitions Contribute a Greater Share to College Revenues?

Student charges now account for only a fraction—and in public I.H.L. for a small fraction—of the current income of the institutions and of the cost of instruction. Whether fees ought to be lifted to higher levels is among the most controversial issues in the field of college finance. Many families find it difficult to finance their children's education at a college of their choice, and some cannot do it at all from their own resources. Higher tuitions would aggravate this situation. On the other hand, there is much doubt that without boosting fees either public or private I.H.L. will be able to raise the funds which they are believed to need in the years ahead.

Public I.H.L. generally want to retain their low-tuition policy and hope for sufficient increases in appropriations from tax funds. Many private I.H.L. feel that they cannot raise their fees much farther above those of comparable public I.H.L. without pricing themselves out of the market. The large tuition differential has already caused a dramatic shift from private to public enrollment in the past fifteen years which threatens the very existence of many private colleges. The disproportionately sharp enrollment growth in public I.H.L. dissipates the appropriation increases they do receive and does not leave enough money for adequate raises in faculty salaries. The private-to-public enrollment shift thus works hardships on both types of institutions, as well as on the taxpayers.

The specter of the qualified student who does not enroll in college for "financial reasons"—which may mean many things besides inability to pay the required charges—acts as a restraint on plans to boost fees. Of course, student aid programs in the form of jobs, loans, and scholarships help many young people of limited means meet essential college costs. The annual amount of such programs was estimated at substantially above $700 million in 1963, and is steadily growing.[39] Some have even placed it at over a billion dollars.[40] No talented student with a strong desire to go to college nowadays is prevented from enrolling merely by inability to meet the essential expenses.

But some observers feel that there is not enough aid available and that it does not go where it is needed the most. Elmer D. West of the American Council on Education wrote: "There is a substan-

---

[39] "Aid to Students at Highest Level," *The New York Times,* February 4, 1963.
[40] Benjamin Fine and Sidney A. Eisenberg, *How To Get Money For College* (Garden City, N. Y.: Doubleday, 1964).

tial opinion to the effect . . . that the neediest segment of the population is not getting the financial aid; in fact, there is considerable evidence to prove that children receiving financial aid come from families with above-average income."[41]

Many of the scholarship programs—such as the National Merit Scholarships—aim more to identify the *talented* student than the *impecunious* one. This is why the average family income of scholarship holders is reported to be far higher than that of student borrowers; the latter do not have to prove superior ability. The high achievement student tends to have parents with a professional or managerial background and of a higher socio-economic status. If he does come from a poor family then he can find help from some of the existing programs. But the student whose talents *and* means are low may not be permitted to hold a job (because his grade average is too low), he may be unwilling to borrow (because his future earning potential is cloudy), and he may be unable to get a scholarship for lack of achievements. He would suffer if tuitions were raised even if the number and amounts of scholarships were substantially expanded. Whether public and institutional policy should focus more on excellence or on bringing up the average or below-average, more on the outstanding or on the mediocre student, is a philosophical and political question which will continue to be argued in the debate over the size of tuitions.

At this time, tuitions and fees are not higher than they were two decades ago when expressed in *constant* dollars, and lower in proportion to the average family income. A projection prepared by the Office of Education in 1962 would double tuitions and fees at public I.H.L. in the 1960's and lift them two-thirds at private I.H.L. It would repeat that process in the 1980's.

This plan would multiply institutional income from tuitions and fees about 3.5 times in the 1960's. Since part of the proceeds would have to be applied to expanded student aid programs, the *net* available revenue might approximately triple during the decade. Present trends do not suggest that this plan will be carried out. Rather, that tuitions will climb at a more leisurely pace and that the institutions' revenues from them will multiply about 2.5 times in the 1960's.

---

[41] West, p. 77.

7 The Donor Helps

The private donor to higher education has always played a far greater role in the United States than anywhere else in the world. He was responsible for the founding of some of the country's leading universities and has continued to contribute generously to the physical expansion and current operations of many hundreds of colleges and universities. With the tremendous growth of tax-supported I.H.L., private giving no longer looms as large as it once did. This has led some observers to predict a steady decline in the role of voluntary support as government assumes major responsibility for higher education. But the postwar period has shown a very healthy growth in gifts to I.H.L. which gives no indication of slackening. Under favorable public and institutional policies, gifts could well maintain their relative role in the support of higher education. It is encouraging that all voluntary giving in the United States has doubled over the past ten years and that education's share of the charity dollar climbed from eleven to seventeen per cent.

The Council for Financial Aid to Education estimated that I.H.L. received $1.1 billion in donations during 1962–63 but that the strong upward surge which characterized earlier periods had somewhat tapered off between 1931 and 1963.[1] About one-fourth

[1] *1962–63 Voluntary Support of America's Colleges and Universities*, Council for Financial Aid to Education, Inc., 1964.

of the support was earmarked for physical plant, about one-eighth each for research and for student financial aid, and one-sixth for other specified purposes. One-third of the funds were unrestricted. The donations came from these sources:

Alumni	24.2%	
Non-alumni	21.6%	
All individuals		45.8%
Foundations		23.4
Business corporations		16.1
Religious bodies		8.8
Other sources		5.9%
		100.0%

One group of large business concerns for which data are available for the years 1953 and 1962 raised its contributions to higher education from 0.19 per cent of profits before taxes to 0.46 per cent.[2] Receipts from business might have grown even more substantially if corporate profits had been able to maintain their share of the national income. The Council for Financial Aid to Education hopes that corporate giving to I.H.L. will climb sharply and within a few years account for one-fourth of all gifts to higher education.

The principal of endowment funds doubled in the 1950's and reached $5.3 billion in 1960, with more than $300 million in new funds added each year. But they no longer loom as large as at the time of the founding and in the early years of some of our major private institutions. More than half the endowments are now invested in common stocks and about one-fourth in bonds, most of them corporate, few governmental. Earnings average close to five per cent per annum when computed on book value and less than four per cent on market value. Boards of trustees differ in their investment policies, with some placing more emphasis on capital appreciation through growth stocks and others more anxious to maximize current income. Earnings from endowment funds have not been growing as fast as other sources and declined from 5.2 per cent of the educational and general income of all I.H.L. in 1950 to 4.4 per cent in 1960.

[2] *After Ten Years,* Council for Financial Aid to Education, 1963. (Also from the same source: *1960 Corporation Support of Higher Education,* 1962.)

Endowment funds tend to be highly concentrated. On last count, half the national total was owned by one per cent of all I.H.L. and about one hundred institutions—or five per cent of all—accounted for ninety-two per cent of the funds. Endowments are not a significant factor in public I.H.L. and, in fact, are so only in a small number of private I.H.L.[3] Under the pressure of urgent needs, the emphasis of institutional administrators and donors has been shifting from endowments to gifts for current purposes, for plant expansion, and for student aid. In 1920 endowments accounted for three-fourths of all gifts received, in 1930 for close to one-half, but in recent years for only about one-third. While the role of endowments and endowment earnings has been shrinking, other private gifts and grants have been coming up. Between 1950 and 1960, educational and general income of I.H.L. grew 155 per cent, gifts 223 per cent. (Converted into *constant* dollars, the increases equaled 108 per cent and 163 per cent respectively.)

Voluntary support plays only a small role in the budgets of public I.H.L.—a mere 4 per cent of the current educational and general income in 1960—but still is of major importance to private I.H.L. In 1960 gifts accounted for 14.7 per cent of the current educational and general income of private I.H.L., endowment earnings for 9.2 per cent, for an aggregate of 23.9 per cent, or almost one-fourth of the total. The success of private I.H.L. in attracting gifts caused public I.H.L. to pay increasing attention to this source of revenue and their efforts are paying off; percentagewise they boasted a faster increase in gifts during the 1950's than private I.H.L. But the total amounts are still quite small. Donations are the source for almost two-thirds of the funds for the construction of academic and general buildings at private I.H.L. They are insignificant in public I.H.L., which derive a comparable share of their construction funds from state and municipal appropriations.

If the rate of growth in voluntary support of higher education which the Council for Financial Aid to Higher Education reported

[3] W. Robert Bokelman, J. Harvey Cain, and Ernest V. Hollis, *College and University Endowment Investments,* a Survey as of June 30, 1958, Office of Education, Circ. No. 579, 1959, p. 5.

over the past four years were to continue through the 1960's, private giving would multiply two and a half times. The Council itself expects funds to more than double, and there seems to be much reason to be optimistic about the outlook. The level of personal income and the number of alumni are steadily rising, public awareness of the need for voluntary support of higher education is widening and deepening, and the various development campaigns and fund drives which, under whatever imaginative name, are being sparked each year by hundreds of institutions and manned by enthusiastic alumni, are intensifying. We may expect that gifts to I.H.L. will at least double between 1960 and 1970 and they could multiply two and a half times.

Endowments are heavily concentrated among old and large prestige institutions. Current gifts also tend to favor big "name" institutions and come largely from wealthy or well-to-do individuals. Our tax laws enable them to be generous in philanthropic activities at less cost to themselves than persons in lower brackets. The Internal Revenue Code permits taxpayers to deduct from their tax base contributions to educational institutions (and to other specified organizations) up to a maximum of 30 per cent of adjusted gross income. Thus the *net* cost of a college donation may equal only 40 per cent or 30 per cent of the *gross* amount to a person in a high tax bracket. But a donor of moderate or low income bears 75 per cent to 86 per cent of the value of his gift.

It is not overly surprising that many alumni and others in low tax brackets donate little if anything to educational institutions. Thus, much of the voluntary support of education rests on a relatively narrow base of affluent individuals. If persons in lower tax brackets were permitted to deduct from their tax liability a greater percentage of their donations—or possibly up to 100 per cent—with a dollar ceiling, they might be more easily persuaded to become regular contributors to college fund drives. Much of the tax relief would go directly to persons in middle or lower income brackets, but the real beneficiaries would be colleges and universities which, most likely, could multiply the number of their supporters and would not have to rely so much on finding wealthy benefactors. Particularly public I.H.L. could turn voluntary support from a minor to a major source of income by impressing upon alumni the fact that their tuitions had paid only a small share of the cost of their education. Many of them do not have a sufficient number of wealthy alumni. But hundreds of thousands of former students would much rather contribute $100 or $200 annually to their alma mater than pay it to the Internal Revenue Service. The American Association for the Advancement of Science advocated such a plan a few years ago, and a group of college presidents suggested in 1963 a 100 per cent tax credit for donations.

The United States Treasury strongly opposes such plans because they would cause a substantial loss of revenue. This appears to be a valid argument at times of substantial budgetary deficits unless the plan advanced were an alternative to other proposals of comparable cost to the Treasury, such as grants-in-aid. There are also other objections to tax credit plans which will be discussed in the ninth chapter.

Summary: The Potential of Voluntary Contributions to I.H.L.

The role of endowments in higher education has shown a long-range decline which is not likely to be reversed. However, gifts for current purposes or buildings maintain a healthy upward trend which may be expected to continue through the 1960's. They may double between 1960 and 1970 and could multiply 2.5 times. Even public I.H.L. are now trying to attract more donations from alumni, corporations, and others. The granting of federal income tax credits for contributions to educational institutions could step up the pace of private giving very considerably.

8 The State Supports — Some

Public colleges and universities depend for three-fourths of the cost of their instructional and general activities (i. e., excluding organized research) and for over four-fifths of capital outlays for academic and general buildings (i. e., excluding residential plant) on appropriations from state and local governments. About ninety per cent of this support comes from the states, the remainder from municipalities for city colleges and from (school or college) districts for junior or community colleges. Except for Pennsylvania, which subsidizes a few private institutions, no state allocates significant amounts of public funds to privately controlled I.H.L.[1]

The citizens of the several states bear a widely differing tax burden for higher education. In North Dakota, for example, the per capita expenditures of state I.H.L. equalled $47.68 in 1963, in Massachusetts $7.84. The explanation is quite simple: 96 per cent of the North Dakota enrollment is in public I.H.L.; 84 per cent of the Massachusetts enrollment is in private I.H.L. A few examples, given in the table below, may illustrate the relationship. The expenditure data include funds derived from other than state taxes but do not include city or other local colleges. But they do

---

[1] A new Maryland program of aid to private colleges has been challenged on constitutional grounds. The case is presently under litigation in the state courts and will probably finally be adjudicated by the United States Supreme Court.

demonstrate how much easier the state tax situation is wherever, for historical, policy, or other reasons, private institutions are a major element in higher education. In 1962–63 Pennsylvania allocated $34.3 million in state appropriations to the state university and colleges and divided $20.8 million among sixteen of the state's 114 private I.H.L. (with three-fourths of the total allocated to the University of Pennsylvania, University of Pittsburgh, and Temple University). With the strong enrollment shift toward public

PER CAPITA EXPENDITURES OF STATE I.H.L. AND PRIVATE
ENROLLMENT PERCENTAGES IN SELECTED STATES

State	Enrollment in Private I.H.L. Fall 1960	Expenditures of State I.H.L. Per Capita of Population Fiscal Year 1963	
		Dollars	Per cent of personal income
U.S. average	41%	$22.52	0.97%
North Dakota	4	47.68	2.07
California	17	38.19	1.37
Michigan	22	35.87	1.51
Minnesota	28	29.90	1.35
Missisippi	19	19.43	1.54
Arkansas	27	18.59	1.26
New York	69	12.57	0.44
Pennsylvania	77	10.42	0.44
Massachusetts	84%	7.84	0.29%

Source: Bureau of the Census, *Compendium of State Government Finances in 1963*, 1964. Office of Education, *Opening (Fall) Enrollment in Higher Education, 1960: Analytic Report*, Circ. 652, 1961.

higher education of the 1950's, which is certain to carry through the 1960's and beyond, the financial demands on state governments have been mounting rapidly and will continue to soar. In response to budgetary requests, state and local government support of public higher education has shown a healthy upward trend. Between 1950 and 1960 it almost tripled in actual dollars and, when adjusted for inflation, multiplied 2.2 times. The crucial question is, of course, whether state and local governments *can* increase their support of higher education at a sufficient rate in the 1960's, and whether they *will* do so.

Do the States Have Sufficient Taxable Capacity?

There is no definite or impartial measurement of fiscal capacity. A staff report to the Advisory Commission on Intergovernmental Relations concluded: "The appraisal of a state's fiscal capacity is a political decision it alone can make; it is not a researchable problem."[2] How much a state can levy in taxes depends on the willingness of its citizens to tax themselves, either in general or for a particular purpose. Many observers of the financial scene, however, have long maintained that the ability of state and local governments to expand their revenues is strictly limited, particularly when compared with the national government. A cursory historical review seems to bear them out: between 1902 and 1964, federal revenues multiplied 185 times, state-local revenues 69 times, and national income 29 times (in *current* dollars). It has been the conventional conclusion that "state and local tax systems are, in some respects, archaic and it is very difficult to keep the revenues from this source growing in step with the economy or with the growing demand for governmental services which an expanding economy creates."[3]

But a closer analysis reveals that federal revenues grew more rapidly than state-local only during shooting wars—that is, between 1916 and 1920, 1940 and 1945, and to a lesser degree, between 1950 and 1952. During the intervening periods, state-local tax collections invariably climbed faster than federal revenues and national income. This has again proved true since the end of World War II:[4]

[2] *Measures of State and Local Fiscal Capacity and Tax Effort, A Staff Report,* Advisory Commission on Intergovernmental Relations, 1962, p. 87.

[3] *The Pursuit of Excellence,* Education and the Future of America, Panel Report V of the Special Studies Project, Rockefeller Brothers Fund (Garden City, N. Y.: Doubleday, 1958), p. 35.

[4] Bureau of the Census, *Historical Statistics on Governmental Finances and Employment,* 1964. Bureau of the Census, *Government Finances in 1963–64,* 1965. Data for 1945 are estimates based on Census Bureau statistics for 1944 and 1946, and the annual *Report of the Secretary of the Treasury.* National income data are from the Department of Commerce, *Survey of Current Business,* July 1964, February 1965, and *National Income,* 1954.

Fiscal Years	Revenues		National Income
	Federal	State-Local	
1945, billions	$ 54	$14	$187
1964, billions	$121	$71	$494
Increase	124%	407%	164%
Increase in constant dollars	22%	173%	44%

* * *

In dollars of constant value, federal revenues have risen 22 per cent since the end of World War II, state-local revenues 173 per cent. This seems to invalidate the argument, to which I referred earlier, that state-local sources grow too slowly. But now the case is being turned around. The Office of Education for example, in a fact sheet attached to legislation proposed for 1965, pointed at the much sharper rate of growth in state-local than in federal receipts to suggest that by their fiscal efforts state and local governments had exhausted their capacity to support education.

Actually, the contrasting trends in war and peace time simply illustrate the basic fact that war inevitably calls for a concentration of the national effort in terms of manpower, materials, and money in the national government, while during peace periods the domestic public services which constitutionally and traditionally are functions of state and local governments expand. So we experience a fiscal centralization in wartime and a decentralization when the country is at peace. During World War II the state-local share in all governmental revenues in the United States fell from 61 per cent to 20 per cent. Since then it has again climbed to 37 per cent (with a temporary relapse during the Korean action). The strength and consistence of this long-range trend suggest that it might well continue; present indications are that it will, at least for several more years.

The federal tax cuts in 1964 and 1965 are likely to be followed by a more rapid expansion of state and local revenues. The Treasury Department estimated that the tax reduction "when fully in effect, would result in the addition of $2.9 billion to the tax revenues of state and local governments. This increase would be over and above the increase in tax revenues which these governments would realize in the absence of federal tax reductions."[5]

---

[5] *Congressional Record*, May 8, 1963, p. 7508.

The most potent restraint on the fiscal capacity of state and local governments is the weight of federal taxation. So, when federal tax rates are lowered, the other governments tend to move in. The last federal tax cut in 1954 was followed by state tax boosts in two-thirds of the states during the succeeding year. Federal tax reduction in 1964 and 1965 could well help repeat this experience in 1965. The majority of governors recommended tax boosts in 1965, and more than half the state legislatures subsequently enacted new or increased taxes.[6] The total could add almost $3 billion to the state tax receipts; the proposed expenditure increases were for education more than for any other service.[7]

Between 1959 and 1963 all but five states raised the rates of at least one of the six major state taxes, and state tax collections climbed from $15.8 to $22.1 billion, or 39 per cent. Then more than half the legislatures meeting in 1963 boosted state taxes by over $1 billion annually, or about 5 per cent.[8] By 1964 state tax collections totalled $24.1 billion. If they continue to expand at their 1959–64 rate they will total more than $41 billion by 1970, an increase of 131 per cent over 1960, and if adjusted for inflation, of 101 per cent. This suggests that state revenues, expressed in *constant* dollars, will double during the 1960's. Some observers, however, have drawn different conclusions from the historical record, as I mentioned earlier. They believe that by their repeated rounds of tax boosts and an extraordinary fiscal effort, state and local governments have exhausted their fiscal capacity and will not be able to expand their revenues much further. States are, it was said, "at the end of their financial ropes."

Does this appear to be sound reasoning? Supposing that state-local governments had only doubled their income instead of more than quadrupling it in the postwar period, or that they had not increased it at all. Would these same observers have concluded that this left state-local governments with a large, unused capacity? Or would they have taken it as proof of their earlier assertions that state-local fiscal capacity was inflexible and that those govern-

---

[6] *Tax Administrators News*, February 1965 p. 1. *State Government*, Winter 1965, p. 6 and Spring 1965, p. 6. *U.S. News & World Report*, July 5, 1965, p. 72.

[7] *Tax Review*, February 1965, p. 5. *State Government*, Spring 1965, p. 73.

[8] *Tax Administrators News*, September 1963, January 1964. *Tax Review*, October 1963.

ments were unable to raise more money under their own power? On closer analysis, their point does not seem to be that state-local governments *cannot* expand their resources, but that it is *undesirable* that they do so. State and local taxes are said to be of an objectionable type, namely, regressive, in contrast to the progressive federal taxes.

Is Increased State Support Desirable?
(State Taxes and the "Class Struggle")

A pamphlet, *The Root of Opposition,* distributed by the National Education Association in 1962, contended that state and local taxes are largely paid by the poor, and federal taxes by the rich, and that suggestions for heavier reliance on state-local tax support of education (rather than federal) were really attempts by rich people to shift their responsibility to the poor. It was "a struggle between people with wealth and people with kids."

This charge relates to the fact that state-local governments depend for revenues largely on sales and property taxes, the national government on individual and corporate income taxes. To be sure, the states were quick in adopting income taxes during the 1930's but, when the federal government raised its income tax rates to near-confiscatory levels during the 1940's, states turned increasingly to other means of raising revenue. The United States at present relies more fully on income taxes and uses sales taxation less than any other industrial country, even if federal-state-local taxes are combined. There are indications that our lopsided tax structure, which is unique in the world, bears a heavy share of the responsibility for our unsatisfactory rate of economic growth. In this volume I cannot deal extensively with the problems of our tax structure and must refer the reader to what I have said elsewhere.[9]

It is now generally recognized that federal personal and corporate income tax rates are too high. In his 1963 Tax Message, President John F. Kennedy declared that "the largest single barrier to full employment of our manpower and resources and to a higher rate of economic growth is the unrealistically heavy drag of federal

---

[9] *Revenue Act of 1963,* Hearings Before the Committee on Finance, U.S. Senate, 88th Congress, 1st S., 1963, Part 3 pp. 1335–97. Roger A. Freeman, *Taxes for the Schools* (Washington, D.C.: The Institute for Social Science Research, 1960), Chapters III through VI.

income taxes on private purchasing power, initiative, and incentive." It is for this reason that Presidents Kennedy and Johnson recommended, and Congress enacted, cuts in federal income tax rates. If the states raised their own income tax rates, they would undo much of the beneficial effect which the federal tax reduction is hoped to produce over the next few years. In view of the federal concentration on—and almost pre-emption of—income taxes, it seems natural that state-local governments focus on other types and thus help provide a better balance in the over-all tax structure.

The claim which I mentioned earlier, that suggestions for greater reliance on state-local support of education are attempts by rich people to shift their responsibility to the poor, is based on a misunderstanding of tax incidence. It exaggerates out of proportion the difference in location of the burden between federal and state-local taxes and, for example, apparently assumes that the corporate income tax is wholly borne by the stockholders. If it were, stockholders would, after federal corporate and individual income taxes, have left between a maximum of 38.4 per cent and a minimum of 4.3 per cent of the profits (1963 rates)—less a few percentage points for state and local corporate and personal income taxes.[10] If that were the case, the American economy would long since have broken down. But there is ample evidence that much or most of the corporate tax is in the long run shifted to consumers in the form of prices. After-tax earnings on net worth were maintained over a period during which the corporate tax rate quadrupled.

That most of the personal income tax rests on the rich was true until a generation ago. But it no longer is, since it turned from a class tax into a mass tax. The bulk of all income in the United States goes to families "in the middle" who cannot escape paying a proportionate share. Taxpayers with an adjusted gross income between $5,000 and $20,000 accounted, in 1962, for 65 per cent of all income and paid 62 per cent of the federal individual income tax. The steeply graduated rate schedule makes for a sharp progression between the upper and lower end of the scale but yields little additional revenue. A flat 20 per cent rate on the reported taxable

[10] Under tax rates effective from 1965 on, stockholders would have left between 14.4 per cent and 41.3 per cent of corporate profits.

income would have brought in 87 per cent of the actual yield. It has been estimated that tax rates over 50 per cent yield less than one billion dollars out of a total yield between $40 and $45 billion annually, and rates over 65 per cent slightly over one-quarter billion (at 1963 rates).

Labor compensation and welfare payments account for a steadily growing share of all personal income; and dividends, business, and professional income for a declining share:

DISTRIBUTION OF PERSONAL INCOME (BEFORE TAXES)
SELECTED YEARS 1929 TO 1964

Year	Labor Income and Transfer Payments	Dividends, Business, and Professional Income	All Other Personal Income
1929	61.1%	17.0%	21.9%
1940	67.5	15.6	16.9
1950	71.4	14.1	14.5
1960	75.9	11.9	12.2
1964	76.2	11.7	12.1
1965 (Jan.—June sea. adj.)	76.4%	11.6%	12.1%

Source: *Economic Indicators,* July 1965, and *1964 Supplement.*

There may be a case in equity against heavy reliance on sales taxation in a country with vast masses of impoverished people. But nowhere else in the world is such a small segment of the population truly poor. The incidence of low-income families has been consistently declining, and the percentage of households with an income under $2,000 (in price-adjusted 1963 dollars) shrank from 30 per cent in 1929 to 16 per cent in 1947, and to 11 per cent in 1963.[11]

About 11 per cent of all personal income in the country accrues to individuals and families in the $25,000-a-year-and-up category and they pay less than one-fourth of the personal income tax. A government that claims 25 per cent of its citizens' income, as the federal government now does, cannot get a major share of its revenue from an upper class that receives 11 per cent of all personal

---

[11] *Survey of Current Business,* April 1964, Table 2. This includes both families and unattached individuals. Only 6.9 per cent of all *families* had an income under $2,000 (same source, Table 5).

income. Only a small share of the federal taxes is paid by the rich, simply because there are not enough of them; and very little of the state and local taxes is paid by the poor. The poor receive much more in various types of welfare payments than they pay in taxes. Most of the taxes in the United States are eventually paid by the great mass in the middle of the income scale.

Since the end of World War II, a growing number of states have been turning to retail sales taxes, and many have been raising their rates or broadening the base of the tax. At this time, sales tax rates are still much lower in the United States than almost anywhere else, and it seems likely that states and cities will expand further in that direction in the years to come.

The argument against state-local fiscal capacity has its roots not so much in economics as in political opportunism. Officeholders and candidates try to avoid any responsibility for raising taxes which might be needed to fulfill their promises to a multitude of claimants for greater public funds. They prefer to shift the onerous task of finding the money to the federal level, where it is possible to increase expenditures and cut taxes at the same time by the simple expedient of letting the budgetary deficit and the national debt rise to higher levels.

Will States Continue to Increase the Support of Higher Education?

The record of school finance during the 1950's is full of gloomy predictions that even some of the wealthiest states would fail to meet their essential educational needs. For example, the executive secretary of the California Teachers Association, Arthur F. Corey, testified before the House Education Committee on May 3, 1955:

> From all sources something over a billion dollars must be spent on school buildings in California by 1960. How much of this can be carried by the local districts depends on factors which are almost impossible to estimate with any accuracy. Suffice it to say that even the alleged fabulous wealth of California will be unequal to the responsibilities placed upon it.[12]

A table Mr. Corey submitted showed that in the succeeding five years, 22,444 additional classrooms would be needed to meet expected needs. As it happened, somewhat over $2 billion was spent

---

[12] *Federal Aid to States for School Construction,* Hearings before the Committee on Education and Labor, H.R., 84th Congress, 1st S., 1955, Part 3, p. 818.

for school buildings in California between 1955 and 1960, and the number of classrooms increased by 43,000. In other words, twice as much was accomplished as was considered necessary and held to be an impossibly big task.

California, the state with the biggest enrollment increase by far of all the states, has since drawn up a Master Plan for Higher Education, which envisages more than a million students in its colleges and universities by 1975, with close to ninety per cent enrolled in public institutions. The official state committee which prepared the plan concluded: "California can and will, as in both the past and the present, provide adequate support for an efficient program of public higher education designed to meet fully the rapidly changing needs of society."[13] The plan was adopted by the California legislature and is now in the process of being carried out.[14]

At least forty states have in recent years explored the growing needs and problems of higher education through state-wide committees created by the governor or the legislature. Selma J. Mushkin summarized, in the Office of Education's report, *Economics of Higher Education*,[15] that "each of the state study groups concludes that their state can afford to finance an enlarged public program of higher education."

Only a few years ago some of our fiscal experts who projected higher educational finances viewed the future of state support with pessimism. Wrote Richard A. Musgrave, then of Johns Hopkins University (now at Princeton University):

> The gain in receipts from state and local governments, on the other hand, will surely be less than would be required to maintain their current share. The same revenue sources which in 1957–58 financed a contribution of $1.2 billion may be expected to yield $1.7 billion by 1969–70, reflecting the growth of the economy and resulting increase in tax base. However, maintenance of the 1957–58 share would require a total of $3.4 billion, thus calling for a significant

---

[13] *A Master Plan for Higher Education in California 1960–1975*, California State Department of Education, 1960, p. 196; also *California's Ability to Finance Higher Education, 1960–75*, 1961, summarized in Joseph O. McClintic, "California's Ability to Finance Higher Education," *National Tax Journal*, June 1962.

[14] Ben Hibbs, "California Builds Big for Education," *The Reader's Digest*, July 1963.

[15] *Bulletin*, 962, No. 5, pp. 243–44.

increase in revenue sources. Given the heavy demands on state and local finances for other purposes, education at lower levels in particular, it seems most unlikely that this total will be forthcoming. A total of $2 billion would seem to be the maximum allowable in a realistic estimate.[16]

This was written in 1959. In 1963, state and local governments contributed over $2 billion to the current operations of I.H.L. and, if current trends continue, they will by 1970 provide about $3.5 billion, and quite possibly more. The earlier underestimates may not be unrelated to the fact that Professor Musgrave and other authors in this field favor federal over state financing. In contrast, I must admit to a preference for the state financing of state I.H.L. This suggests that I must particularly guard against letting my judgment of what is *likely* to happen be swayed by what I would *like* to see happen.

The major factors controlling the size of state funds for I.H.L. are the magnitude of state revenues and the proportion that will be allocated to higher education. That the tax receipts of state governments have been showing a strong and continuing upward trend, I showed earlier. That the share devoted to higher education also is consistently growing, is apparent from the following table:

STATE TAX COLLECTIONS AND CURRENT FUNDS DISTRIBUTED TO I.H.L. SELECTED YEARS 1940 TO 1962

Year	State Tax Collections	Current I.H.L. Funds from State Governments	State I.H.L. Funds as Percentage of Tax Collections
	Million	Million	
1940	$ 3,313	$ 154	4.6%
1950	7,930	500	6.3
1960	18,036	1,389	7.7
1962	20,561	1,689	8.2%

Source: Bureau of the Census, *Historical Statistics on Governmental Finances and Employment*, 1964, Table 5. Office of Education, *Financial Statistics of Institutions of Higher Education, 1959–60*, 1964, Table 2. Office of Education, *Digest of Educational Statistics*, 1964 edition, Table 79.

16 Richard A. Musgrave, "Higher Education and the Federal Budget," in *Higher Education in the United States: The Economic Problems*, ed. Seymour E. Harris (Harvard University Press, 1960), p. 98.

In 1962, state funds for the current purposes of I.H.L. equalled 8.2 per cent of state tax receipts, not including capital outlays which would add at least another two percentage points, nor counting local government support, which would increase the total by one-ninth.

There is every likelihood that the percentage of state tax receipts channeled into higher education will continue to go up. The three major claimants on state funds, which account for at least four-fifths of the total, are: education, welfare, and highways. Highways are in almost all states financed from special highway user taxes and seldom compete with education for general state revenues. Public welfare has been absorbing a declining share of state resources. Public assistance payments from state funds equalled: 15.4 per cent of state tax receipts in 1940, 13.4 per cent in 1950, 7.5 per cent in 1960, and 6.6 per cent in 1964. The Public Welfare Amendments of 1962, though substantially increasing public assistance outlays in the long run, shifted a greater share to the federal government whose percentage of the total cost has steadily climbed, from 26 per cent in 1940 to 45 per cent in 1950 and to 56 per cent in 1964.[17] The state share is almost certain to keep shrinking.

The public schools have been the major competitors of I.H.L. for the state tax dollar, with higher education gradually gaining. In 1954, the schools received 2.36 times as much as state I.H.L. expended. Ever since, the ratio has been declining, to 1:2.05 in 1958, and to 1:1.61 in 1964.[18] That this trend will continue appears almost certain. Enrollment in the public schools grew 43 per cent between 1953 and 1963 and is projected to rise only 15 per cent between 1963 and 1973. During the balance of the 1960's, the annual growth rate of the public schools will drop to one-third of what it had been in the preceding ten years. But enrollment at I.H.L. will expand substantially in the second half of the 1960's. Under those circumstances, legislatures most certainly will boost appropriations for I.H.L. at a faster rate than for public schools.

---

[17] Computed from: *Indicators*, July 1965, Department of Health, Education, and Welfare, Table S–23 and Census Bureau reports cited in footnote 4.

[18] Computed from: Bureau of the Census, *Compendium of State Government Finances in 1954*, 1955; *Compendium of State Government Finances in 1964*, 1965.

With their enrollments expanding at a slow rate, schools can be expected to become less dependent on state support than they were during the past fifteen years when they obtained, in the national average, a steady 39 per cent of their revenues from state appropriations.

Can the property tax be expected to carry a greater share of the cost of the public schools and community colleges? The property tax has long been maligned as being stagnant and not expanding with general economic growth. But nothing could be further from the truth. Over the past ten years, collections increased: property taxes, 114 per cent; all other taxes combined, 49 per cent.[19] Even in the state-local picture, property taxes grew at a more rapid rate than the aggregate of income, sales, and other taxes.

Most of the increase in property tax receipts came from a growth in tangible wealth. The 1962 Census of Governments made some interesting comparisons possible with developments since the 1957 Census: the sales or market value of all locally assessed taxable real estate increased 40 per cent over the five-year period during which national income grew only 21 per cent.[20] The growth was due largely to the addition of almost $200 billion in new private construction and rising land values. The homeowner understandably is often appalled at the size of his local tax bill. He seldom stops to realize that, on the average, he offsets at least two-thirds of it on his federal and state income tax through the deductibility of the property tax and mortgage interest and the nontaxability of the return on his equity.[21]

The trend of rising property tax receipts does not appear to be ending. Collections in calendar year 1964 increased seven per cent over 1963.[22] Considering the trend shown in the table on page 127, it is difficult to avoid the conclusion that current state funds for I.H.L. will equal at least nine per cent of state tax receipts by 1970, and probably more. If state taxes then totalled $41 billion,

19 Computed from: Bureau of the Census, *Historical Statistics on Governmental Finances and Employment,* 1964, Table 2, and Bureau of the Census, *Governmental Finances in 1963,* Table 1.

20 Computed from: Bureau of the Census, *Taxable Property Values, 1962 Census of Governments,* 1963; same publication: *1957 Census of Governments.*

21 For details see: Roger A. Freeman, *Taxes for the Schools, Appendix D.* "Income Tax Relief for the Homeowner."

22 Bureau of the Census, *Quarterly Summary of State and Local Tax Revenue, October-December 1964,* March 1965.

as I estimated earlier, the institutions would receive at least $3.7 billion from state governments, and about $4 billion from state and local governments combined.

How realistic is this prospect? What is the situation in the states as of 1965? Recent developments permit much optimism. A summary of the governors' legislative messages in 1963 concluded:

> Education received far more attention in the messages than any other public service. . . . Virtually all the messages recommended record appropriations for state higher educational institutions. Proposals for increased faculty salaries were specific in a number of them, and large provisions for campus construction were widespread.[23]

A summary of state budgets submitted in 1963 concluded:

> The upward movement in state expenditures is distributed among all functions, but educational costs remain the principal factor raising budgetary levels. In recent years, appropriations for education, which account for about a third of state spending, have risen a tenth annually. The shift in school enrollments toward college-age brackets has increased appropriations for higher education at a somewhat faster rate than aid to public schools.[24]

Between the fiscal years 1960 and 1962, state funds for the current purposes of I.H.L. rose 21 per cent. An inquiry about action at the 1963 legislative sessions brought responses from all but five state budget offices which may be summarized as follows: States on a *biennial* budget basis raised current appropriations for higher education 23.5 per cent between 1961–63 and 1963–65. States which budget *annually* increased appropriations 28.5 per cent between 1962 and 1964, and 29.4 per cent between 1963 and 1965. A combination of these data suggests a two-year increase for all states of 26.3 per cent.

This closely agrees with findings in two surveys that Professor M. M. Chambers of the University of Michigan conducted for the

[23] "Trends of State Government in 1963 as indicated by the Governors' Messages," *State Government,* Spring 1963.

[24] Leon Rothenberg, "State Budgets—1963," *State Government,* Spring 1963.

[25] M. M. Chambers, *Appropriations of State Tax Funds for Operating Expenses of Higher Education 1963–1964,* Joint Office of Institutional Research, Washington, 1963; same report for 1964–65. See also: "More Money—More Needed," *The New York Times,* December 15, 1963; "College Money," *U.S. News and World Report,* December 23, 1963.

Joint Office of Institutional Research in the fall of 1963 and 1964.[25]
Actual expenditure data for the 1933–65 biennium are not available
at this writing—and will not be available for some time—but the
state budgets submitted in January 1965 indicate that the upward
trend continues unabated, as I mentioned before. A biennial rise
of 26.3 per cent corresponds to a decennial increase of 221 per cent
and, when adjusted for an annual 1.5 per cent loss in the value of
the dollar, of 177 per cent. This suggests that if present trends
continue, state funds for the current operations of I.H.L. will rise
from $1.4 billion in 1959–60 to $3.8 billion (1960 $) in 1969–70.

In relation to the Gross National Product, current state funds
for higher education rose from 0.19 per cent in 1950 to 0.28 per cent
in 1960, and to 0.31 per cent in 1962. A ratio of 0.40 per cent or
0.45 per cent would appear reasonable by 1970. This would suggest
a total of between $2.8 and $3.4 billion, depending on the growth
of the economy. When we consider the various methods of projection and try to form a composite judgment, we may well arrive
at the conclusion that current state support of higher education
will be in the neighborhood of $3.5 billion (1960 $) by 1969–70,
and could be higher.

Construction Funds and Bonds

Statistics on higher educational construction by the Office of
Education are several years behind, but reports of the Bureau of
the Census enable us to follow the progress in recent years. Capital
outlays at state I.H.L. multiplied 5.2 times between 1954 and 1964.

CAPITAL OUTLAYS IN STATE I.H.L. IN EVEN YEARS 1954 TO 1964

| | | As Percentage of | | |
Year	In Millions	All New Construction in U.S.A.	State Tax Collections	G.N.P.
1954	$ 243	0.6%	2.2%	0.07%
1956	380	0.8	2.8	0.09
1958	598	1.2	4.0	0.14
1960	675	1.2	3.7	0.14
1962	854	1.5	4.2	0.16
1964	$1,260	2.0%	5.2%	0.21%

Source: Bureau of the Census, *Compendium of State Government Finances in 1954;
1956; 1958; 1960; 1962; 1964. Construction Review,* October 1963, March and
August 1964, February 1965.

Even when adjusted for the rise of construction prices, they more than quadrupled during the ten-year period (increase in constant $: 312 per cent).

It is apparent that construction at state I.H.L. has been rapidly growing not only in absolute terms, but also relative to other measures such as total construction in the United States, state tax collections, or Gross National Product. If building at state I.H.L. were only to maintain its ratio to those aggregates, it would total about $1.5 billion by 1970. In 1960, state institutions accounted for 57 per cent of building at all I.H.L. Assuming that, by 1970, that ratio will stand at least at 60 per cent (because of the relatively heavier enrollment growth in public I.H.L.), all building in higher education would amount to about $2.5 billion. It could be slightly less if efforts to eliminate waste and improve space utilization on U.S. campuses are successful in the second half of the 1960's.

The prospect that public I.H.L. will be able to obtain the necessary funds and authorizations to construct about $1.5 billion worth of facilities annually by 1970 appears good. It seems reasonable to assume that the effort for public higher educational construction will not diminish during a major enrollment increase which, in terms of numbers, is unprecedented. The past record suggests that efforts will increase. Moreover, a decline in the need for building public schools will leave more leeway for constructing academic facilities at I.H.L.

The building needs of public elementary and secondary schools during the 1960's were estimated at 600,000 classrooms in the President's education messages in 1961 and 1962. During the first four years of the decade, construction proceeded at the rate of 70,000 classrooms per year. With annual enrollment increases expected to drop to half their former size, it appears certain that public school construction will soon fall to between 50,000 and 55,000 classrooms a year or less. (Replacement needs are low because more than half the present school plant is of recent date, having been built since the end of World War II.) A cut in annual public school construction by 15,000 to 20,000 classrooms means a saving—in current funds or in borrowing—between $500 and $800 million a year. Part of this could certainly be used for I.H.L.

Methods of financing state I.H.L. vary widely. Some states appropriate funds annually from current revenues. Others issue state bonds, either redeemable from general revenues or with specified tax revenues earmarked for the annual debt service. In some states, such as Georgia or Pennsylvania, a state authority builds the facilities from the proceeds of its bonds which are redeemed from annual state appropriations. In Louisiana, the state earmarks certain taxes and other university income for the redemption of improvement bonds, which do not require approval by the voters. And in many other states the legislature may authorize the university or college board of trustees (generally or in specific cases) to issue its own bonds and retire them from future tuitions or other receipts. The New York legislature raised tuitions in 1962–63 for the service of bonds to be issued through a State University Construction Fund.

Bonds play an important part in the financing of public higher educational construction. The aggregate volume of state and local debt financing has been sharply increasing, and some observers have expressed the concern that it may sooner or later bump against a ceiling in the market or in voter acceptance. Sales of state and local securities averaged $5.7 billion annually during the 1950's, hit $7.2 billion in 1960, $8.7 billion in 1962, and soared to a record $10.6 billion in 1964, with the uptrend continuing in 1965.

Voters showed no resistance to bonds in 1964 and approved 78 per cent of the amounts submitted to them. Moreover, there is a vast backlog because almost half of the state and local bonds approved at elections since 1956, for a total of $17 billion, were not yet sold at the end of 1964. State and local indebtedness jumped from $24 billion in 1950 to $70 billion in 1960, and reached $92 billion at the close of the fiscal year 1964. It is likely to exceed the $100 billion mark sometime in 1965 and will thus have multiplied more than six times since 1946.

There certainly is no sign of voter resistance to bonds for college and university construction. The citizens of California approved a $270 million issue in November 1962 (of which at least 80 per cent is to be used for I.H.L.), and a year later the residents of Ohio approved $175 million, those of Florida $75 million, in bonds for the construction of I.H.L. The rejection of a college bond issue is a rare event, while most votes have been showing thumping majorities favoring the issue. In fact, 90 per cent of all state and local bonds on the ballot in November 1963 were approved, if we disregard a New Jersey proposal which had little economic justification and heavy political overtones. In November 1964 more than $2 billion in bonds were authorized by the voters and the failure of some issues seems to have been related to local controversies. Nor does the bond market, which offers a sensitive and usually reliable yardstick, seem to regard state and local debt to be overextended. The prices of state-local bonds have held up well, and yields as computed by Standard & Poor's have *declined* in relation to those on Federal securities:

AVERAGE YIELD OF HIGH GRADE MUNICIPAL BONDS AS A PERCENTAGE OF
THE YIELD ON FEDERAL TAXABLE BONDS, 1959–1965

(Annual Averages)

1959	96.8%
1960	92.8
1961	88.7
1962	80.5
1963	81.0
1964	77.6
1965 (Jan.–June)	76.2%

Source: *Economic Indicators*, July 1965.

Help for the Low-Income States?

States differ in their economic circumstances and capacity to support public services. Those in the lower per capita income categories sometimes find it more difficult to meet their educational requirements than the wealthier states. But there are some offsetting factors. Per capita income has been growing more rapidly in the poorer states and the range among the states has been shrinking. For example, the ratio in per capita income between New York and Mississippi declined from 1:4.0 in 1940 to 1:2.4 in 1960 and to 1:2.2 in 1964. Measured in "disposable" income the ratio stood at 1:2.0 in 1964. Mississippi's per capita income equalled 37 per cent of the U.S. average in 1940; by 1964 it had advanced to 57 per cent and there is no sign that this trend is about to end.

Most of the increases in school enrollment occurred in the higher income states, largely because of the massive and continued migration from poorer to more prosperous areas. Projections indicate that most of the enrollment increase in higher education will also take place in the states with above-average economic and fiscal capacity. Moreover, differences in per capita income do not necessarily reflect a proportionate difference in ability to finance education. Wage and salary levels, prevailing living standards, and the cost of building facilities differ among states and between metropolitan, small town, and rural areas, which tends to reduce the effect of dollar differentials. The progressive federal tax system also helps to shrink the difference in resources available for state and local taxes. On the average, progress in meeting educational needs has been more rapid in low-income states. But they do undeniably have a more difficult problem than the wealthier states.

Various proposals have been advanced for distributing a small share of federal tax collections to the states, with relatively larger amounts going to low-income states. I suggested such a system of fiscal grants to the Joint Economic Committee in 1957[26] and later pointed at a similar program initiated in Great Britain.[27] The (then) chairman of the Council of Economics Advisers, Walter Heller, recommended a program of that type in 1964 but failed to find adequate support for it. Still, if it is felt that some states, or all states, lack adequate fiscal capacity to support their essential public services, including education, a redistribution of federally collected taxes under some such plan would be an effective way of meeting the problem.

Summary: The Outlook for State Support Is Bright

State and local government support of higher education has been steadily increasing, and a continued upward trend has been strongly in evidence in the first half of the 1960's which, by all indications, should persist throughout the decade and beyond. The rate of growth in state-local funds for the current operations of I.H.L. equalled 123 per cent (in *constant* dollars) during the 1950's and is not likely to be lower between 1960 and 1970. It could run as high as 150 per cent. Current state and local support of higher education would then total $3.5 billion or more in 1970, construction at public I.H.L. close to $1.5 billion. State and local

---

[26] *Federal Expenditure Policy for Economic Growth and Stability,* Papers submitted by panelists, 85th Congress, 1st S., 1957. pp. 1100ff., Hearings, p. 587ff.
[27] Roger A. Freeman, "Grants Without Strings," *National Civic Review,* June 1959.

tax rates were boosted many times during the postwar period, largely for the benefit of education, and more such tax increases may be expected in the years immediately ahead, following the federal income tax cut of 1964. The share of state funds allocated to higher education is likely to keep growing.

An increase in state support of 125 per cent between 1960 and 1970 would approximately parallel the rate of enrollment growth in public I.H.L. Earlier—in Chapter 2—I estimated that higher educational enrollment would almost double during the 1960's. But the ever-widening discrepancy in the size of tuitions is causing a drastic shift from private to public higher education. The number of students may climb less than 50 per cent in private I.H.L. but is likely to jump 125 per cent in public I.H.L. State and municipal colleges accounted for half of all higher educational enrollment in 1950, but will be called upon to carry at least 70 per cent of the load by 1970, and 80 per cent by 1980 or earlier if present tuition policies continue without a significant change.

If enrollment and state appropriations at public I.H.L. were to rise at approximately the same rate—about 125 per cent on a decennial basis—salary increases and expansion of services would have to be financed either through savings by greater efficiency of operations or through substantial boosts in tuitions and fees. Some have suggested federal support for college instruction as an alternative. This will be discussed in the next chapter.

The shift in responsibility from individuals and families to government and the resulting disproportionate rise in the cost of public higher education may strain the willingness of taxpayers to approve a rate of growth in appropriations which materially exceeds enrollment expansion. It is conceivable that state legislatures and voters could become tired of ever-higher taxes and appropriations. There certainly is a good possibility that legislative committees will closely scrutinize all requests for enlarged funds, whether from education or from other claimants—particularly when they call for higher taxes or bond issues. It will not become easier to have legislatures approve increases in appropriations of ten per cent or more each year, and the institutions will have to present conclusive evidence that the added funds are essential and cannot be secured from other sources. The public and the legislators may insist that I.H.L. give evidence of more efficient use of available resources. A continuation and spreading of such student riots as took place in the latter part of 1964 could also have an adverse effect on the willingness of legislators to increase appropriations. But there is no reason to doubt that higher education will in the future, as it did in the past, receive a sympathetic hearing from state and local governments.

9 Uncle Sam to the Rescue?

In his address opening the finance session of the White House Conference on Education on November 30, 1955, Lieutenant Governor Frank C. Moore remarked that the conference participants could be divided into two groups: those who feared that they would not have an opportunity to discuss federal aid and those who feared that they would not have an opportunity to discuss anything else. This turned out to be a cogent observation, at the time.

At the succeeding White House Conference on Education in July 1965 it was amply evident that the first group no longer had anything to fear and the second group was conspicuous by its absence, not having been invited. Nowadays, discussions of problems in education invariably focus on federal action, serve as a vehicle for featuring it, or lead up to it on a more or less circuitous route. Discussants at professional meetings or in the educational literature no longer consider whether federal aid is necessary or desirable but concentrate on the practical task at hand: how to get more of it.

It has been said time and again that the question whether we ought to have federal aid to education comes far too late, that we have long had it in large amounts, and that the only appropriate subject for discussion at this time is how much of it we should

139

have and in what form. Opposition to federal aid has been called "as unrealistic as a moral assault on the multiplication tables."

Presidential Assistant McGeorge Bundy, a former Harvard dean, complained that "too many of us are acting as if federal participation in the higher learning were still an uncertain experiment, instead of the stable and growing reality which it is . . . generalized hostility to federal money is as senseless as titlting at a windmill. The windmill is here to stay, and it is no man's enemy."[1] Based on the premise that the principle has long been established, hundreds of proposals were advanced in recent years which aimed to increase the number and type of federal educational programs, with amounts ranging from a few million dollars to several billions. The National Science Foundation's deputy director, John T. Wilson, commented early in 1963 that it seems obvious "that the future will see an even greater involvement of the federal government in higher education than has been the case heretofore."[2] Actions of the 88th and 89th Congresses appear to confirm this forecast.

How Much Federal Aid Does Higher Education Now Get?

Everything in this area is controversial, and even the actual magnitude of federal spending for education is more a matter of definition and personal opinion than of record. The budget which the President submitted in January 1963 showed actual expenditures for education in the fiscal year 1962 at $1.1 billion, the House Education and Labor Committee a few months later reported them at $2.2 billion,[3] while the Legislative Reference Service of the Library of Congress earlier had listed 440 federal educational activities costing at least $3.8 billion.[4]

A compilation by the U.S. Office of Education estimated federal appropriations for education in the fiscal year 1965 at $4.9

---

[1] McGeorge Bundy, "Of Winds and Windmills: Free Universities and Public Policy," in *Higher Education and the Federal Government, Programs and Problems,* ed. Charles G. Dobbins, American Council on Education, 1963, p. 94.

[2] John T. Wilson, "Higher Education and the Washington Scene: 1963," *The Educational Record,* April 1963.

[3] *The Federal Government and Education,* Committee on Education and Labor, H.R., 88th Congress, 1st S., 1963, p. 115.

[4] *Federal Educational Policies, Programs, and Proposals,* prepared in the Legislative Reference Service of the Library of Congress by Charles A. Quattlebaum, Committee on Education and Labor, H.R., 86th Congress, 2d S., 1960.

billion, but the President's budget simultaneously listed them at
$1.5 billion.[5] If we think that we have difficulty analyzing Soviet
statistics on educational outlays when we try to compare them
with ours, then we ought to sympathize with Soviet economists
who attempt to derive correct and meaningful data from our official
documents.

Several reports have stated that the federal government now
underwrites nearly half the budget of some of our largest universities. But the head of the College and University Administration
Branch in the Office of Education, Ernest V. Hollis, asserted in
1962,

> that to date the federal government has done very little to strenth-
> en or otherwise genuinely aid our more than 2,000 public and pri-
> vate higher education institutions. With the further exception of
> the transfer of government surplus property and extending the
> benefits of federal borrowing power through the College Housing
> Loan Program, federal money has done little more than purchase
> research and training services its agencies needed and aid indi-
> viduals to attend college.[6]

The person seeking information is inevitably confused by such
conflicting statements. It may help him little to learn that the
discrepancies are caused by differing views and definitions of what
is "education" and what is "federal aid."

To its alumni who were surprised to learn that nearly half of
Princeton University's income comes from the federal government, President Robert F. Goheen explained that virtually all was
"payments in support of particular research or training undertakings," that 69 per cent of the federal funds go into the development and operation of three major research areas in the Forrestal
Research Center: the Plasma Physics Laboratory, the Princeton-
Pennsylvania Accelerator, and Aeronautical Engineering. Another
29 per cent carries other research programs and the remaining
2 per cent are for R.O.T.C., graduate fellowships, tuition payments

[5] Office of Education, *Federal Funds for Education: Estimated Appropriations by Agency for Fiscal Year 1965*, mimeo.
   The Budget of the U.S. Government, fiscal year ending June 30, 1966, Part 1, p. 124.
[6] Ernest V. Hollis in: *Proceedings of the Fifty-Fifth Annual Conference on Taxation*, National Tax Association, 1963, p. 486.

for military officers, etc. "Except for the student loan funds, the entirety of these receipts is for specific services received."[7] Almost no federal funds are available for undergraduate instruction.

Researchers who reviewed the record in recent years and analyzed federal educational programs concluded that "what is often described under the heading of federal aid, either present or proposed, is not aid but either payment for services rendered or aid to individuals" (President David D. Henry of the University of Illinois),[8] that "legislation affecting higher education has been a by-product of some other well established concern, such as agriculture, or public health, or the disposal of public lands or military needs" (Alice M. Rivlin of the Brookings Institution),[9] and that "major federal programs in higher educations have seldom been passed for the sake of higher education" (Congressman John Brademas).[10] The Commission on Intergovernmental Relations found that "most federal activities in support of education have been incidental to other national objectives,"[11] and President Lee A. DuBridge of the California Institute of Technology concluded that "almost no federal support is given to the regular tasks of undergraduate education other than certain limited funds available for the purchase of scientific laboratory equipment."[12] The fact is that no program for the *general* support of common schools or of higher education from federal funds has ever been enacted, and the aim of the continuing fight, in the words of one of its spokesmen in Congress, is to "place on the statute books the *principle* of general federal aid to education" (emphasis supplied).[13]

The history of many programs relating to education bears out

---

[7] Robert F. Goheen, "Federal Financing and Princeton University," *Princeton Alumni Weekly*, April 19, 1963.

[8] David D. Henry, "The Role of the Federal Government in Higher Education," *The Educational Record*, July 1959.

[9] Alice M. Rivlin, *The Role of the Federal Government in Financing Education*, The Brookings Institution, 1961, p. 118.

[10] John Brademas, "Higher Education and the 87th Congress," *Higher Education*, April 1961.

[11] *The Commission on Intergovernmental Relations*, A Report to the President for Transmittal to the Congress, 1955, p. 186.

[12] Lee A. DuBridge, "Private Higher Education," *Engineering and Science*, January 1964.

[13] *Congressional Record*, May 22, 1961, p. 7958, also p. 7964; also September 11, 1961, p. 17803. That principle may have been established by the 1965 school aid bill. Views differ though on whether it constitutes general support.

Representative Brademas' statement that federal programs are seldom passed for the sake of higher education. Even so, many of the programs faced much resistance. The Morrill Act authorizing land grants to the states for colleges for the agriculture and mechanic arts, passed by Congress in 1859, was vetoed by President James Buchanan for reasons which, with one exception, still constitute main objections to federal aid to education a hundred years later: (1) the U.S. Treasury is running a deficit. (2) To subvent states will unduly centralize power in the national government. (3) It will lead to land speculation. (4) It will not accomplish its objectives. (5) It will interfere with colleges not benefited by the program. (6) Education is not among the constitutional powers of the federal government.[14]

But federal aid to higher education has, and long has had, its firm advocates. Today their case is largely based on the proposition that I.H.L. need far larger funds than they are now getting and that the money is not likely to be forthcoming from any source save the national government. The idea is not new. More than half a century before the passage of the Morrill Act, George Washington mentioned the possibility of a national university in his first annual report to the Congress. Thomas Jefferson suggested, in his sixth annual message on December 2, 1806, to apply to public education and public improvements some of the surplus which he expected to accumulate in the Treasury (the Treasury did indeed produce a surplus in each year except one between 1800 and 1811). He added: "I suppose an amendment to the Constitution by consent of the states, necessary, because the objects now recommended are not among those enumerated in the Constitution, and to which it permits public moneys to be applied."[15]

No such amendment was ever seriously considered although educational appropriations were approved by Congress in later years. Like some other major changes of the U.S. Constitution, this change was brought about without going through the cumbersome process of formal amendment. President Franklin D. Roosevelt remarked in the 1930's that the Constitution "is so simple and

---

[14] James D. Richardson, *A Compilation of the Messages and Papers of the Presidents*, Bureau of National Literature, New York, 1897, Vol. VII, pp. 3074–81.

[15] Saul K. Padover, *The Complete Jefferson* (New York: Duell, Sloan and Pearce, 1943), pp. 425–26.

practical that it is possible always to meet extraordinary needs by changes in emphasis and arrangements." The matter was never adjudicated, but subsequent decisions of the U.S. Supreme Court on related matters indicate beyond doubt that the Court would uphold the appropriation of federal funds for educational purposes if it were ever questioned.

Three years after the Buchanan veto, during the Civil War, Congress approved and President Lincoln signed the Morrill Act. It was changed from land grants to a cash program in 1890 and now distributes $14.5 million annually among sixty-eight institutions. As of 1965 it still is *the only federal grant* which can be spent by I.H.L. for their *general operating purposes, according to their own discretion with but few restrictions.*

Research Funds for Higher Education

By far the largest and fastest growing amounts of federal money for I.H.L. are awarded in the form of research contracts and grants. Those funds were of insignificant size prior to World War II, totalled less than $200 million in 1950, and have shown an explosive growth in recent years. A subcommittee of the House Education Committee listed federal research funds for I.H.L. in 1962 at $613 million. The National Science Foundation, using a broader concept of research and development, reported far larger sums for the last three fiscal years: $1,358 million in 1962, $1,633 million in 1963, and $1,961 million in 1964.[16] One study projected all organized research outlays at I.H.L. to climb from $1.2 billion in 1960 to $4 billion or more in 1970, with close to three-fourths of the funds coming from the federal government.[17]

Most of the projects are in the natural and life sciences, and are conducted on behalf of the Department of Defense, Atomic Energy Commission, National Aeronautics and Space Administration, and the National Institutes of Health. I.H.L. account for 12 per cent of all federal research and development outlays, industrial and commercial organizations for 65 per cent, and the remaining 23 per cent of the work is carried out by the professional staffs of federal agencies directly.

---

[16] *Federal Funds for Research, Development and Other Scientific Activities,* Fiscal Years 1962, 1963, and 1964, National Science Foundation, Table C-1.

[17] Herbert H. Rosenberg, "Research and the Financing of Higher Education," *Higher Education,* October–November 1961.

Research grants to higher education are highly concentrated. "Of all funds for research in fiscal year 1960, 68 per cent went to 25 universities, 82 per cent went to 50, and 94 per cent went to 100."[18] Within the institutions, grants were highly concentrated in a few departments and, within the departments, on a few projects. In some of our largest and best-known institutions, federal funds now account for close to (or even more than) half their total income, as for example:[19]

California Institute of Technology	48%
Stanford University	47
University of California at San Diego	76
Massachusetts Institute of Technology	43
Princeton University	42%

The Carnegie Foundation report from which these data were taken and a simultaneous Brookings Institution study[20] reported that the institutions they investigated regard the grants to be "highly beneficial." Federal funds enabled university departments to hire many outstanding scientists, boost their salaries, attract and support talented graduate students, vastly expand the scope of operations and experimentation and, on the whole, raise themselves to higher levels in the subject fields of the projects.

Some of the ill effects of the research funds have been in the field of teaching. President Clark Kerr of the University of California complained:

> Federal project funds are increasingly being used to bid salaries and allowances up and bid teaching assignments down. How much further such competition can go without raising grave policy problems for federal agencies is problematical. The market is sufficiently active without this added inflationary stimulus and the universities are sufficiently in trouble with internal inequities and reduction of teaching time.[21]

Coming from the head of an institution which can and does outbid most others, this is a remarkably frank statement. The

---

18 *A Survey of Federal Programs in Higher Education,* by J. Kenneth Little, Office of Education, Bulletin 1963, No. 5, p. 7.

19 "Twenty-six Campuses and the Federal Government," *Fifty-Eighth Annual Report,* Carnegie Foundation for the Advancement of Teaching, 1962–63, Table 3.

20 Harold Orlans, *The Effect of Federal Programs on Higher Education,* The Brookings Institution, 1963.

21 Clark Kerr, "The Realities of the Federal Grant University," *The Educational Record,* April 1963.

"projectitis" which has infected faculties all over the country has downgraded teaching, made it a less-respected and much-avoided assignment, and widened the cleavage between the status and rewards of the faculties in the sciences and in the humanities. It has turned the classroom into a place where the outstanding scholar—except in the humanities—is found with growing infrequency. Students complain that they can talk to the "jet set professor" only on his way to or from the airport. This "flight from teaching" may soon precipitate a faculty crisis, warned John W. Gardner in his 1964 presidential report to the Carnegie Foundation for the Advancement of Teaching.

Commenting editorially on the mentioned Brookings report, the *New York Times* concluded that "the enormous extent of governmental subsidies for scientific research may be seriously weakening the teaching of science in American universities and colleges, and thus in some ways damaging the nation's future scientific prospects."[22] One mathematics department head was quoted as saying:

> As far as the average undergraduate is concerned, the well-qualified professor is nearly extinct. . . . He may be in the laboratory or the library doing research, in Washington advising the government, or giving guest lectures elsewhere . . . and, as a result, spending only a small part of his time with his own students.[23]

The fact that almost all federal research money is concentrated among five per cent of all I.H.L. does not mean that it has had no impact on the other ninety-five per cent of the institutions which, of last account, shared among themselves no more than six per cent of the total funds. The Brookings study found:

> The direct effects of the federal programs have been profound and beneficial in the sciences, noticeably more imbalanced in the social sciences, and negligible in the humanities. Federal programs have *not* notably affected the relative proportion or quality of faculty or students going into the sciences, but *have* concentrated a large number of faculty and many of the best students at a few leading institutions.[24]

---

[22] "Damage to Science Teaching," *The New York Times,* January 3, 1964, commenting on: Harold Orlans, "Federal Expenditures and the Quality of Education," *Science,* December 27, 1963.

[23] John G. Kenney, "Once a Professor was a Teacher . . . ," *New York Times Magazine,* June 2, 1963.

[24] Harold Orlans, p. 293.

Federal research and development funds are highly concentrated in a few states and in 1963, for example, California received 38.4 per cent, New York 9.2 per cent, Massachusetts 4.6 per cent, and together these three states received over half the federal research and development money. That Midwestern institutions feel unhappy about this situation is not surprising and President Elvis Stahr of Indiana University complained that "the result of current federal policy has been almost inevitably a brain drain on most areas."[25] The resulting departmental, institutional, and geographical imbalances are causing growing concern. Arthur F. Engelbert, dean of the college at Washburn University, wrote that

> present grant and contract practices are creating a serious manpower situation in colleges and universities. This is true, first of all, in the relatively few institutions blessed with generous federal grants, because much of the research talent is apparently being siphoned away from the mainstream of institutional operations into highly specialized grant programs. Second, it is even more serious in the less-favored institutions that receive little or no grant support, because the decimated departments of the large, favored universities are looking to the smaller colleges and universities to supply the faculty strength of which they have been deprived.[26]

Mr. Engelbert arrived at what he called the "painful conclusion" that

> Federal research and development grants and contracts are neither aids to higher education, nor do they serve the national interest, if they tend to undermine the ability of many colleges and universities to train large numbers of people prepared to move into research fields.

The result of the system of awarding research grants is, as presidential science advisor Jerome B. Wiesner expressed it at the centennial celebration of the National Academy of Sciences in October 1963, that "the rich get richer and the poor get poorer."[27] But the alternative, Mr. Wiesner sadly observed—to abandon quality standards in the award of contracts—might lead to political favoritism.

Some of the recipient institutions have complained about the imbalance and restrictions in the programs, harassment by federal

[25] Quoted in *Congressional Record*, March 2, 1965, p. 3852.
[26] Arthur F. Engelbert, "Short-Term Grants and Long-Range Goals: The Dilemma of Federal Policies," *The Educational Record*, April 1963.
[27] "Science Aide Asks New Grant Policy," *The New York Times*, October 24, 1963.

auditors, inadequate reimbursement for indirect ("overhead") costs, and the lack of concern on the part of the sponsoring agencies for the educational aspects which are the primary task of the universities. Ernest V. Hollis of the U.S. Office of Education wrote that federal research funds *through* instead of *to* institutions not only do not assist with the education of students, they use faculty and facilities that otherwise might be used for educational purposes.[28] Possibly the sharpest criticism of the system was aired by the publisher of *Scientific American*, Gerard Piel, in a paper presented at the annual meeting of the American Philosophical Society in April 1965. Mr. Piel charged that federal research contracts have undermined the independence of the nation's major universities and have turned many professors into "mercenaries of science and scholarship," that they reduce the integrity of higher education, downgrade the teaching function and weaken the universities' role as "agents of free inquiry" and as "centers for the independent criticism and surveillance" of federal policies.

On the whole, however, spokesmen for the recipient I.H.L. welcome and praise the federal funds ("The Blessing that is Federal Aid"[29]), try to get them increased and restrictions relaxed, and shudder at the thought that they might some day be cut or discontinued. In this attitude they do not differ from industrial contractors who regard federal orders for goods or services as highly desirable and (hopefully) profitable business propositions which have become vital to their operations. But those contractors do not call federal orders "federal aid." Neither should I.H.L.

The rapid and steady growth of federally supported research led most observers to believe that funds would continue to multiply. But out of nowhere a storm blew up in 1963 which, though not likely to reduce the size of operations, will make further increases harder to come by. When the Rules Committee of the House of Representatives proposed a thorough investigation of federal research programs, "including grants to colleges and universities as well as scholarship grants," it found enthusiastic

---

[28] *Proceedings of the Fifty-Fifth Annual Conference on Taxation*, p. 484.
[29] This is the title of an article by McGeorge Bundy, former Harvard dean now a presidential assistant, in the *Princeton Alumni Weekly* for February 1, 1963, which produced a flood of critical letters to the editor.

support on both sides of the aisle and the resolution establishing a Select Committee to undertake the task was approved with one of the rare roll call votes without even one dissenting vote. The House debate on September 11, 1963,[30] and the hearings which started on November 18, suggested that Congress was in an angry mood and that, in the words of one member, "the honeymoon is over." The conclusion was inevitable at the annual meeting of the American Association for the Advancement of Science in December 1963, that science in America is "in trouble with the Federal government, with a sizable segment of the general public and, to a large extent, with itself." "A sense of disquiet over the internal health of science" prevailed at the same meeting one year later and it was reported that "Scientists are worried whether science today is being corrupted by affluence."[31]

Even the National Science Foundation, which had enjoyed great prestige and always been treated with kid gloves and even with reverence, did not escape. It had originally been established because Congress lacked confidence in the Office of Education and was averse to giving that office broad research grant authority. But the NSF budget request was, in the words of one professional report, bludgeoned by the House in October 1963. Scientists, not surprisingly, blamed the fact that ' something has gone very wrong on the congressional scene" on Congress itself.[32]

Ten reports issued by the Select Committee expressed its frustration in trying to devise corrective action.[33] A new committee was then established by the 89th Congress, with a somewhat changed emphasis as the title of its first report suggests: *Conflicts Between the Federal Research Programs and the Nation's Goals for Higher Education.* Research fund requests may be more closely scrutinized in the future and the amounts may level off, at least, for some time. The outlook for an easing of restrictions or approval of institutional instead of project grants is dim and it could even be that controls will be tightened. Members of Congress

---

[30] *Congressional Record,* pp. 15867-77.
[31] "Hostility Toward Science," *The New York Times,* December 29, 1963. "The Integrity of Science," *The New York Times,* December 29, 1964.
[32] *Science,* October 18, 1963, pp. 368-370.
[33] *Congressional Record,* January 19, 1965, p. A 210; *Congressional Record,* March 16, 1965, p. 4991.

seem to suspect that some "boondoggling" is going on and that a liberal grant policy may be conducive to a "leisure of the theory class."

I.H.L. can hardly look to research funds for any sizable share of the operational support they need in the years ahead. Some of their spokesmen have long sought for a *raison d'être* for federal funds other than specific projects and have proposed or demanded general grants in aid.

Federal Grants in Aid to Higher Education

To describe the numerous federal programs which, in one way or another, affect higher education would fill a book—in fact, it filled several books. The Committee on Education and Labor of the House of Representatives reported federal expenditures for education in the fiscal year 1962 at $2.2 billion, largely for higher education, and listed such diverse grant and loan programs as military academies ($129 million), cost of educating government personnel at other I.H.L. ($167 million), student support including veterans ($257 million), surplus property disposal ($376 million at acquisition cost), etc.[34] The Commissioner of Education, testifying before the Senate Subcommittee on Education, reported:

> In 1961–62, higher education institutions received approximately $1.4 billion from the federal government and its departments and agencies. More than 80 per cent of this total was for the purchase of research. The balance included appropriations to land-grant colleges, payments for tuitions and fees of eligible veterans, payment for training of service personnel, payments to Howard University and Gallaudet College, and support of the service academies. The total amount of $1.4 billion excludes various loan funds such as the college housing program and student loans under the National Defense Education Act.[35]

For our purposes it might be best to follow the *functional* classification in the U.S. Budget. The budget which the President submitted in January 1965 estimated expenditures for "Assistance to Higher Education" in 1965 at $428 million, of which 83 per cent

---

[34] *The Federal Government and Education,* Committee on Education and Labor, H.R., 88th Congress, 1st S., June 1963, pp. 115ff.

[35] *Education Legislation—1963,* Hearings before the Subcommittee on Education, Committee on Labor and Public Welfare, U.S. Senate, 88th Congress, 1st S., 1963, Vol. V, p. 2537.

was in the form of loans and $71 million or 17 per cent were grants (see following table). The subventions to two *local* institutions

ASSISTANCE FOR HIGHER EDUCATION IN 1964 AND 1965

	Estimated Expenditures (millions) Fiscal Year	
	1934	1965
Grants in Aid	$ 56	$ 71
Morrill Act (land-grant colleges)	15	15
Gallaudet College-Howard University	14	17
National Defense Education Act		
Fellowships	21	29
Language Area Centers	6	7
Construction of academic facilities	—	3
Loans	327	357
College housing	219	229
Student loans	$108	$128
Grand total—grants and loans	$383	$428

in the District of Columbia—Gallaudet College, a school for the deaf, and Howard University, established in 1867 for Negroes—should long have been transferred to the budget for the District of Columbia. Not counting fellowships which are aid to graduate students, this leaves grant-in-aid expenditures to I.H.L. in 1965 as follows: $15 million to 68 "land-grant" institutions, $7 million to 127 language and area centers, $3 million for construction of academic facilities, for a grand total of $25 million. This equals about one-fortieth of 1 per cent of the U.S. Budget and one-fourth of 1 per cent of the combined budgets of all I.H.L. in the United States. This is truly an insignificant contribution.

The estimate for 1965 includes amounts for several programs which were newly enacted or expanded in 1963 and 1964 and will substantially increase federal participation in the financing of higher education in future years:

a) Grants averaging $58 million annually for the construction or rehabilitation of medical training facilities and $10 million in loans to medical students;

b) Construction grants averaging $278 million annually, divided as follows: $48 million for graduate schools, $50 million for public junior colleges, and $180 million for undergraduate facilities especially designed for instruction or research in the natural or physical sciences, mathematics, modern foreign languages, or engineering, or for use as a library. Further, $120 million annually in loans for academic facilities;

c) Extension and expansion of the National Defense Education Act which changes the nature of the program from an emergency statute, passed after the Russians orbited the first sputnik, to a regular support program, including: a gradual increase between 1964 and 1968 in the ceiling for student loans from $135 million to $195 million annually; an increase in the number of fellowships from 1,500 to 7,500; a boost in the language development program from $8 million to $18 million, etc.

Moreover, the President recommended further expansion of aid to higher education early in 1965: an additional $179 million annually in grants for college construction, an additional $25 million for 4,500 more graduate fellowships, an additional $110 million for basic research and to promote science education, a system of scholarships and loan guarantees, funds for a work-study program, etc. Congress was clearly anxious to aid higher education and approved most proposals, enlarging some of them.

The authorization for "obligational authority" for higher education, requested for the fiscal year 1966, totals $1,184 million ($854 million in grants, $330 million in loans) of which $782 million are expected to be actually expended in that year. The major share of the requested authorization—$523 million—is for grants to specified types of construction, listed under *b* above. It cannot be used for general classrooms or academic buildings. The use of all other funds is also closely earmarked and subjected to strict control by the U.S. Office of Education.

The new funds are evidently quite substantial. But even so, the grants available to the institutions themselves—not counting scholarships which will not ease and may, in fact, aggravate their budgetary difficulties—will equal only between 5 per cent and 7 per cent of the $7 to $11 billion increase in institutional funds expected between 1960 and 1970. This leaves between 93 per cent and 95 per cent of the increase to be financed from other sources—

presumably the traditional sources of higher educational support.

The new funds are to be provided on a matching basis and the purposes to which they are to be applied are therefore likely to receive priority in the allocation of local or institutional funds so as to earn the matching money. This may well work to the disadvantage of programs not specifically benefited. None of the amounts are to be made available to I.H.L. to be used according to the judgment and in the discretion of their boards of trustees or administrators or to help in the areas which need strengthening most urgently: salaries and operations. Students of higher educational finance, however, have repeatedly stressed the priority which ought to be accorded to the current operational needs of the institutions.

Richard A. Musgrave wrote that "the most crucial issue will not be met until the problem of direct assistance to the operating costs of institutions of higher education comes to be faced."[36]

Alice M. Rivlin declared, in a report for the Brookings Institution: "If the increased federal money is to do any real good, it must be directed toward support of the instructional functions of higher education."[37]

The National Science Foundation stated: "The situation appears to call for general aid to U.S. universities patterned somewhat after that provided universities in the United Kingdom by the University Grants Committee. In any event, the question arises of direct subsidy to educational institutions in order to increase the overall strength of their departments and to provide greater flexibility in their administration.[38]

The Association of State Universities and Land Grant Colleges and the State Universities Association testified at congressional hearings in 1963 that "the highest priority of colleges and universities, both public and private, is for general operations support and particularly for faculty salaries."[39]

---

[36] Richard A. Musgrave, "Higher Education and the Federal Budget," in *Higher Education in the United States, The Economic Problems,* ed. Seymour E. Harris, Harvard University Press, 1960, p. 101.

[37] Alice M. Rivlin, *The Role of the Federal Government in Financing Higher Education,* p. 173.

[38] National Science Foundation, *Annual Report, 1960,* 1961, p. 16.

[39] *National Education Improvement Act,* Hearings before the Committee on Education and Labor, H.R., 88th Congress, 1st S., 1963, p. 166 and p. 755.

Although the priority claim of operational needs is widely recognized, suggestions to establish general aid to higher education have not been seriously considered. A memorandum prepared in the Office of Education in 1961 said: "No significant group of higher education institutions ever requested or recommended federal subvention of faculty salaries. In part, this negative sentiment is believed to stem from a desire to avoid possible diminution of institutional autonomy."[40] This leaves us to ponder why institutional autonomy would be jeopardized by federal aid for broad institutional purposes within the discretion of the governing boards while that autonomy is regarded as safe from federal interference under programs which not only specify in great detail the select purposes to which the funds may be applied but also minutely prescribe the administrative practices that must be followed and the supervisory powers of the U.S. Office of Education.

To be sure, several presidential commissions in recent decades, and a task force of the President-elect in 1960, recommended large federal programs of grant-in-aid for the operation or construction (or both) of colleges and universities. But no President ever transmitted such proposals to Congress. Nor did Congress advance or enact any of the numerous plans of general support for I.H.L. which were introduced in bill form by individual members.

One reason for this absence of action was considerable dissension within the ranks of higher education, until quite recently, whether federal aid was desirable and, if so, in what form. When President Truman's Commission on Higher Education in 1946–48 proposed gradually rising amounts of federal grants to public I.H.L., the Association of American Universities sponsored the Commission on Financing Higher Education which flatly opposed such a program and declared: "This Commission has reached the unanimous conclusion that we, as a nation, should call a halt at this time to the introduction of new programs of direct federal aid to colleges and universities."[41] At that time, and for a few years

---

[40] *Aid for Higher Education,* Hearings before the Subcommittee on Education, Committee on Labor and Public Welfare, U.S. Senate, 87th Congress, 1st S., 1961, p. 165.

[41] *Nature and Needs of Higher Education: The Report of the Commission on Financing Higher Education* (New York: Columbia University Press, 1952), p. 157.

after, a poll of college and university presidents (or boards of trustees) would have returned a decisive vote against *direct* federal aid. This does not apply to *indirect* aid such as federal income tax credits for tuitions which were then actively sought by the American Council on Education, Association of American Colleges, and other major organizations. But when that drive did not succeed and enrollments and financial needs soared, college presidents grew weary of spending much of their time on endless rounds of cajoling state legislators into higher appropriations or wheedling gifts from private donors. They saw Congress triple grants in aid for a widening range of state services—from $2.4 billion in 1950 to $7 billion in 1960—found the small amounts of federal funds which began to trickle into institutions much to their taste, and thirsted for more. Many of those who did not share in the manna from heaven became envious. Opposition to federal aid crumbled, and by the early 1960's a substantial majority of institutional heads seemed to favor it. As one report put it:

> When the Association of American Colleges held its annual meeting at Boston, early in 1960, the college officials present generally were leery of the idea of federal construction grants for their institutions. Not quite a year later the association, whose membership includes large state schools but is heavily weighted with relatively small, private liberal arts colleges, sent members a questionnaire on such grants. The result: Of the 70 per cent replying, 84 per cent said they now favored government contributions to their building programs.[42]

During the American Council on Education meeting in October 1960, "the ghost of federal aid appeared like an uninvited, not quite welcome but very prominent guest."[43] But three months later the Council submitted a broad program for federal action which had been agreed on by a substantial majority of its members.[44] Two events may account for this change in attitude. Homer Babbidge, Assistant Commissioner of Education and later vice-president of the American Council on Education (now president, Uni-

---

[42] "More Educators Shift Views, Urge Broader Aid from Government," *The Wall Street Journal*, December 29, 1961.

[43] "College Costs," *The New York Times*, October 9, 1960.

[44] *A Proposed Program of Federal Action to Strengthen Higher Education*, American Council on Education, January 1961.

versity of Connecticut), and his aide, Robert M. Rosenzweig, described the turn of events in 1960 as follows:

> The Washington representatives of higher education associations realized that their groups were in danger of losing the sympathy of influential political leaders in both the administration and the Congress if they continued to take the position that they could not comment responsively on legislative matters in the absence of approved positions formally adopted by their entire membership.[45]

So they decided to act on their own in agreeing with some members of Congress on an action program ("making it clear to all concerned that they were not speaking for their associations"). "What their associations and organizations had been unable to work out, these realistic agents had been able to develop almost overnight," commented Babbidge, and explained further why the executive secretaries had been effective and the institutional heads had not:

> Educational leaders had presumed to decide what was good for the nation. What distinguished the national organizations from their Washington representatives and what may distinguish them from national organizations in other walks of American life, is that they regard themselves not as a group seeking the assistance of the government in meeting their needs, but as a group of educators gathered together to mold public safety.[46]

In other words, then, the college and university presidents viewing public policy were uncertain in their minds whether adoption of broad-scaled federal aid to higher education was in the national interest, but the Washington staffs of their associations were not plagued by such thoughts and regarded the issue from a more practical or realistic angle. As the American Council on Education's administrative head, Logan Wilson, later explained: "To borrow a phrase from a recent Carnegie *Quarterly*, there is a growing 'inseparability of politics and education,' and it is for us to make the most of this fact of modern life."[47]

While the initiative by the association secretaries advanced the cause of federal aid to higher education, the event that probably changed the attitude in many I.H.L. was the outcome of the

---

[45] Homer Babbidge, Jr., and Robert M. Rosenzweig, *The Federal Interest in Higher Education* (New York: McGraw-Hill, 1962), pp. 107 ff.

[46] *Ibid.,* p. 111.

[47] Logan Wilson, "A Better Partnership for the Federal Government and Higher Education," *The Educational Record,* April 1963.

election in November 1960: Not in a generation had the political situation and prospects appeared brighter for a huge expansion of federal activities in many areas, and if other services were to get large chunks of federal money, higher education might as well get its share.

No unanimity appeared likely on grants for current purposes—salaries and operations—because private institutions saw little chance of being included in such a program. But a resolution was agreed on by the members of the American Council on Education in January 1961, demanding $1 billion in aid for academic construction—70 per cent grants, 30 per cent loans—on a 50:50 matching basis, an increase in the number and amount of fellowships, a new program of federal scholarships, etc. All programs were to benefit public and private I.H.L. alike.

But President Kennedy's message on education of February 20, 1961, recommended construction aid in the form of loans only and made no reference to grants. At hearings of the House Education and Labor Committee, the spokesmen for I.H.L. declared that loans would be of little value to them and that what they needed were outright grants. The House was responsive and, a year later, on January 30, 1962, passed a bill which, besides construction loans, authorized $180 million in annual grants for academic facilities in public and private I.H.L. with up to one-third federal matching. This was a long way from the $700 million with 50:50 matching, for which the institutions had asked, but it amounted to more money than Congress had ever approved for I.H.L. However, the Senate and its Labor and Public Welfare Committee found grants to private institutions objectionable. On February 6, 1962, the Senate approved construction *loans* only, in addition to scholarships. The House, in turn, found this unacceptable, and when its conference committee agreed to a compromise—in violation of its instructions and promise—the House summarily rejected it on September 19. Both the Senate and the House versions of aid to higher education died with the adjournment of the 87th Congress, the first of three, each of which has been called the "Education Congress."

President Kennedy transmitted a comprehensive message on education to the 88th Congress on January 29, 1963, together with an "omnibus" education bill which proposed twenty-four programs, more than half of them new. Again, the President recommended no grants for academic construction, only facility loans averaging $333 million annually over the three succeeding years. He did propose various other new grants in higher education, such as for community colleges, library acquisitions and construction, graduate schools, technical education, etc., with an authorization aggregating $130 million, and grants for teacher education totalling $52.5 million in the following year.

Again, the two Houses passed bills which differed though by less than in the preceding year. The conference committee arrived at an agreement which the House approved on November 6. But there was such serious dissension in the Senate that, according to newspaper reports, as of December 6, "the Democratic high command in Congress despaired of getting the education bills through this year."[48] Part of the House-Senate friction was over the distribution formula in the pending vocational education bill—whether low-income states should receive proportionately more than wealthy states and, if so, how much—and part over certain details in the college construction bill. At that point President Johnson, who had been in office barely two weeks, went into action:

> In personal contacts and telephone discussions with key members of the House and Senate, the President made it clear that he wanted two bills enacted before Congress went home for the holidays. His appeals were issued over the December 7-8 week end. On the following Monday morning, Senate and House conferees reached quick agreement on differences that had seemed irreconcilable on the previous Friday.[49]

On December 10, the Senate passed the House-approved college construction bill which "gave the Executive Branch its most impressive congressional victory this year."[50] Upon signing the Act on December 16, the President noted that "it contained the first broad assistance program for colleges since the land grants act a century ago." He declared: "This is the most significant education bill passed by the Congress in the history of the republic," and

---

[48] "Conferees Agree on Aid to Education Bills," *The Wall Street Journal*, December 10, 1963.

[49] "Report from Washington: Johnson Touch Frees Education Bills," *Nation's Schools*, January 1964.

[50] "Senate Sends White House College-Aid Bill for Public, Private, Church-Run Institutions," *The Wall Street Journal*, December 11, 1963.

predicted that "this session of Congress will go down as the Education Congress of 1963."[51]

There can be little doubt that the Act established a new principle and is a landmark in the more than century-old struggle for federal aid to education. It is less certain by how much it will help alleviate the financial stress in higher education. The aggregate of both programs approved in 1963 equals barely more than two per cent of the prospective budgets of I.H.L. in 1970.

Federal funds from the college construction and medical facilities acts will total $348 million annually and require a minimum of $590 million in institutional (or state and local) matching funds. The latter amount probably exceeds present spending for the eligible types of facilities. Since the availability of federal matching funds offers a strong incentive, I.H.L. might well expand their building of engineering, physical and natural science, etc., facilities. The big question is whether this will draw funds that otherwise might have gone for general classroom construction which, normally, accounts for a far larger volume than the benefited types. Many liberal arts colleges never had (nor have use for) special engineering or physical science buildings and may or may not decide to expand in that direction so as to get a slice of the federal funds. At this writing it appears likely that most of the federal construction money will be allocated to state institutions with only small amounts going to private colleges or universities. It remains to be seen whether the two bills will simply add $348 million annually to academic construction, whether they will increase the flow of other funds into higher educational building, or whether they will channel monies into the benefited categories which otherwise might have gone for classrooms and other facilities in categories not eligible for federal matching.

It is of course conceivable that Congress will in future years enlarge the amounts authorized by these programs. But this would be of limited help. What the I.H.L. need is not just more money for engineering and science, etc., buildings, but more classrooms for all purposes, general facilities and, above all, larger operational funds. The struggle over construction aid in the congressional committees and between the two Houses suggests that it will be

---

[51] *Congressional Record*, December 18, 1963, p. 23886.

extremely difficult, if at all possible, to liberalize the provisions restricting federal aid to a few specified categories, and that prospects for operational grants are dim indeed for as long as we can see ahead.

Two roadblocks stand in the way of unrestricted or less restricted federal grants for the general purposes of I.H.L.: the conflict over the participation of private, particularly church-connected, colleges and the issue of federal control of education and centralization of government. I shall discuss these subjects in the next two sections.

Aid to Private Colleges and the Church-State Issue

The most intensely argued issue in the battles over federal aid to education in the postwar period has been: should the funds be channeled exclusively to state and other public institutions, or should benefits be available to *all* students, regardless of the type of school they attend. Ever since the school bus controversy broke into the headlines with the Everson case in 1947, the church-state issue has been in the forefront of the aid-to-education debate and has decided the fate of many bills proposing funds for elementary-secondary schools or for colleges and universities. Some members of Congress will not vote for an educational grant program if it *includes* private schools and colleges, and others, if it *excludes* them. The resulting impasse has blocked many educational proposals, from the Taft and Barden bills in 1947–48 to parts of the President's omnibus bill in 1963.

A vast literature has developed on the church-state issue in education, which explores the legal, economic, social, moral and other aspects of the question.[52] I cannot possibly review all of it

---

[52] To name just a few of the better-known books: Virgil C. Blum, *Freedom of Choice in Education* (Glen Rock, N. J.: Paulist Press, 1958), rev. ed. 1963—by the same author, *Freedom in Education* (Garden City, N. Y.: Doubleday, 1965); Robert Drinan, *Religion, the Courts, and Public Policy* (New York: McGraw-Hill, 1963); William Brickman and Stanley Lehrer (eds.), *Religion, Government, and Education* (New York: Society for the Advancement of Education, 1961); Dallin H. Oaks (ed.), *The Wall Between Church and State* (University of Chicago Press, 1963); Joseph Tussman (ed.), *The Supreme Court on Church and State* (New York and London: Oxford University Press, 1962); Paul Blanshard, *Religion and the Schools: The Great Controversy* (Boston: Beacon Press, 1963); National Education Association, *The State and Sectarian Education*, Research Bulletin XXXIV, No. 4, December 1956.

within the frame of this volume. But I shall try to summarize the most significant facts and views as they appear in the extensive congressional debates and in some of the more important relevant books and articles.

Out of 2,139 colleges and universities in the United States, 762 are "public," i. e., owned and operated by states or municipalities, and 1,377 are private, i. e., nongovernmental. Of the latter, 507 are under nondenominational auspices, 870 are church-connected. Not only do private I.H.L. account for two-thirds of the national total, but they also include some of the country's oldest and most eminent institutions from which some of our leading scholars, statesmen, and businessmen graduated. Two-thirds of the private I.H.L. list themselves as adhering to a particular religious faith or church.

Historically, the federal government has made no distinction between public and private I.H.L. For example, the original land-grant colleges, authorized in 1862, included several private non-denominational colleges and one Baptist college. Virtually all the other federal programs benefit public and private I.H.L. alike. But in recent decades the question has been raised with much force whether colleges not under governmental control are entitled to share in federal funds. The constitutional issue hinges on the interpretation of the opening clause to the First Amendment: "Congress shall make no law respecting an establishment of relig-ion, or prohibiting the free exercise thereof." Did the authors intend this to mean only what it says, namely that Congress could not create a national church—in contrast to the motherland and some of the colonies which *had* established official churches—nor give any religion a preferred status? Some so believe. But others aver that it intended to outlaw any type of congressional aid to religion. Still others contend that it is of little relevance what the authors may have had in mind, more than 170 years ago, even if this could be clearly established, and that the clause ought to be interpreted in the light of the circumstances and general attitude in the second half of the twentieth century.

A 5:4 majority of the U.S. Supreme Court agreed with an opinion written by Mr. Justice Black in the Everson case: "The establishment-of-religion clause of the First Amendment means at least this: Neither a state nor the federal government can set up a church. ... No tax in any amount, large or small, can be levied to support religious activities or institutions, whatever they may be called, or whatever form they may adopt to teach or practice religion."[53] Some believe that this outlaws the channeling of any public funds to church-connected institutions, regardless of the purpose to which the money may be applied. Others hold that it forbids only the tax support of denominational activities, i. e., the teaching or practice of a religion, but does not apply to secular or civic activities of church-connected institutions. Since by far the major part of the time and resources of most schools and colleges, except divinity schools and seminaries, is devoted to teaching the customary range of secular subjects, from English to mathematics and the natural sciences, and thus to a *public* function, this would leave church-connected institutions free to receive public funds, provided that those funds are restricted to nonsectarian activities or used only for specifically named subjects.[54]

Another suggestion advanced a cost-accounting approach: if, for example, eighty per cent of the time and resources of a school are devoted to the Three R's and other secular subjects, eighty per cent of its expenditures could be supported by the same formula as the public schools. Opponents base their objections on the fact that denominational schools tend to weave religious themes into secular subjects and permit them to permeate much of the curriculum.

A program of aiding private nondenominational or independent I.H.L. while excluding *church-connected* colleges from the benefits is hardly conceivable. Some of the reasons are technical, because the degree of church control varies and is sometimes hard to determine. More importantly, two-thirds of the nonpublic I.H.L. list themselves as being church-related and would be left in the cold by such a program. To exclude them from benefits would offer institutions a premium for cutting their religious ties and turning secular. This would be tantamount to a government reward for abandoning religion and come close to imposing a penalty upon

---

[53] *Everson v. Board of Education*, 330 U.S. 1 (1947).
[54] See: "The Constitutionality of the Inclusion of Church-Related Schools in Federal Aid to Education," Legal Department of the National Catholic Welfare Conference, *The Georgetown Law Journal*, Winter 1961.

the exercise of religion. Such action would fly in the face of long and firmly established American tradition that church and state should be separate but certainly not hostile to each other. It may be well to recall the oft-cited words of the Northwest Ordinance of 1787 which emphasized the interdependence of religion, education, and good government: "Religion, morality, and knowledge, being necessary to good government and the happiness of mankind, schools and the means of education shall forever be encouraged." There is little doubt that an overwhelming majority of Americans agree with the U.S. Supreme Court's pronouncement in the Zorach case (1952) that "we are a religious people whose institutions presuppose a Supreme Being," and with the Court's statement that the state is following the best of our traditions when it encourages religious instruction.[55] It is very unlikely that Congress would seriously consider a plan of offering an incentive to nongovernmental educational institutions for abandoning religious instruction. In all probability it will not distinguish between church-connected and independent (secular) private I.H.L.

Neither side to the church-state issue in education fully accepts all of the opinions and *obiter dicta* of the U.S. Supreme Court contained in the leading relevant decisions in the Everson, McCollum, and Zorach cases. Both sides believe that the Court, at least in part, misunderstood or misinterpreted the meaning of the U.S. Constitution, although both acknowledge the basic principles pronounced by closely divided majorities in the mentioned cases. The Court, to be sure, has never adjudicated the appropriation of federal funds to church-connected schools or colleges. But it is generally agreed that the Court, as presently composed, is unlikely to uphold across-the-board allocations for the current operations of I.H.L., including denominational institutions, if called upon to render a decision. There may be doubt whether even restricted operating funds would get the Court's approval. But many—and apparently a majority in Congress—are of the opinion that construction funds for all I.H.L., if sufficiently limited in their application to secular subjects, are constitutional and would get the Court's nod, if a case arose.

Until recently the possibility of such a case appeared remote

---

[55] *Zorach v. Clauson*, 343 U.S. 306 (1952).

because the Court had, in a leading case, denied the right of an individual citizen or a state to litigate the constitutionality of a federal expenditure ("we have no power per se to review and annul acts of Congress on the ground that they are unconstitutional").[56] But by an unusual set of circumstances it now appears likely that such a case may reach the U.S. Supreme Court. In 1962 and 1963 the Maryland legislature voted $2.5 million in matching grants for buildings at four church-connected colleges (two Catholic, one Methodist, one United Church of Christ). A group of present and former top officials of the National Education Association and of the Council of Chief State School Officers challenged the constitutionality of the law in the Maryland courts, and the decision of the Maryland Supreme Court, whatever it may be, will probably be appealed to the U.S. Supreme Court. The federal Court can hardly avoid accepting jurisdiction under the circumstances, since a substantial federal constitutional question clearly is involved. It may then, for the first time, pronounce its interpretation of the meaning of the First Amendment in regard to the use of public funds in church-connected educational institutions.

However, the concern of those who object to the allocation of federal funds to church-connected colleges is not only whether it is unconstitutional and would be so held by the Court but whether it is good public policy. Several large organizations and many individuals hold that to supply tax funds to sectarian institutions would promote the cause of the benefited religious denominations and violate the principle of separation of church and state, even if the Court, because of legal technicalities, were to uphold the statute.

The opponents to the inclusion of private I.H.L., even for limited purposes, declare the provisions which had been suggested to be mere subterfuges and call them ineffective "paper" restrictions. Supposing a college can apply federal funds only to secular subjects or even only to engineering, science, or library buildings. Do not those federal funds substitute for and release institutional funds which otherwise would have to be used to construct such

---

[56] *Massachusetts v. Mellon* and *Frothingham v. Mellon,* 262 U.S. 447 (1923).

buildings? And cannot the college then use its own funds, so saved, to build classrooms for religious instruction or chapels? Moreover, while under the Higher Education Facilities Act of 1963, buildings must be especially *designed* for science, mathematics, etc., purposes, there is nothing in the law to prevent an institution from *using* such buildings for any other purpose, as soon as they are completed.

Evidently, the opponents say, the restrictions would merely change the accounting procedures but not the fact that federal funds could help a religious order to promote and expand its sectarian activities. What they object to is not merely a breach of the *words* of the First Amendment, but what they regard as a violation of its *spirit*. They are not satisfied with resolving the constitutional question through a sophisticated legal formula. They believe that it is morally wrong for government to aid sectarian activities, no matter in what form or under what pretense.

The other side is no less deeply committed to its cause. To exclude private I.H.L. from the benefits of the law, it holds, would discriminate against parents and students who exercise their right of choice of institution, and would gravely disturb the balance in and freedom of education. It would restrict the growth and jeopardize the very existence of hundreds of colleges and, in the long run, of private education in America. If the exclusion of private colleges from federal benefits were to lead to the eventual closing of hundreds of institutions, as it well might, it would not only save no public funds but throw upon the taxpayers an added burden which could run into the billions of dollars.

The groups which demand that federal funds be available to all institutions and individuals regard it as morally wrong to place a severe financial penalty upon parents and students who follow the command of their conscience to acquire a religious education, in addition to secular training. Their spokesmen insist that the state interferes with the free exercise of religion if it makes it economically difficult or impossible for parents of moderate means to have their children attend a school in which the tenets of their faith are being taught. They point to the U.S. Supreme Court decision in the Seventh Day Adventist case, which found that the state may not exclude members of various religious denominations from receiving the benefits of public welfare legislation because of their faith or lack of it.[57]

In that case the denial of benefits would have forced the complainant to choose between her religion and her livelihood. Why should a student of modest means, who would like to acquire his education at an institution of his own faith, be forced, by the denial of benefits, to attend a public school or college, or none? If federal action in education aims to aid the welfare of the benefited individuals, why should some be excluded because they follow the tenets of their religion?

Those who demand the inclusion of all I.H.L. in a federal program point out that the federal government, particularly in higher education, has never distinguished between public, independent, and church-connected institutions; that private colleges labor under more severe financial handicaps than public colleges; that enrollment has been shifting from private to public institutions, largely for financial reasons, for the past fifteen years; and that a new federal program, aiding public but not private I.H.L., would lead to increasing difficulties and the eventual demise of many private institutions. They insist that federal benefits of any type must be available to all students on equal terms, or to none.

Some of the strongest objections to the inclusion of private I.H.L. in a federal grant program have come from organizations representing the administrators and employees of the public elementary and secondary schools. It is significant that the above-mentioned Maryland case, though it involves colleges, was taken to court by individuals active in the common schools. When the academic facilities bill was in conference between the two Houses in the fall of 1962, the National Education Association sent telegrams to all members of Congress opposing its passage. This may have been a contributing factor in the bill's failure. At a hearing of the Senate Labor and Public Welfare Committee on May 14, 1963, the president-elect of the National Education Association stated unequivocally that by aiding nonpublic schools, the federal program "would proliferate the whole elementary process" and

[57] *Sherbert v. Lerner,* 374 U.S. 398 (1963).

would be a detriment to the general forward movement of education."[58]

The N.E.A. opposed the inclusion of private I.H.L. because it believed that this would set a precedent for the schools at the lower levels. The subsequent enactment of the academic facilities bill probably does set a precedent. In the elementary-secondary schools, enrollment at private institutions has been growing much faster than at public, and the N.E.A. and its affiliated groups fear— not without cause—that federal funds aiding all schools would enable more parents to send their children to private rather than to public schools. There also seemed to be an element of competition between levels of education involved. The N.E.A. told members of Congress: "We insist that school construction and the teacher's salary bill come before the higher education bill."[59] Spokesmen for higher education, on the other hand, felt that "a better case can be made for federal aid on higher than on lower levels."[60]

The National Education Association soon found itself on the receiving end of sharp criticism for having helped defeat the higher education bill. It still took an uncompromising stand at congressional hearings in February and May 1963, but slightly eased its position on federal aid to private I.H.L. at its annual convention in July 1963, which may have aided the final success of the college construction bill. However, some allied organizations such as the American Association of School Administrators, the National Council of Chief State School Officers, the National Congress of Parents and Teachers, and the National School Boards Association remained adamant in their opposition to federal benefits for private colleges.

The Department of Health, Education, and Welfare prepared a memorandum in March 1961 which concluded that inclusion of church-connected institutions in a federal grant program was

---

[58] *Education Legislation—1963*, Hearings before the Subcommittee on Education of the Committee on Labor and Public Welfare, U.S. Senate, 88th Congress, 1st S., 1963, p. 621.

[59] *Congressional Record*, September 19, 1962, p. 19015.

[60] Logan Wilson, "A Better Partnership for the Federal Government and Higher Education," *The Educational Record*, April 1963.

clearly unconstitutional in the elementary-secondary school field but permissible in higher education.[61]

This attempt to find a distinction in the constitutionality of grants by levels of education, in a constitution which does not even mention education, has received acid criticism as legal legerdemain. One commentator referred to the "magic age of seventeen and one half" at which point a student of Grade 12 stands ineligible for federal benefits but in Grade 13 suddenly becomes eligible. In fact, some hold that a better case might be advanced for making federal aid to the lower schools available to public and private schools alike, because attendance at that level is compulsory, rather than in higher education where participation is discretionary and a personal decision.

Organizations of *public* I.H.L. have generally favored the recommendations of the presidential Commission on Higher Education in 1946–48 (Zook Commission) which proposed to distribute federal grants to state and municipal colleges only, and have looked with a jaundiced eye on proposals to include private I.H.L. in federal grants. But they have not taken as uncompromising a stand as the representatives of the lower schools, possibly because enrollment in higher education has been shifting very strongly toward the public institutions anyway—in contrast to trends in the elementary-secondary schools.

After years of fruitless efforts to obtain federal grants for public institutions exclusively, the state institutions realized that they would be unable to secure aid for themselves without letting private institutions participate. So they refrained in recent years from outright opposition to the inclusion of private I.H.L., although they never supported it in their congressional testimony. The legislative program of the Association of State Universities and Land Grant Colleges, presented to Congress in 1963, would have allowed private institutions *which participate in general state aid for construction* to participate in federal funds.[62] This would, of course, have made barely a handful of private colleges eligible out of a

---

[61] *Constitutionality of Federal Aid to Education in Its Various Aspects,* Senate Document No. 29, 87th Congress, 1st S., 1961, pp. 5ff.

[62] *National Education Improvement Act,* Hearings before the Committee on Education and Labor, H.R., 88th Congress, 1st S., 1963, p. 755.

total of 870. However, Congress ignored this suggestion when it framed the Higher Educational Facilities Act of 1963.

The fight over the church-state issue does not appear to be quite as fierce or carry such high emotional overtones in the field of higher education as in the lower schools. One reason may well be that about 90 per cent of the nonpublic elementary-secondary schools are under Catholic auspices, while private institutions in higher education represent a broader cross-section of American life: 507 are nonsectarian and of the 870 church-connected institutions, 483 are Protestant, 361 Catholic, 8 Jewish, 4 Latter-day Saints, and 14 from other denominations or interdenominational. Thus, the battle-lines are not drawn along the same division as in the school fight, and a compromise is more easily reached in higher education than in the schools. To be sure, no compromise is likely to be reached in regard to federal grants for salaries and operations. For, as far as we can see ahead, the church-state issue alone—aside from other considerations—will prevent the enactment of a program of direct aid for the current (operational) requirements of I.H.L.

A compromise in regard to construction was arrived at in the fall of 1963 after long, protracted, and often stalemated negotiations. To permit federal construction aid to public and private I.H.L. excepting only facilities used for worship or religious instruction seemed acceptable to the House but objectionable to the Senate. The Senate insisted on specifying the curricula subjects, limiting them to the natural and physical sciences, mathematics, modern foreign languages—only foreign, no English!—and engineering and to library buildings. It yielded on the twenty-year use restriction which it originally demanded and was satisfied if the buildings were "especially designed" for the named purposes.

On the whole, a greater willingness than in years past seems to have developed in Congress, in higher education circles, and among the general public to recognize the claims of the patrons of nonpublic institutions and to arrive at a compromise formula that is acceptable to all parties concerned. It is conceivable that some of the limitations in the 1963 construction program might be liberalized in future years. However, a compromise in regard to salary and operational funds does not appear to be in the cards.

Does Federal Aid Lead to Federal Control?

Some observers hold it to be self-evident that "he who pays the piper calls the tune," and that the enactment of major federal aid programs would inevitably lead to eventual federal domination of our educational system. Proponents of federal aid ridicule this proposition, which they call a smokescreen to hide the real motives of the opposition. They insist that we have had federal aid to higher education for over a century (the land-grant act), that it has not brought federal control, and that newly enacted programs are no more likely to result in federal control than the Morrill Act. They say that Congress and the Office of Education harbor no ambition to wield power over colleges and universities, that they could not exercise control even if they tried, that alert institutional management can prevent undue influence, and that the specter of federal bureaucrats riding herd on education is the figment of too lively an imagination. "Federal control" is a straw man, they assert, which opponents use to hide the absence of a cogent, persuasive, and provable case against federal aid.

Whether or not federal aid leads to federal control is to some extent hypothetical. We can, of course, draw conclusions from experience with research grants, from dealing with the federal government in general, and from programs outside the field of education. But the real question is: What *would* happen if large programs of federal grants to education *were* enacted?

At the present time, under very limited programs the national government provides funds for certain curriculum subjects or specified areas within them, but not for others, and demands that states or institutions match the federal money 1:1 or even 2:1. This results in a strong influence, to say the least, of federal agencies on the composition and relative emphasis in the curriculum, and even in the selection of the faculty and upon the use of the university's own funds. On the whole, however, I.H.L. are subjected to less control by the national government in the United States than in most other countries. Also, less of their support is derived from the national government in this country than virtually anywhere else. This could be a coincidence or may be a case of cause and effect.

Some institutions complain that existing federal grants, mostly for research purposes, tend to warp academic programs and to imbalance the curriculum. The "project grants" system works to the disadvantage of subjects in which federal agencies have little or no direct interest, of institutions which are not specialized in those subjects, and of scholars who work on other problems or happen to be *personae non gratae* with the particular federal bureau. Some college departments or scientists have tended to shift their interest to subjects which offer a better chance for obtaining federal funds. Institutions have hired or promoted scholars who had an "in" with or were favored by agencies controlling the funds.

It is inevitable that federal agencies look with a more friendly eye upon project requests from scholars whose views agree with those of the decision-making officials or whose findings tend to support the legislative program of the department. They are more likely to pass over proposals from researchers whose past record has not been one of aiding the department's program or political objectives. Such influence on the results of scholarly work is dangerous, particularly in the field of the social sciences. President Clark Kerr of the University of California said:

> A university's control over its destiny has been substantially reduced. [Federal] funds . . . commit some of the university's own funds; they influence the assignment of space; they determine the distribution of time as betwen teaching and research; to a large extent they establish the areas in which a university grows the fastest; almost imperceptibly a university is changed.

President Kerr further charged that federal funds have split the campus community: "To student versus faculty, assistant versus tenure professors, faculty versus administrators has been added a new hierarchical point of tensions—that between humanists and scientists."[63] He also complained about the controls imposed on the allocation of college construction aid funds *within* states: "I question whether the federal government should go into such details and take the judgment away from the states." It is interesting that the president of the largest state university "feared the private colleges would get the short end" under the point system mandated by the U.S. Office of Education.[64]

Harvard University President Nathan Pusey warned that gov-

---

[63] "Federal Money Stirs Dispute in Colleges," *Los Angeles Times,* October 13, 1963.
[64] "U.S. Fund Red Tape Ires Kerr," *San Francisco Examiner,* September 30, 1964.

ernment agencies show "an increasing desire to say how things are to be done in laboratories, and who may or may not appear in them."[65] Richard W. Pratt, director of the Harvard Office for Research Contracts, was quoted as telling the Atomic Energy Commission: "You've been telling us about your rules, but we've been around longer than the government, and we think it's time you gave some consideration to our rules."[66] President Lee A. DuBridge of the California Institute of Technology related control to the source of funds: "It goes without saying that the reason an independent institution can remain independent is that its endowments, its physical plant, and its operating funds are provided largely or wholly from non-government sources."[67] As an institution comes to depend increasingly on getting its funds from government agencies, it becomes less able to resist suggestions, influence, and demands.

In the 1963 Report of the Carnegie Foundation for the Advancement of Teaching (p. 9), its president, John W. Gardner, warned:

> With more than $1 billion annually flowing to the colleges and universities, it would be idle to argue that there is no problem of federal control. Universities testify that the government has behaved with great propriety, but none would deny that the huge influx of dollars has produced changes in these institutions that the faculty and administration might not have chosen under other circumstances. *Thus the future of the colleges and universities may be molded by the collective weight of the government decisions on the flow of federal funds* [Emphasis supplied].

Harold Orlans summarized this report on the effects of federal programs on higher education based on a study of 36 representative institutions: "Their wish for greater federal aid has blinded many educators to the very real dangers: (1) that academic values and objectives will be surrendered to those of a business enterprise or the more important goals of the nation, and (2) that some form of political control will, indeed, follow federal aid."[68]

Many I.H.L. and their organizations are painfully aware of these overt and covert influences and blame the resulting distor-

---

[65] In the *Harvard Alumni Bulletin;* quoted from *Time,* July 27, 1962.

[66] Cal Brumley, "Harvard Talks Back," *The Wall Street Journal,* July 3, 1963.

[67] Lee A. DuBridge, "Private Higher Education," *Engineering and Science,* January 1964.

[68] Harold Orlans, *The Effects of Federal Programs on Higher Education,* Brookings Institution, 1962, p. 292.

tions on the practice of granting federal funds for specific projects rather than for the general support of institutions. But unrestricted grants are unlikely to be forthcoming, as I pointed out earlier, and the new programs of 1963, 1964, and 1965 are detailed to a previously unheard-of extent. Moreover, in higher education there is a good chance that we shall repeat the experience in some of the grant-in-aid programs in other fields where federal rules, regulations, and supervision were gradually tightened, and the recipients became less and less able to resist federal directives. The Carnegie Foundation suggested in its 1956–57 report (p. 17) that even general operations ("lump sum") grants to I.H.L., such as used in Great Britain, offer no safeguard against government control: "Given the strong tendency for the federal government to regulate the activities which it supports, this form of grant would seem to be the most direct avenue to possible federal control of higher education." Whether a system such as that administered by the British University Grants Committee is possible and could operate successfully in the United States has been questioned. The well-known economist, David McCord Wright of the University of Georgia (formerly of McGill University), told the Senate Eduction Subcommittee:

> I submit on the basis of observation of such grant systems in Canada, the United Kingdom, and in Europe, that an academic grants committee, over the years, will come to be a greater danger to the development of thought, if possible, than the overt prejudices of a Congress. At least Congress acts openly, and usually consciously. The expert grants committee acts secretly and may, with the most high-minded intentions, damn and smear an innocent man, or a creative man, beyond any possibility of remedy.[69]

Professor Wright pointed out that grants committees are no less likely to impose their own views on others and to bring about a stultifying uniformity than any other form of organization. Similarly, C.I.T. President Lee A. DuBridge charged committees of scientists with suppressing "daring ideas":

> The chief threat of control has come not from the government agencies who administer the funds, but from the panels and advisory committees (composed largely of professors) who pass upon projects and budgets before they are accepted . . . a type of bureaucratic committee control has grown up which suppresses daring ideas and

---

[69] *Education Legislation—1963*, p. 1224.

takes administrative control out of the hands of the universities themselves.

As a long-time faculty member myself, I can pray fervently that both I and my faculty may be delivered from dictatorship by government faculty committees. . . . Scientists when they get into government are their own worst enemies. When they have control over activities of their colleagues, through the administration of research grants, they become autocrats of the most difficult kind.[70]

The experience with federal participation in the financing of education during the emergency of the 1930's led to a study and report on federal control by the Problems and Policies Commission of the American Council on Education and the Educational Policies Commission of the National Education Association and the American Association of School Administrators. In a joint policy statement in 1945 they said:

It is the mature conclusion of the commissions responsible for the issuance of this report that a continuance of recent and current trends in federal-state relations in education will, within a measurable period of time, transfer predominant responsibility for the control of education in the United States from the states and localities to the national government. Already we have traveled further along this road than is generally realized. . . .

If education becomes federalized in the United States it will not be because the people want this to happen. At no one time will they clearly and decisively take action to make the national government the predominant agent of educational control.

Rather, national control of schools will come by a process of accretion and infiltration. This is how it has happened thus far. It will come, not because the people approve a policy of gradually shifting predominant educational control from the states and localities to the nation. Rather it will result from responses to many small emergencies and from the pressures of many special interests. . . . Increasing federalization of education has also been brought about in recent years by groups anxious to secure public funds for various undertakings and purposes. Washington has furnished a setting favorable to the accomplishment of their ends. Through political maneuvering they have been able to obtain federal funds for undertakings and purposes which the states and localities have not been willing to finance.[71]

[70] Lee A. DuBridge, "Basic Research and the Private University," in *Symposium on Basic Research*, ed. Dael Wolfle, American Association for the Advancement of Science, 1959, pp. 113–14.

[71] *Federal-State Relations in Education*, American Council on Education and National Education Association, 1945, pp. 10–15.

This is as accurate a description today as when it was written in 1945.

A few years later the Commission on Financing Higher Education of the Association of American Universities warned that expansion of federal grants in aid in higher education would jeopardize the institutions' freedom, diversity, and independence:

> Such independence will be threatened if higher education is subjected to further influence from the federal government. That influence flowing from present support is already a cause for concern. Its withdrawal or its unwise administration would produce grave results for our institutions. But in our view, as things are now, such exigencies as these can be weathered. *We are convinced that they would be fatal were federal support to be substantially extended* [Emphasis supplied].[72]

The Commission's executive director, John D. Millett, who for some time administered the Academic Facilities Act of 1963 in the Office of Education and is now Chancellor of Ohio's Board of Higher Education, wrote that "the conclusions of the Commission on Financing Higher Education have not been outdated either by events or by further analysis."[73]

For close to a hundred years the National Education Association has been aiming its major effort at obtaining general and unrestricted federal grants for the public schools. Suffering defeat after defeat, it seems now, judging by a report it published in 1964, to have resigned itself to the fact that the only form in which the schools can get federal funds is "categorical" aid, that is, grants for specific projects or programs, determined by Congress or the U.S. Commissioner of Education.[74] This seems to be confirmed by the passage of the 1965 school aid bill. Moreover, the record of federal grants in such fields as public welfare, highways, urban renewal, etc. shows that federal administrative agencies gradually tighten their control and that this often comes about when abuses occur or policy disagreements arise between federal and state officials, as inevitably they must, sooner or later. Such parallels are too close to be overlooked.

---

[72] *Nature and Needs of Higher Education*, pp. 158–59.
[73] John D. Millett, "Financing Higher Education: Ten Years Later," *The Educational Record*, January 1963.
[74] *Educational Responsibilities of the Federal Government*, Educational Policies Commission, National Education Association, 1964.

The experience in those other fields may or may not be repeated as larger grant-in-aid programs are enacted in higher education. The federal control question is only part of several broader issues which tend to come up when federal aid to education is being considered. Some of them were cited in President Buchanan's veto of the Morrill Act in 1859 (see first part of this chapter). Above all, there is the question of big and ever-growing government, of the centralization of governmental power, of the gradual fading of the principle of federalism and home rule as more and more authority is shifted to the national government, as communities and private institutions yield control over their affairs in return for "free" federal money, and the gradual relinquishment of personal responsibility. The problem of segregation also has injected itself into the debate on federal aid to education as has the consideration that large-scale grants in aid may tend to weaken efforts at making fuller and more efficient use of available resources. In any case it is obvious that the prospect for general subvention of higher education without control—the enactment of sizable federal grants which could be spent according to the judgment of institutional governing boards—is extremely dim.

Federal Building Loans for Higher Education

I mentioned earlier that President Kennedy recommended in 1961 and 1963 to aid I.H.L. through loans for the building of academic facilities and that such a program for an authorized total of $120 million annually was approved late in 1963. It is still too early to evaluate how effective this program will be. A federal loan program for college housing has been quite successful since 1950 in promoting and assisting in the building of dormitory and dining halls and other auxiliary structures. Federal funds totaling $2.8 billion have been committed in the past 15 years in 2,500 projects and Congress authorized in July 1965 a gradual increase to $4 billion by 1968. The loans are being repaid from room and board charges and other revenues. However, most witnesses who testified at congressional hearings voiced serious doubts whether a loan program would be of much help in building academic facilities and, in fact, that it would be of *any* help to most I.H.L.

Long-term borrowing is employed for the financing of many types of construction but is not widely used to build academic facilities. No bonds for that purpose have been sold by private I.H.L. for some years, and public institutions borrow for academic facilities only as a last resort, if they cannot persuade their parent governments to appropriate or borrow the needed funds. Residence and dining halls and student union buildings are commonly debt-financed because they produce sufficient income to service the securities, which therefore constitute no drain on general revenues and are considered self-financing. But the only income which academic buildings may be held to produce directly are the fees of additional students whom the new structures accommodate. Those fees do not even meet the costs of instruction.

State constitutional and statutory restrictions prohibit most public I.H.L. from incurring general debt without the approval of the legislature and the voters. The institutions usually are reluctant to raise tuitions and pledge the proceeds for revenue bonds. State institutions, as a rule, finance their expansion from current state appropriations or through state bond issues and, to a limited extent, by issuing their own general obligation bonds. Many public two-year colleges which are organized on an area basis like school districts often sell bonds to finance academic buildings.

Because interest on state (and state institutional) bonds is exempt from federal income taxes, those bonds usually bear lower interest rates than federal loans, which run at 3.5 per cent p.a. In the summer of 1963, for example, the University of California and the California state colleges sold $42 million in 26-year bonds at an average rate of 2.98 per cent; the Oregon State Board of Higher Education sold $9.6 million 30-year bonds at an average rate of 3.059 per cent; the University of Cincinnati, $9 million 35-year bonds at 3.186 per cent. Taxable bonds of the U.S. Government were then yielding 4.0 per cent, Aaa-rated corporate bonds 4.3 per cent, high-grade municipal bonds 3.3 per cent. Because public I.H.L. were able to sell bonds at lower rates than those offered by H.H.F.A. Congress reduced the interest rate for student housing bonds to a maximum of 3.0 per cent in July 1965.

Private I.H.L. have shied away from debt-financed academic construction programs, because debt retirement and interest would cut into the funds available for salaries and operations in future years. If institutions wished to engage in debt financing, they probably could sell substantial amounts of bonds in the market at reasonable interest rates. But private I.H.L. have been suppliers more often than borrowers of funds in the money market; their endowment and other funds totalled $5.6 billion in 1960 and are growing at the annual rate of over $300 million, which must be invested. What I.H.L. need is not a market for bonds but additional revenues, revenues the federal loan plan would not provide.

To finance expansion, private I.H.L. prefer to rely on available funds and on donations, which often are much easier to obtain for the construction of permanent—and name-bearing—buildings than for operations. They put on a fund drive when they plan to expand and keep the volume of building within the frame of the incoming or pledged amounts. The experience with loan funds set aside for private schools under Title III of the National Defense Education Act (for equipment) is enlightening: at least 90 per cent of the authorization lapses each year for lack of applicants. Fifty-year terms offered under the new federal program may tempt some colleges to avail themselves of the opportunity. Some institutions with an astute financial management could conceivably take advantage of the federal 50-year 3.5 per cent loans for building, instead of using their own funds, which they often would invest at higher rates of interest. On the whole, it seems that loan programs for academic facilities offer little help to most I.H.L. and no help to many.

Federal Student Aid Programs (Loans, Work-Study, Scholarships, Fellowships)

Until a few years ago not many students borrowed to finance their college education. But the generous terms and forgiveness features of the National Defense Education Act of 1958, which commercial institutions could not quite match, broke the ice. Borrowing became respectable and even highly popular on campuses throughout the country, particularly when some of the terms were further liberalized. An undergraduate can borrow up to $1,000 a year—and up to $5,000 in total—and is expected to start repaying the loan in ten annual instalments one year after he leaves college. No interest is charged during college attendance, and later on the rate is only three per cent p.a., which is considerably less than what savings and loan associations now pay for savings deposits.

Three-fourths of all I.H.L. participate in the program, with the college supplying ten per cent of the funds, the federal government the rest. Rapidly growing demand led to several increases in the amount of the federal authorization, from $90 million in the early years to $195 million for 1968, with further boosts leading up to a total of $275 million by 1971 pending at this time. More than 600,-000 students had borrowed about $450 million by 1964.

It appears that some students, because of a misunderstanding about the nature of a federal "loan" or otherwise, are attempting to push the foregiveness features somewhat beyond the terms of the law. A survey by the Office of Education in 1964 found one in every six due loans to be delinquent. This is ten times as high a delinquency rate as in instalment loans of commercial banks where it averages only 1.7 per cent. With the number of maturing loans sharply rising, the situation may grow worse in the years ahead.

Earnings from part-time or summer jobs have always provided a substantial share of the support of many students and most I.H.L. assist their students in finding such jobs, on-campus or off. It has been estimated that college-paid undergraduate employment now totals about $145 million and provides 425,000 students with average earnings of $350 a year each. The national government entered the work-study picture with the Economic Opportunity Act of 1964 (Poverty Program). It makes $72 million annually available to pay from 50 per cent to 90 per cent of the wages of students from low-income families for up to 15 hours of work a week, either on-campus or on off-campus jobs with public or nonprofit agencies. Pending plans will raise the federal share to $129 million in 1966. Since many or most of the students for whose wages the college (or other agency) will receive part-reimbursement would have been working anyway, and they do render services to their employers, it could be argued whether this program constitutes aid to students or subvention of colleges and other agencies. In any case it is likely to expand employment opportunities for students who need and want gainful employment.

The President also proposed early in 1965 that the federal government guarantee loans to students by nonfederal lenders, a service which has so far been rendered by some statewide plans and by United Student Aid Funds, a national nonprofit organization. The federal government would also pay up to two percentage points of the interest cost for insured student loans.

But the most significant part of the higher education bill passed in September 1965 is a federal scholarship program. Such a program has repeatedly been proposed over the years, either for its own sake, to aid students, or as a substitute for general aid to I.H.L. which kept running into insuperable roadblocks. The only major program of this type enacted, the "G.I. Bill of Rights," provided educational subventions for veterans of World War II and the Korean War and war orphans. It was conceived as a bonus in kind or as "the twentieth century equivalent of 'forty acres and a mule.'" More than ten million men and women participated, with about one third of them enrolling in I.H.L.

It was realized from the outset that regular tuitions would not cover the costs of instruction and that the addition of millions of students, instead of helping the institutions, would put an extra burden on them. So, several devices were tried, such as an additional $350 grant per student to private institutions, or letting public I.H.L. charge veterans the much higher "out-of-state" tuition fees. Those measures alleviated but never satisfactorily solved the problems and distortions which the federal program brought about. Similar plans in recent years, offering scholarships without requiring veteran's status, ran into the church-state issue—because federal supplemental payments would go to public and private institutions directly.

A majority of the veterans enrolled in private I.H.L. and thus confirmed an experience in regard to student preference of many other scholarship programs which pay for all or most of the tuition charges and leave the choice of institution to the student. In 1961 it was found that eighty per cent of the students under the National Merit Scholarship Program attended private I.H.L.

Land-grant colleges and state universities became disenchanted with federal scholarships which seemed to make it easier for students to enroll in private institutions, and their spokesmen testified at congressional hearings in 1958 and 1963 that they were "opposed to the inauguration of a federal scholarship program."[75] The Association resolved at its annual meeting in November 1964 that

> our association has for a number of years consistently opposed a general federal scholarship program and continues to do so. Opposition to a federal program has been based on two principal factors: (1) Continuing lack of evidence that any national scholarship program will have any marked effect in assuring college attendance of an appreciable number of students who cannot now enroll under existing programs; and (2) the fact that higher education has higher priority needs requiring federal financial assistance.

Early in 1965 however the White House which had persuaded the House and Senate to recede from long-held positions also succeeded with the state I.H.L. They were given to understand that student grants were part of a federal package which they would have to accept *in toto* if they derived any benefits at all. So the association's executive committee reversed itself early in 1965 and so testified at congressional hearings at which it implied that the institutions wanted "to be at the trough no matter what."[76]

For some years the rapid growth of state and private scholarships and loan programs seemed to take the edge off federal scholarships, and they moved into the background after the enactment of the federal student loan program in the National Defense Education Act. The Senate tacked a scholarship program onto the academic facilities bill in 1962, but the House instructed its conference committee, as a condition of agreeing to a conference with the Senate, not to accept it. When the conferees nevertheless returned with a bill containing scholarships, the House forthwith killed the bill.

Elmer D. West, Director of the Office of Statistical Information of the American Council on Education, subsequently presented a strong case for a federal scholarship program. He charged:

---

[75] *Science and Education for National Defense,* Hearings before the Committee on Labor and Public Welfare, Senate, 85th Congress, 2d S., 1958, p. 693. *National Education Improvement Act,* Hearings before the Committee on Education and Labor, H.R., 88th Congress, 1st S., 1963, p. 760.

[76] *Higher Education Act of 1965,* Hearings before the Special Subcommittee on Education, Committee on Education and Labor, H. R., 89th Congress, 1st S., p. 631.

> There are economic barriers, and particularly socio-economic barriers, which deprive capable students of a higher education and deprive the nation of their services at the level at which they could perform. . . . The task is not yet being done satisfactorily by the states, by private individuals and organizations, or by the colleges and universities. The data show conclusively that there is a segment of the population with insufficient funds to educate their children to the maximum level of capability.[77]

However, James W. Arnold and Ralph E. Weber, in a new book which outlines the various possibilities of financing a college education, arrived at a different conclusion: "Despite rising college costs, almost every student—with the desire and ability—can manage higher education through a combination of savings, scholarships, jobs, and loans."[78]

An enlightening exchange on this subject took place in the U.S. Senate on February 5, 1962, between Senators Lausche and Morse. When Senator Lausche said that students who really wanted to go to college could borrow the money and that he did not believe that a highly intelligent student would not go unless he received a scholarship, Senator Morse replied that the argument was effective before an audience of self-made men and women, that the members of the Senate had made great sacrifices to attain their positions, but that they should not judge others by their own standards, and that "we would be running a risk that some young men and women would not be willing to borrow the necessary amount to go to college, as we did, for example." To this Senator Lausche replied: "A student who refuses to attend an I.H.L. unless he is given an outright grant, instead of a loan, in all probability does not possess the moral fabric to justify making the grant to him."[79]

---

[77] Elmer D. West, *Financial Aid to the Undergraduate: Issues and Implications,* American Council on Education, 1963, p. 125. For a collection of arguments pro and con, see: *Guaranteeing an Opportunity for Higher Education to All Qualified High School Graduates: Should the Federal Government Participate?* Selected Excerpts relating to the National College Debate Topic 1963–64, Legislative Reference Service, Library of Congress, House Document No. 164, 88th Congress, 1st S., 1963.

[78] James W. Arnold and Ralph E. Weber, *Admission to College* (Milwaukee: Bruce Publishing Co., 1964); quoted from prepublication article by the authors, "What It Costs to Go to College," in *Ave Maria,* February 8, 1964.

[79] *Congressional Record,* February 5, 1962, pp. 1506, 1633.

The Office of Education justified the need for federal scholarships in 1965 by pointing out that the cost of college attendance
had risen 31 per cent in public and 39 per cent in private I.H.L.
over the past decade.[80] It did not mention that about half of this
increase had been caused by inflation—prices rose 15 per cent to
21 per cent, depending on which price index we use—and that
average family income had expanded 48 per cent over the past ten
years.[81] This means that the cost of attending college has declined
in proportion to family income, as I showed in Chapter 6. Of course,
the income of *some* families did not grow at the average rate. But
the number and percentage of low-income families have been
shrinking while the number and amount of scholarships and other
student aid programs have been growing.

Reports suggest that there are, in the mid-1960's, sufficient
scholarships available to meet the essential needs of gifted and
ambitious students which cannot be met in any other way. But
mediocre and marginal young people of low motivation may have
difficulty finding adequate financial assistance in the form of
grants. Opinions differ on whether this situation needs to be cor-
rected by the enactment of a large federal scholarship program.
The failure, by a narrow margin, of a proposed educational tax
credit program in the Senate in February 1964—which will be discussed in the next chapter—rekindled interest in federal scholarships among those who are opposed to tax credits.

Elmer West's earlier cited study also showed that available aids
tend to be won by students from middle-income families with only
a small share going to those from the lowest income groups. This is
so largely because scholarships are now commonly awarded com-
petitively by academic achievement, and young people from low
socio-economic backgrounds frequently do not show up well in
tests or attain scholastic standing in high school. How to interpret
this well known fact is and will remain controversial, at least until
studies, now taboo, also reveal the distribution of ability and motivation. But the findings led to demands for channeling more student aid to the very poor and eventually to the President's program

---

[80] *Congressional Record,* February 1, 1965, p. 1611.
[81] Bureau of the Census, *Current Population Reports,* Series P-60, No. 43, Table B.

of "educational opportunity grants" in 1965 which award between $200 and $800 a year to about 130,000 "exceptionally needy" students.

The number of fellowships for graduate students, either privately sponsored or under the auspices of a number of federal agencies, has been increasing rapidly and will, by all appearances, continue to grow. However, a group of distinguished scientists argued before the House Committee on Science and Astronautics on January 23, 1963, that the number of fellowships available in science and technology already exceeded the supply of competent graduate students.

Summary

Large federal funds are flowing into higher education, mostly for specified research purposes. They have, on the whole, had beneficial effects on the small number of institutions—or departments within institutions—among which most of the project monies are concentrated, but also led to serious imbalance and raised grave problems. They tend to make "the rich richer and the poor poorer." Undergraduate instructional programs have not been helped by the research grants and, in many institutions, may have been hampered. Federal research funds appear to have reached a plateau and will probably not expand substantially in the next few years. But even an increase in such funds would offer no answer to the financial problems of I.H.L.

The federal government is not now aiding the instructional programs in higher education by grants for salaries and operations, nor is it likely to do so for as long as we can see ahead. The roadblocks appear to be insuperable, at least for a long time.

Federal grants for certain selected types of construction were enacted in 1963 and assist in the building of the benefited types of facilities, i. e., in the natural and physical sciences, mathematics, foreign languages, engineering, and libraries. Federal construction loans are helpful in the building of student housing but are of limited value for other types of needed facilities.

On the whole, then, it seems that in the next few years the support of colleges and universities, for current operations and for plant expansion, will continue to rest largely on the established four major sources: tuitions and fees, state and municipal appropriations, endowment earnings and gifts, federal research grants and contracts with limited amounts of other federal funds added.

Projections of sources of revenue for current operations appear in the table at the end of this chapter. They assume that (a) tuitions and fees will be substantially raised, both in public and private I.H.L.; (b) state and local appropriations will rise at a faster rate in the 1960's than they did in the 1950's, which will require major tax boosts in many states; (c) private donors will continue to raise their level of giving under the impact of intensive fund drives; (d) the federal government will moderately increase its grant and loan programs in higher education.

These projections do not suggest that I.H.L. will find it easy to finance their activities adequately during the balance of the 1960's. Quite the contrary. The assumption of substantial boosts in state (and local) taxes, tuitions, fees, and enlarged donations presupposes not only that institutions will exert extraordinary efforts, but also that they will, on the whole, be successful. Only the future can tell whether this assumption is justified. Money-raising efforts will inevitably run into many obstacles and road-blocks and some needs may not be met. The resistance of taxpayers and legislators could well grow stronger. Private institutions may have reached the limit which students and their families are willing or able to pay, if state institutions offer comparable programs at a fraction of the cost and if the tuition differential continues to grow. An accelerated shift from private to public institutions could lead to a grave crisis both in public and private colleges and universities.

Strong pressure will inevitably continue for increased support and some form of general assistance from the national government. While attempts to secure direct grants of significant size appear to be stalled by major roadblocks, there are other ways in which the national government could materially aid higher education. They are discussed in the next and last chapter.

REVENUES OF I.H.L. IN 1950, 1960, AND 1970

	Millions of 1959–60 Dollars		Per Cent Increase	Billions of 1959–60 Dollars		Per Cent Increase	
	1949–50	1959–60	1950–60	1969–70 Low	High	1960–70 Low	High
Student fees	$ 864	$1,165	35%	$ 2.7	$ 3.7	132%	218%
Gifts and endowment earnings	264	590	123	1.2	1.5	103	154
State and local governments	690	1,541	123	3.1	3.8	101	147
Federal research	232	912	293	1.9	2.9	108	218
Federal, other	37	125	238	0.3	0.5	140	300
Other	180	380	111	0.7	0.8	84	111
All educational and general	$2,267	$4,713	108%	$ 9.9	$13.2	110%	180%
Auxiliary activities and student aid	666	1,100	65	2.0	2.4	82	118
All current revenues	$2,933	$5,813	98%	$11.9	$15.6	105%	168%
Plant funds	650	1,312	102	1.7	2.1	30	60
All Revenues	$3,583	$7,125	99%	$13.6	$17.7	91%	148%

Notes

  1970 figures projected.

  Does not include additions to endowment funds principal.

  Student fees include those derived from federal veterans program (G. I. Bill). Those fees amounted to $378 million in 1950 (1960 dollars) and to $4 million in 1960. If those amounts are excluded, revenue from student fees increased 139 per cent between 1950 and 1960.

  Historical data derived from: Office of Education, *Financial Statistics of Higher Education, 1959–60,* 1964, Table 7.

10 More Than One Way to Skin a Cat

A study of the dramatic congressional battles over federal aid to higher education in recent years suggests certain conclusions in regard to the future prospects of such proposals: *The enactment of grants for the general institutional purposes of colleges and universities, for undergraduate education or for salaries and operations, appears highly improbable. Construction grants for selected types of facilities now authorized for the next three years are likely to be extended, amounts may be enlarged, and some of the restrictions might be eased, if not very substantially; research grants will not continue to grow at the rate at which they have been increasing and, in any case, are of significant benefit only to a tiny fraction of I.H.L.; loans to students and for student housing may keep expanding; other types of loans are of only limited value; a federal scholarship program of modest proportions has been enacted and may subsequently be expanded.*

On the whole, then, it seems that higher education cannot expect, through any or all of the mentioned programs, aid from the federal government which is significant in terms of its prospective budget of $15 billion or more by the end of the current decade. Yet it is obvious that the idea of federal assistance pervades much of the current discussions of higher educational finances. Some believe that other sources, public or private, do

not have a sufficient capacity to meet essential goals; others hold
that state and local taxes or tuitions and fees are less wholesome
sources than federal taxes, and that a boost in those sources is
undesirable; still others feel that the growing imbalance in the
structure of higher education calls for some corrective action.

The expressed or implied hope seems to be that a "magic
formula" will be found which will enable the national government
to bypass the obstacles which have blocked innumerable proposals
in the past and which will permit it to come to the assistance of
higher education. Such a "magic formula" may take the shape of
indirect aid. If the government cannot aid the colleges through
direct appropriations—for reasons set forth in the preceding chapter—then it can possibly do so in an indirect manner, by helping
to ease the burden of those who now provide much of the support.

The most obvious indirect way leads through the tax system.
Virtually all agree that the heavy taxes which the national government now imposes bear a major responsibility for the inability—or
at least diminished ability—of state governments, families, and
individuals to supply higher education with larger funds. The 1964
tax cut eased this condition only slightly and was too broadly
distributed to be of sufficient help in this area. Alleviative measures
would have to aim specifically at those who now foot the bill for
higher education.

Tax Relief for Education

Aiding education through exemption from or abatement of
taxes has long been an established practice in the United States.
Tangible property of schools and I.H.L. used for educational purposes is generally exempt from property taxes, and the income
and transactions of educational institutions are not subject to
federal or state income taxes nor most other state and local taxes.
The federal government, some years ago, widened the range of
excise taxes from which schools and colleges are exempt.

With virtually all activities of I.H.L. already free of taxation,
there is not much left that government could exempt. But it can
give tangible recognition to those who support education. Donations to educational institutions are deductible from adjusted gross
income for up to thirty per cent of an individual's adjusted gross

income or up to five per cent of a corporation's taxable income. It is less well known that the tax law permits a double personal exemption for many college students: they can claim a personal exemption on their own return while their parents, if they supply over half the student's support, may also claim it on their return. Furthermore, income from scholarships or fellowships is not considered income for tax purposes.

There have been many suggestions that the national government should go further along the road of providing indirect tax benefits to higher education. The Twelfth General Assembly of the States, on December 4, 1954, urged the national government to grant private I.H.L. the privilege of issuing tax-exempt bonds, a right that state and municipal I.H.L. enjoy as a matter of course. Such recognition of private educational contributions to the public responsibility, the resolution declared, would prevent a heavier load of needed construction from falling upon the states. This method would avoid any possible governmental interference with private educational policy.[1] The request was not granted, and Congress preferred to extend and expand the College Housing Program of loans for the construction of dormitories, dining halls, etc., and, a few years later, an academic facilities program at public and private I.H.L. Those programs assure the two federal departments involved an influence on the planning and execution of campus construction while the grant of tax-exemption for bonds would have given them no such privilege. It would have lowered the interest rates for private college bonds.

The largest nonpublic revenue source of I.H.L. is tuitions and fees. In the early 1950's the idea started gaining popularity that some tangible acknowledgment should be given through the federal income tax to the special burdens that students in higher education, and their parents, bear for four or five years or longer. In recognition of the fact that society as a whole and not only the student himself benefits from higher education, it was felt that he or his parents should be granted some tax concessions. The thought behind the proposal was, however, that a shift of part of the cost of tuition from the family to the federal government would make it easier for institutions to raise the level of tuitions. So, while the

---

[1] *State Government*, January 1955, p. 27.

plan was widely announced as offering relief to students and their families, it was also intended as a device by which I.H.L. could augment their revenues without unduly increasing the burden on student families.

The idea caught on, and the number of educational tax relief bills soared from 15 in the 83rd Congress to 56 in the 85th and to more than 100 in the 87th. Close to 150 bills were introduced in the 88th Congress which provide for some type of tax benefits for students and their families. Altogether, there have been close to 500 such bills in the past twelve years. Some sponsors deem the tax-concession approach superior to the grant method; others regard it as a necessary supplement to grants; and still others feel that it should serve as a substitute, as long as direct operational grants are not or cannot be enacted. Few types of legislation, if any, have ever been advanced in so many simultaneous proposals in both Houses of Congress and by members of both political parties. The large and ever-growing number of bills and several polls which indicated overwhelming support suggest that there is widespread and growing public sentiment for this type of aid to education. The proposals can be divided into three major types: deductions, exemptions, tax credits.

Deductions for Educational Expenses

The simplest and most frequently advanced plan would add another category to the deductions from adjusted gross income which are presently permissible, such as state and local taxes, interest, medical costs, charitable contributions, etc. It would let the student or his parents deduct tuitions and fees and, under some bills, also other expenses, such as books, supplies, board and room, etc. The deduction would be available only to full-time students at a public or private college or university—under some bills also to those in other schools—to his spouse, or to a taxpayer who pays for the college expenses of his dependent children, other relatives, or nonrelated persons. As a rule there is an upper ceiling, running anywhere from $600 to $2,000 per student.

None of the many congressional sponsors of educational tax relief plans has been more articulate and fought harder for the idea than Senator Abraham A. Ribicoff. Immediately after resigning as Secretary of Health, Education, and Welfare to run for the Senate, he advocated such a program on the TV show "Meet the Press," on June 17, 1962, and declared the enactment of such a plan essential in two speeches in the Senate on May 2 and August 6, 1963, as well as on various other occasions.[2] He introduced a bill (S 1567) to permit students enrolled at I.H.L. to deduct up to $1,500 in college expenses from their (or their families') income for tax purposes.

Senator Barry Goldwater's "Educational Opportunities Act" (S 991, 87th Congress; S 181, 88th Congress) would have allowed the deduction of higher educational expenses up to $2,000 but placed an effective income ceiling of $12,000 for single and $22,000 for married persons on the availability of these benefits. Other bills on educational tax deductions were introduced by Senators Magnuson, Randolph, Byrd (W. Va.), Mundt, Scott, Symington, Fulbright, Long (Missouri), Prouty, Keating, Smathers; Representatives Fogarty, Chamberlain, Judd, Westland, May, Bow, Hall, Langen, and many others.

Additional Exemptions for College Students

The deduction method would give no benefits to persons using the standard deduction on their income tax returns. This would be remedied by bills which permit a student or his parents to claim one or two *additional* personal exemptions or to increase the personal exemption from $600 to $1,000 or more. Senator Fulbright has submitted proposals of this type (and also several others of a slightly different type) in every Congress since the 84th and declared that it is more efficient to encourage individual payment of educational expenses than for government to assume the burden of educating its citizens.[3]

Senator Smathers, who co-sponsored a similar bill, originally introduced by Senator Cannon, together with Senators Johnston, Hartke, Randolph, Byrd (West Virginia), Allott, and Young, stated: "I cannot help feeling that this is a better way in which to educate the young people of America, or to make it possible for

---

[2] *Congressional Record,* May 20, 1963, pp. 8500 ff. Related articles in: *U.S. News and World Report,* June 3, 1963; *Time,* May 31, 1963; *The New York Times,* May 26, 1963, etc. *Congressional Record,* August 6, 1963, p. 13396.

[3] *Congressional Record,* January 9, 1957, p. 352.

their parents to educate them, rather than to talk about loan or grant programs or other proposals of that type, although I am in favor of loan programs."[4] Other bills of this type were introduced by Senators Hill, Scott, Johnston, Dodd, Hruska, Carlson, Pearson, Hartke, McCarthy; Representatives Elliott, Teller, Multer, and many others. Several state legislatures, including those of Illinois, Colorado, South Carolina, etc., memorialized Congress in recent years to adopt such a plan.[5]

Tax Credits for Educational Expenses

Deductions and exemptions (which are in effect fixed-dollar deductions) have been criticized for giving the greatest benefit—up to 70 per cent—to persons in high brackets and only 14 per cent to those of moderate income (using tax rates effective from 1965 on). A tuition boost would cost a student or his family of low income 86 per cent net, while the cost to those in high brackets would be only 50 per cent or as little as 30 per cent. This would largely defeat the purpose of granting tax concessions in higher education, which is to help institutions and students from moderate income families. So a method was conceived to provide more equal benefits to persons in all tax brackets by permitting them to deduct a fixed percentage of their educational expenses *from the tax liability itself,* rather than from the adjusted gross income (the tax base). Bills of this type were introduced by Senators McCarthy, Wiley, Dominick, Thurmond; Representatives Boggs, Roosevelt, Laird, Curtis (Missouri), Frelinghuysen, Cleveland, Thompson, Perkins, Byrnes, Stratton, Zelenko, Rhodes, Jackson, and numerous others. Representative Schwengel combined tax credits with the purchase of certificates in what he called the "Iowa Plan."[6]

The Taxation Section of the American Bar Association, in cooperation with the American Council on Education, devised a plan in 1954 under which a student or his family could deduct thirty per cent of educational expenses up to a maximum of $1,500

---

[4] *Congressional Record,* September 5, 1962, p. 17493.

[5] *Congressional Record,* March 7, 1961, p. A 2559; April 15, 1963, p. 6162; April 26, 1963, p. 6766; etc.

[6] *Congressional Record,* May 25, 1961, p. 8296; September 27, 1961, p. A 7909; August 20, 1962, p. 16014; January 7, 1963, p. 519.

(that is, up to a maximum credit of $450).[7] Several other organizations, such as the Association of American Colleges, the American Alumni Council, the U.S. National Student Association, etc., joined the American Council on Education which testified on behalf of the plan before the House Ways and Means Committee and conducted a vigorous campaign for it.[8]

The Republican platform, adopted on July 27, 1960 in Chicago, suggested "consideration of means through tax laws to help offset tuition costs"[9] and the platform adopted on July 14, 1964 in San Francisco pledged "tax credits for college education" and "tax credits for those burdened by the expenses of college education." The Association for Higher Education, a department of the National Education Association, passed a resolution in 1957 asking that tax credits be granted only to persons who are enrolled in tax-exempt (i.e., state or municipal) institutions.[10]

Deduction, Exemption, and Flat Percentage Credit Bills and Their Shortcomings

Hundreds of bills of the described types were introduced in the past twelve years but no positive action was taken by either House of Congress on any of them. None of them was seriously considered by a single committee or ever brought to a vote. On closer analysis it must be said that there were reasons for this lack of attention: the bills would not have accomplished much of what they set out to do.

Under the deduction and exemption plans, persons in high income and tax brackets would have recovered up to 91 per cent of their educational expenses (under the tax rate scale in effect until 1963), up to whatever ceiling was imposed, while persons in modest circumstances would have recouped only 20 per cent of their outlays. So, low-income families would have had to bear 80 per cent of tuition and fees, wealthy families only a small frac-

---

[7] *A Proposed Tax Credit Plan to Aid Students in Institutions of Higher Learning,* American Council on Education, 1955.

[8] *General Revenue Revision,* Hearings before the Committee on Ways and Means, H.R. 85th Congress, 2d Session, 1958, pp. 1061 ff and 1092 ff.

[9] *Aid for Higher Education,* Hearings before the Subcommittee on Education of the Committee on Labor and Public Welfare, Senate, 87th Congress, 1st Session, 1961, p. 154.

[10] *Higher Education,* April 1957, p. 158.

tion. This, of course, can be explained as the effect of our steeply graduated income tax schedules which permit the relatively greatest benefits of deductions and exemptions to persons in high brackets and thus offset, to a very minor and on the whole insignificant degree, some of the excessive progression in the rate scale. But to give the highest educational tax benefits where relief is needed the least, namely to wealthy families whose offspring, if otherwise qualified, would have enrolled in college anyway at no particular financial sacrifice, would have defeated the very purpose of the plan: it would have given little aid to families in moderate circumstances and helped the institutions not much if at all. Even the 30 per cent tax credit plans would let the student and his family foot 70 per cent of the expenses and of increases which the colleges might subsequently impose; it would be of very limited assistance.

These technical shortcomings of the various pending educational tax relief plans were more widely realized as time went on and were demonstrated by Allan M. Cartter, vice-president of the American Council on Education.[11] The President's Committee on Education Beyond the High School (Josephs Committee) recommended in 1957 that tax benefits be granted in higher education and that "provisions be included which will grant proportionately greater tax benefits to those least able to afford those expenditures.[12] But no such plan was developed for several years. The earlier enthusiasm for tax relief in educational circles faded when no action was forthcoming from Congress after several years of intense efforts. Gradually interest shifted to other, and seemingly more promising, ways of aiding college finances.

One Hundred Per Cent Tax Credits for Educational Purposes

The apparent inadequacy of the tax deduction and exemption plans led to the idea that more truly effective aid could be rendered if educational expenses were permitted to be offset against the tax liability itself rather than against the tax base. In other words, the tax would be reduced, dollar for dollar, by the amount of tuition, fees, etc., up to a specified ceiling. Senator Strom Thurmond, for

---

[11] Allan M. Cartter, "Tax Reliefs and the Burden of College Costs," *The Educational Record,* October 1963; also: *Congressional Record,* July 19, 1963, pp. A 4623 ff.

[12] The President's Committee on Education Beyond the High School, *Second Report to the President,* 1957, p. 56.

example, introduced such a bill that would have set the ceiling at $100.[13] This seemed somewhat too low a figure and a group of twenty college presidents developed a plan which would have set it at $300. The proposal was presented to the Subcommittee on Education of the Senate Committee on Labor and Public Welfare by President John A. Howard of Rockford College and President Landrum Bolling of Earlham College on May 16, 1963, in hearings on the President's Omnibus Education Bill.[14] This plan, obviously, would be of very substantial aid. It would, in effect, make higher education tuition-free for most students at I.H.L. whose fees total $300 or less, and would reduce the cost by that amount for those at higher-priced I.H.L. Alternatively, it would permit institutions to boost their fees by $300 without added cost to their users.

Bills to implement this plan were introduced by Representatives Wright, Cabell and others but, despite their undeniable appeal, have led to no congressional action. The idea of a 100 per cent credit, or full offset of expenses against taxes, struck many members as going too far and made them reluctant to support it. The setting of the ceiling posed a problem. If it were set low it would be of only modest help. If it were set high it would, in effect, establish a tuition minimum and might favor high-cost institutions. Considering the actual size of tuitions in 1965, a ceiling of $300 is probably as good a compromise as can be devised. Still, there has been little response in Congress to the bills advancing that plan.

A Sliding Tax Credit Plan

In the spring of 1963 the Senate Committee on Labor and Public Welfare asked me to testify on pending bills for aid to education. It seemed to me that none of the various grant and loan proposals would give higher education the effective assistance it needed or had much chance of being enacted, with the exception of restricted construction aid. Nor did most of the pending tax relief plans provide adequate assistance and good legislative prospects. It appeared that tax credits offered the most promising

---

[13] S 3483, 85th Congress, *Congressional Record*, March 14, 1958, p. 4396.

[14] *Education Legislation–1963*, Hearings of the Subcommittee on Education of the Committee on Labor and Public Welfare, U.S. Senate, 88th Congress, 1st Session, 1963, pp. 1127 ff. This plan was implemented in H.R. 8539 by Rep. Griffin; *Congressional Record*, January 22, 1964, pp. 904/5, and others.

method of effectively helping to finance higher education but that a compromise formula would have to be found to bring the various interests into balance: high-cost vs. low-cost, public vs. private institutions, institutions vs. students and parents, etc.

When I testified before the Committee on May 27, 1963, I suggested to resolve the problem by enacting a graduated or sliding tax credit schedule as follows:[15]

Tuitions and Fees	Credit
First $100	100%
Next 400	30
Next 1000	20%

Maximum net tax credit: $420.

Senator Barry Goldwater inserted my testimony in the *Congressional Record* and introduced a bill to implement it (S 2269—88th Congress).[16] Representative Thomas B. Curtis introduced a companion bill in the House (H.R. 8981—88th Congress).[17] One week after I testified, Senator Hubert Humphrey, then assistant majority leader, delivered a speech in the Senate in which he adopted the sliding tax credit schedule as a "sensible and workable system of federal assistance":

> It is essential that an across-the-board tax credit program be initiated to assist every person currently facing the considerable expenses associated with higher education. . . .
>
> I have sponsored similar tax credit legislation for many years. However, the bill I introduce today is, in my opinion, a significantly improved measure over all earlier versions.
>
> Tax deductible, additional exemption, and tax credit bills share a common purpose: first, to assist persons financing a college education and second, to provide indirect assistance to the institutions of higher education.[18]

---

[15] *Education Legislation—1963*, pp. 1265 ff; *Congressional Record*, May 27, 1963, pp. 8928 ff.

[16] *Congressional Record*, October 30, 1963, pp. 19495 ff.

[17] *Congressional Record*, October 30, 1963, pp. 19625 ff.

[18] *Congressional Record*, June 6, 1963, p. 9676.

Senator Humphrey then cited from my testimony before the Senate Committee on May 27 and continued:

> The sliding tax credit schedule provides a sensible and workable system of federal assistance that helps every student, indirectly helps both public and private institutions, and does so in a manner that in no way interferes with individual or institutional freedom or policies. This bill, providing for a declining tax credit for expenditures on tuition, fees, books, and supplies mitigates the distortion found in the large majority of bills that rely on tax deductions, additional exemptions, or non-variable tax credit. . . .
>
> While this tax credit proposal would not solve all the financial problems related to higher education, it would represent a significant contribution well within our national means. It would provide this assistance in a manner that avoids any argument about federal control of education and also the nagging question of church-state relations. Moreover, it would provide this aid without having to expand the Federal bureaucracy to administer the program.
>
> Support in the Congress has been growing for this general approach to the problem of federal aid to higher education. I know the appropriate committees in both Houses are giving these proposals careful scrutiny and consideration. I hope that the Administration will consider seriously requesting such legislation from the Congress.

Senator Humphrey thought that the 100 per cent credit which I suggested in the lowest bracket might not be acceptable and lowered it to 75 per cent, while slightly increasing the percentages between $100 and $1,000. He proposed this schedule:

Tuitions, Fees, Books, and Supplies	Credit
First $100	75%
Next 400	40
Next 500	30
Next 500	20%

Maximum net credit: $485.

Senator Humphrey's proposal was described as a potential life saver for private higher education by one of the most effective and prolific writers in the field of educational finance, the Reverend Virgil C. Blum, S.J., head of the Political Science Department at Marquette University:

The enactment of the Humphrey bill would probably make possible the survival and improvement of most private colleges and universities. Unless some such program is adopted to relieve the private college of the burden of so heavily subsidizing its students, Louis T. Benezet's dire prediction may well come to pass: "We may expect to see the monumental construction of state university metropolises on the one hand and on the other the disappearance of most of the private colleges—perhaps in a state junior college system, or possibly into mental hospitals, another growing public need.[19]

That a legislative action plan in a highly controversial field such as aid to education could find the support and the sponsorship of two senators of such widely differing political philosophies as Barry Goldwater and Hubert Humphrey—who were then respectively the leaders of the conservative Republicans and of the liberal Democrats in the Senate and were soon to be the Presidential and Vice Presidential candidates on the two opposing tickets in the 1964 election—was quite unusual. It suggested that the proposal had considerable merit and broad appeal independent of political considerations, and represented a compromise solution to an intricate problem which seemed acceptable on the left as well as on the right side of the political fence. Support for the plan was gaining in both parties and numerous newspaper reports and editorials commented favorably on it.

Under congressional rules, however, the Education Committee has no jurisdiction over this type of legislation. When a tax relief amendment was proposed during the debate of the College Construction Bill, the bill's floor manager and chairman of the Education Subcommittee, Senator Wayne Morse, commented: "I suggest that the amendment is a far more appropriate vehicle for consideration before the Senate Finance Committee, for the amendment contemplates changes in the internal revenue of the government. The Committee on Labor and Welfare really has no jurisdiction in this area."[20] We may also surmise that Senator Morse, who is personally opposed to educational tax relief, expected the Finance Committee to be less favorably inclined toward such plans than an education committee.

---

[19] Virgil C. Blum, "Senator Humphrey's Tax-Credit Bill," *Journal of Higher Education,* December 1963. Dr. Benezet is quoted from an address delivered before the Association of American Colleges, January 12, 1960.

[20] *Congressional Record,* October 21, 1963, p. 18869.

The proper way to advance the tax credit plan in Senator Morse's undoubtedly correct interpretation was then to proceed through the Finance Committee which at that time had a general tax reduction and reform bill under consideration (H.R. 8363) which had already passed the House and later became the Revenue Act of 1964.

Thus when the Senate Finance Committee invited me to testify on the then pending tax bill, I added to my comments on the House-approved changes in the Internal Revenue Code a section in which I again proposed a sliding tax credit plan as a means of aiding higher education.[21] When I testified before the committee on November 6, 1963, Senator Ribicoff announced that some of the Senators who had introduced educational tax relief bills were in the process of agreeing on a uniform approach and that "you and I and most Senators interested in this field are about on the same track today."[22] This meant that Senator Ribicoff and several of his colleagues had shifted from the tax deduction or exemption plans which they had previously advocated to the sliding tax credit method as the preferred or most promising solution.

Two weeks later Senator Ribicoff introduced an amendment (No. 329) to the pending tax bill to implement the sliding tax credit plan,[23] which was co-sponsored by ten other Democratic and six Republican Senators.[24] These Senators decided to change the percentage scale slightly from the formula used by Senator Humphrey:

Tuitions, Fees, Books, and Supplies	Credit
First $200	75%
Next 300	25
Next 1,000	10%

Maximum net credit: $325

---

[21] *Revenue Act of 1963*, Hearings before the Committee on Finance, U.S. Senate, 88th Congress, 1st Session, 1963, Part 3. My testimony begins on p. 1335; the section dealing with educational tax credits appears on pp. 1394–97.

[22] *Ibid.*, p. 1369.

[23] *Congressional Record*, November 21, 1963, p. 21490.

[24] Co-sponsors were: Senators Brewster, Byrd (W. Va.), Cannon, Dodd, Dominick, Gruening, Humphrey, Keating, Long (Mo.), Moss, Prouty, Randolph, Scott, Beall, Jordan, and Edmondson.

Newspapers reported and commented on these efforts, and a growing number of individuals and organizations rallied to support them. From the nucleus of twenty college presidents who earlier in the year had advocated a 100 per cent tax credit for higher education tuitions and fees up to $300, a Citizens National Committee for Higher Education was formed "to conduct research into and propose ways and means of increasing the flow of national income into higher education," to promote the expansion of services and encourage voluntary giving to higher education, etc. The Committee viewed tax credits for college expenses and donations as the most promising immediate means of strengthening higher educational finances and backed the Ribicoff amendment. It arranged an organizational meeting in Washington on January 14, 1964, during the 50th annual convention of the Association of American Colleges, at which Senators Ribicoff and Dominick spoke. Senator Ribicoff explained his proposal as follows:[25]

> This amendment provides an income tax credit to any person who pays for college tuition and certain related expenses, such as fees, books and supplies. The credit is available to parents, to students themselves, if they pay or contribute to their own tuition, and also to any other person who may decide to finance the higher education of a deserving young man or woman. . . .
> [The] percentage formula was used to recognize the fact that tuition at most public colleges is less than at private colleges. By giving a proportionately greater credit to low tuitions, we have sought to equalize the relative benefits of the credit between those who pay tuitions at public and private colleges.
> The credit is reduced by one per cent of the amount by which the taxpayer's adjusted gross income exceeds $25,000. This means the credit is reduced by $50 for each $5,000 of income over $25,000. Under this provision the man in the $30,000 bracket gets less tax benefit than the man in the $10,000 bracket, and the man in the $60,000 bracket gets no benefit at all.
> This feature of the amendment is designed to meet the objection to other tax relief plans that they waste benefit on the very rich who do not need it and they prefer the upper income groups. Our amendment provides no benefit to the very rich and prefers the middle and lower middle income groups. . . .
> I support this amendment to the tax code because I believe the heavy burden of a college education is just as entitled to be lessened through our tax laws as the heavy burden of medical expenses

---

[25] *Congressional Record,* January 15, 1964, pp. 468–469.

or casualty losses. College costs hit a family in a comparatively short span of years and hit with an impact that hurts. A $3,000 college expense is a staggering burden for a man earning $8,000, $12,000, or $15,000. It is no answer to say that the cost can be anticipated. Medical expenses, too, can be anticipated, yet our tax laws even provide tax relief for the cost of health insurance.

Senator Dominick defined the aim of the plan: to enable a student's family to use its *pre-tax* earnings to pay for his college education.

At the concluding session of the Association of American Colleges convention two days later, its legislative and resolutions committees recommended a resolution which would have withdrawn past endorsement of the tax credit plan "in principle" and established a committee to study it. But on a motion from the floor, the membership reversed its committees and endorsed the tax credit by a four-to-one standing vote:

Whereas the Association has in former years endorsed in general terms the principle of an income tax credit for personal expenditures for higher education, and
Whereas legislation to effect such an aim is pending in Congress, and
Whereas there is now a greatly increased interest in the entire subject,
Be it resolved that the Association commend the members of this Congress who are now seeking to obtain the enactment of legislation to implement this principle.

A few days later, however, on January 21, 1964, the Senate Finance Committee rejected the Ribicoff amendment with a vote of 10:7. Interestingly, while the amendment had been sponsored, as mentioned earlier, by eleven Democrats and six Republicans, all Democrats in the Senate Finance Committee except Senator Ribicoff voted against it, although four of them had earlier introduced similar bills—and all Republicans voted for it.

There is a plain explanation for this strange reversal of positions: the Treasury Department had long opposed proposals of tax relief for higher education, during the Eisenhower Administration when the idea first came up and even more strongly under the Kennedy Administration. It had been successful in having the President support its stand. There were indications in the fall of 1963 that the Administration might be willing to compromise, in view of the proposal's great popularity in Congress. However, the tragic events in Dallas changed this. President Johnson was determined that his budget for 1965, as submitted in January 1964, should show the smallest possible budget deficit and took an adamant stand in regard to proposals which would have reduced revenues below those in his budget. He used all means at his command to assure a defeat of the plan and made a vote against the Ribicoff amendment a matter of party discipline.

After debating the Ribicoff amendment for several hours on February 3, 1964, the Senate proceeded to vote on February 4th.[26] *The Wall Street Journal* described the events: "The Ribicoff forces gained a quick lead as the Senate roll was called. A number of Democrats held back until it became clear that their votes were needed to beat the plan. Three of the last minute 'no' votes came from Democrats Humphrey of Minnesota, Moss of Utah, and Robert Byrd of West Virginia, who were among the Ribicoff plan's co-sponsors."[27]

As finally recorded, 5 Republicans joined with 43 Democrats in defeating the Amendment, while 19 Democrats joined 26 Republicans in voting for it. The *Washington Post* reported:

> This key roll call closed in breathtaking finish, with Democratic leaders producing the winning margin against the Amendment in the last few minutes of the tally. . . .
> The leadership heat was really on, following a morning legislative conference on the tax bill at the White House. At least three "loyal" Democrats, who were listed as co-sponsors of the original Ribicoff college education amendment, cast their votes with the leadership to defeat it on the showdown.[28]

The final vote of 45:48 included among the negative votes besides the mentioned 3 co-sponsors of the amendment, another 6 Senators who had previously introduced similar bills (Fulbright, Hartke, Johnston, McCarthy, Smathers, and Thurmond).[29]

---

[26] *Congressional Record,* February 3, 1964, pp. 1699–1735, February 4, pp. 1747–58.

[27] "Senate Rejects 2 Tax-Relief Plans for Allowing College-Cost Claims," *The Wall Street Journal,* February 5, 1964.

[28] "Dividend Credit Loses in Senate Vote on Tax Bill," *The Washington Post,* February 5, 1964.

[29] Republican Senators voting against it were: Aiken, Javits, Miller, Saltonstall, and Smith. Senator Young (N. Dak.) was paired against it with the absent Senator Dirksen, who favored it.

U. S. News & World Report gave a dramatic description and evaluation of the defeat of the Ribicoff amendment:

> The cost of a college education is a growing force in politics that seems on the way to influencing tax policy. . . .
> The final vote—and the backstage maneuvering preceding it—demonstrated that college aid in some form is going to be increasingly difficult to deny. . . .
> Barriers raised against the plan were on a rare scale. The Johnson Administration used every ounce of influence it could muster. . . .
> The final 48-to-45 count did not reveal the full strength of the drive for aid to parents of college students.
> As the roll call neared its end, the tally stood 44 to 44, then 45 to 45. It was at this point that the drive was halted by Administration supporters who, though backing the plan, had pledged their votes against the amendment if those votes were needed to block the bill. These Senators quickly went to the floor and cast the "no" votes that defeated the Ribicoff amendment.[30]

It appears likely that the defeat of the Ribicoff amendment on February 4, 1964 was not the end but the beginning of the fight for educational tax credits. This was the first time that Congress ever had considered tax relief for higher educational expenses and voted on it. It was only a few months after the idea of a sliding scale credit had first been proposed, yet a clear majority in the Senate was favoring it and it missed passage by only two votes. The events of that day merely go to prove that nowadays a President who is determined to use all the powers of his office and knows how to use them can impose his will on Congress, at least temporarily.

That the proponents were not discouraged was indicated by Representative Seymour Halpern (N. Y.) in a speech in the House on February 10, 1964.[31] Mr. Halpern said that the closeness of the vote in the proposal's first congressional test

> convinces me that by continuing to push relentlessly for legislation of this kind, we can pass a bill which would not only afford students

---

[30] "Eventually, a Tax Subsidy for College Education?" *U.S. News and World Report,* February 17, 1964.
[31] *Congressional Record,* February 10, 1964, p. 2734.

and parents relief from the growing cost of education but would provide the greatest spur ever given to higher education in this country. There is no reason whatsoever, Mr. Speaker, why the objectives of this amendment still cannot be achieved through separate legislation along the lines of my bill, H.R. 5719, or the language of the amendment offered by Senator Ribicoff.

Senator Ribicoff, speaking in San Francisco on February 14, 1964, announced that he intended to pursue his tax credit plan, "year in and year out," to final success and that other members of Congress in both political parties planned to do likewise. He reintroduced his bill in the 89th Congress as S 12, cosponsored by 17 Democratic and 17 Republican Senators.[32]

An identical proposal was incorporated in the Educational Incentives Act of 1965 (H.R. 6349) by Representative Ayres, which was announced as the "Republican Proposal for Aid to Education."[33] That bill would also allow tax credits for elementary- secondary schools which I had recommended at House and Senate committee hearings on February 1 and 4, 1965.[34] The Republican Conference of the House issued a unanimous report in June 1965 strongly recommending the Ribicoff-Dominick plan.[34a] By that time, 64 Republican and many Democratic members of the House had introduced such legislation. Tax credits were also suggested as preferable to Administration proposals in the minority report on the higher education bill of 1965.[34b]

What Would Educational Tax Credits Accomplish?

All of these plans would permit a taxpayer to deduct from his federal income tax an amount which is related to the tuition and fees—or also books and supplies—which he pays for himself, his dependents, or somebody else. The plans compare as follows:

---

[32] *Congressional Record,* January 6, 1965, pp. 190–193.

[33] *Congressional Record,* March 16, 1965, pp. 4967–70, 4972–73.

[34] *Aid to Elementary and Secondary Education,* Hearings before the Gen. Subcommittee on Education, Committee on Education and Labor, H.R., 89th Congress, 1st S., 1965, pp. 1383 ff. *Elementary and Secondary Education Act of 1965,* Hearings before the Subcommittee on Education, Committee on Labor and Public Welfare, U.S. Senate, 89th Congress, 1st S., 1965, pp. 2757 ff.

[34a] *Congressional Record,* June 28, 1965, pp. 14360–64.

[34b] Higher Education Act of 1965, H.R., 89th Congress, Report No. 621.

Howard-Bolling	Freeman	Humphrey	Ribicoff-Dominick
100% credit to $300	100% for first $100 30 for next 400 20 for next 1,000	5% first $100 40 next 400 30 next 500 20 next 500	75% first $200 25 next 300 10 next 1,000

Maximum Credit

$300	$420	$485	$325

The credits would equal the following amounts:

Credit Base*	Amount of Credit			
	Howard-Bolling	Freeman	Humphrey	Ribicoff†
$ 100	$ 100	$ 100	$ 75	$ 75
200	200	130	115	150
300	300	160	155	175
400	300	190	195	200
500	300	220	235	225
600	300	240	265	235
700	300	260	295	245
800	300	280	325	255
900	300	300	355	265
1000	300	320	385	275
1100	300	340	405	285
1200	300	360	425	295
1300	300	380	445	305
1400	300	400	465	315
$1500	$300	$420	$485	$325

* Tuitions, fees, in some bills also books and supplies.
† Reduced by one per cent of the amount by which the taxpayer's adjusted gross income exceeds $25,000.

The effect of the tax credit on the *net* cost to the student of subsequent tuition increases depends on the level of the new tuition. Let us just show two examples:

1) Present tuition and fees, $300—increase, $200—new tuition, $500. The *gain* to the college is $200 per student, less additional

scholarship aid (or tuition abatement). The net *saving* to the student *after the tuition increase* is:

Howard-Bolling	$100
Freeman	20
Humphrey	65
Ribicoff	$ 75

2) Present tuition and fees, $1,000—increase, $300—new tuition, $1,300. The gain to the college is $300 per student, less additional scholarship aid (or tuition abatement). The net *saving* or *cost* to the student *after the tuition increase* is:

Howard-Bolling	None
Freeman *(saving)*	$ 20
Humphrey *(saving)*	85
Ribicoff *(net cost)*	$ 25

The aggregate saving to taxpayers—and revenue loss to the Treasury—can only be tentatively estimated:

The saving under the Howard-Bolling plan was placed at $860 million by Rutgers University economist C. Harry Kahn. Kahn estimated that a 100 per cent credit with a $100 ceiling would net $253 million; with a $500 ceiling, $1,066 million.[35] In my testimony before the Senate Finance Committee, I estimated the net savings under my schedule at $700 million or more. The Treasury Department prepared the following estimates:[36]

	Millions of Dollars	
Calendar Year	1964	1970
Freeman plan	$725	$1,400
Humphrey plan	800	1,500
Ribicoff plan	750	1,300

The Treasury estimates for 1970 appear to me to be somewhat too high, but all such estimates depend on a number of assump-

---

[35] Memorandum to the Foundation for Voluntary Welfare.
[36] *Congressional Record*, February 3, 1964, p .1726.

tions which may or may not be borne out by subsequent developments.

The effect of tax credits is a reduction in the cost of higher education for students and their parents. This is true whether I.H.L. raise their tuitions or not, unless the institutions increase their fees by a greater amount than the total of the credit and *by more than they otherwise would have raised them.* Tuitions and fees have been going up year after year and there is every reason to believe that this trend will continue. The expenses of the institutions will keep climbing rapidly and it appears unlikely that governments or private donors will boost their support at a sufficiently steep rate to make further tuition increases unnecessary. Rising prices and a steady increase in personal income also give the I.H.L. justification for uplifting their charges.

I showed in Chapter 6 that tuitions and fees at public I.H.L. increased only 5 per cent in constant dollars between 1940–41 and 1960–61, and 21 per cent in private I.H.L. As a percentage of family personal income they *declined* in public I.H.L from 4.1 per cent in 1940–41 to 2.6 per cent in 1960–61, and in private I.H.L. from 13.4 per cent in 1940–41 to 9 8 per cent in 1960–61. The total cost of attending college—including room and board—declined both in constant dollars and as a percentage of family personal income.

It is of course possible and in fact quite likely that many boards of trustees will have a better conscience about raising tuitions if they know that the students and their families simultaneously receive tax credits which equal the increase or at least diminish its net cost. Thus, some increases will take place which otherwise might have been postponed, in spite of the unfavorable effect which such a delay might have on the institutional program or the faculty.

Thus, there will be a savings to the students and their families except in the very unlikely case mentioned above, namely, that I.H.L. boost tuitions by more than they otherwise would have done, by an amount greater than the tax credit.

In my testimony before the two Senate committees, I mentioned that three-fourths of the tax credits—or a total of about $500 million a year—might be recouped by the institutions. The new funds could be used to lift faculty salaries. Or they could finance a program of *general* construction (which will not benefit from the highly restricted federal program enacted in 1963).

Supposing the I.H.L. were to issue $5 billion in 25-year serial bonds. About two-thirds of the bonds would be issued by state institutions and be tax exempt at an average interest rate of (presently) slightly over three per cent. Private institutions might have to pay up to five per cent unless the federal government were to grant them the same tax exemption that public institutions enjoy or buy the bond issues at a lower interest rate. The annual service cost would be:

	Million
Retirement of principal	$200
Average annual interest during the 1960's	160
Average annual principal and interest during the 1960's	$360

Obviously, subsequent tuition boosts would not be identified as having been imposed because of the tax credits nor would the additional funds be distinguishable from other revenues. It is thus impossible to estimate with any degree of accuracy just what tax credits would do for the institutions, but it is a likely assumption that they would help them to improve faculty salaries and to expand their physical facilities. However, as we have seen, educational tax credits have engendered sufficient opposition to enable the Administration to defeat the proposal in February 1964. Thus, it seems appropriate to review and analyze the objections that have been raised to educational tax credits.

Objections and Opposition to Tax Relief for Higher Education

The major arguments against educational tax credits may be summarized under six headings:
a) They would cause a large loss to the Treasury.
b) They would not help students and their families but institutions.
c) They would benefit well-to-do families but not help the needy ones.

d) They would break down the separation of church and state.
e) They would discriminate against public I.H.L. in favor of private I.H.L.
f) They would surrender control over public tax funds to private individuals.

Let us explore these arguments, one by one.

a) "Tax credits would cause a large loss to the Treasury." The Treasury Department has long opposed education tax relief and given the resulting revenue loss as a major reason for its position. In a story on the Senate debate on February 3 and 4, 1964, the *Washington Post* reported: "During spirited debate on the Ribicoff amendment, Democratic leadership objections were aimed mainly at the costs. The Treasury had estimated it would lose $750 million annually in revenue at the outset and that this loss soon would climb to $1.3 billion."[37] Other opponents such as the land-grant college association and the National Education Association stressed the same point.

This is undoubtedly a justified concern at a time when multi-billion dollar budgetary deficits seem to have become the rule and during a period which has seen a spectacular rise in the rate of federal spending for nonwar connected (i.e., domestic) purposes; over the past ten years (1954–64) those expenditures grew 232 per cent compared with a simultaneous growth in population of 18 per cent and of the gross national product of 67 per cent. The objection to tax credits would have to be accepted at face value if it were directed with equal force against other measures which cause, or contribute to, budget deficits. But the Treasury—and others who raised the same point—did not testify against an $11 billion tax cut which was recommended and enacted in a fiscal year when the budget was running $8 billion in the red with several more deficit years in the offing. Nor did they protest against numerous new or increased *spending* plans which were simultaneously advanced by the Administration. *The objections were raised only when it was proposed to aid education by reducing taxes rather than by increasing public spending.*

Most of the opposition to tax credits comes from individuals

---

[37] *The Washington Post*, February 5, 1964.

and organizations which have long been demanding sharply increased federal spending for purposes in which they have a direct stake or interest. Their attitude seems to be conditioned less by concern over the condition of the Treasury or of the budget than by the fact that tax credit plans would run counter to their aims to tax and spend *more* rather than to tax and spend *less*. It is basically the question whether government should grow ever bigger in proportion to the private economy or smaller. The fact is that most of those who are troubled by the phenomenal growth in the domestic activities of government in recent years, and who give balanced budgets a high priority, support educational tax credits, as an analysis of the Senate vote shows.

The revenue loss to the Treasury would not mean a loss to the general taxpayer, as has been asserted, but could result in substantial savings to him, because 1) State institutions could boost their tuitions *without placing an additional burden on their students* and thus would not have to depend so heavily on state appropriations. 2) Aid to students in private institutions could slow down the drastic enrollment shift from private to public I.H.L. and save taxpayers huge sums—far larger than the amount of the tax credits —which otherwise would have to go for construction and operation of vastly expanded state college campuses.

b) "Tax credits would not help students and their families but the institutions." In a circular letter dated February 27, 1963, the secretary of the Association of State Universities and Land-Grant Colleges wrote: "While the plan has been 'sold' to many parents as means of getting financial relief from the Federal treasury for the cost of sending children to college, it was in origin and is in its primary intent, a plan to siphon off substantial amounts from the federal Treasury for support of colleges and universities." The National Education Association, Division of Federal Relations, stated in a *Flash* bulletin of January 7, 1964: "It seems clear that, rather than a tax saving to the taxpayer, the 'tax relief' type of education legislation would accelerate rapidly rising student fees, especially in private institutions, which would be encouraged to capture the so-called tax saving."

The charge that a plan would "siphon off substantial amounts from the federal Treasury for the support of colleges and universities" and that it might, in the *end*, help to improve their finances comes in particular ill grace from the two groups which have long been leading the campaign to channel large federal funds into education—provided that their member institutions, and no others, were the only beneficiaries. That a proposed plan would help colleges and universities in the financing of their educational programs does not seem to be too grave an indictment at this particular time, considering the current problems in higher education.

So it is not surprising to find that some of the opponents of education tax credits use exactly the reverse argument. Wrote Fred Hechinger, education editor of *The New York Times:* "But a more fundamental objection to tax credits is that this is not aid to education at all—merely aid to parents."[38] A few paragraphs later, however, Hechinger who, like his newspaper, strongly supports federal grants in aid to education added that "The effect of the measure might well be to shift the major burden of state university support from the states to the federal government." That this sounds confusing to the reader is not surprising. So is the whole argument over whether the benefits would accrue to parents or to institutions. It is artificial, irrelevant, and specious. As long as a substantial part of the support of higher education is derived from fees, it is immaterial for the benefit question at what point in the stream the funds are added.

Yet the opponents try to make it appear as if there were a dichotomy among the proponents, that some such as Senator Ribicoff present it as a tax relief to parents while others, including myself, see it as a means of improving the financial health of the institutions. Most major opponents who participated in this debate in early 1964 quoted from my statement before the two Senate committees in which I used an illustration of the effect tax credits would have on college finances if the institutions absorbed three-fourths of the tax saving.

This was taken as proof that what I really intended to do was to help institutions more than parents. I may as well admit that I do not regard the aim to aid colleges and universities at this point in time to be of a sinister nature nor a nefarious plot which needs to be unmasked. I can see nothing wrong with helping students and

[38] Fred M. Hechinger, "Federal Aid Issue," *The New York Times,* May 26, 1963.

their families support the college of their choice. Aid to parents and to institutions are simply two sides of a coin which cannot be divided though some may pretend that the one side they are looking at is the whole coin. There is no basic disagreement among the advocates of educational tax credits on what they will accomplish, save in the imagination of some of the opponents.

A short historical glance may give us a better perspective at this point. When educational tax relief proposals were first seriously advanced in the early 1950's it was mostly individuals who testified before congressional committees and they stressed, understandably, the relief-to-parents aspect which has a potent political appeal. But it was clear from the outset that this did not imply a reduction in the then existing level of college expenses borne by the parents, but rather a cushion against the increases which were known to be inevitable.

The American Alumni Council passed a resolution in July 1954, unanimously approving tax relief for tuition as a means of aiding colleges and universities to effect necessary increases in their tuition charges without placing an unbearable burden on the parents who pay them. This has remained the basic case for educational tax relief ever since. The Reverend Virgil C. Blum wrote in his earlier-quoted article in December 1963: "The prime purpose of the tax credit is to help the student pay a bigger share of the actual cost of his education." The American Council on Education and related groups vigorously pursued tax credits in the 1950's because they saw in them a means of helping to finance higher education. When no congressional action ensued they turned to other, presumably more promising plans. Now that it is becoming increasingly obvious that the national government will not, or cannot, aid higher education through direct grants-in-aid—except in a very restricted way such as construction aid for selected types of facilities—interest is shifting back to tax credits as a practicable way in which the objective can be accomplished.

Tax credits may in some cases mean an actual dollar reduction in the net college expenses of students, at least temporarily. But to most it will mean a reduction (or total offset) of increases which they would otherwise have to bear. The suggestion of tax credit opponents that boards of trustees would raise tuitions to "raid the

Treasury" and to make sure that students and their families get no benefits from the credits is preposterous. The purpose of tuitions and the policy in setting them is not to soak the students or the public or anybody else but to meet essential college needs. Boards boost fees when the financial situation of their institutions demands it and when the alternative is a cutback or deterioration of services which they are unwilling to make. Tax credits would enable them to boost tuitions without placing a corresponding *additional* burden on the students and their families. I.H.L. do not like to boost tuitions under any circumstances. Private colleges do not like it any better than public, and probably less so, because many of them are under heavy competitive stress. But their only choice is often between raising fees and not meeting essential needs.

Some colleges might postpone or forego needed boosts, at the expense of their program or of the faculty and of the caliber of the faculty they can hire and keep. A tax credit may cause some boards to approve a hike which otherwise might have been deferred. If so, the credit will help to build more classrooms or hire additional faculty and pay them higher salaries. Are these necessarily undesirable objectives? Or are they desirable only if it is the government rather than the student and his family who select the institution? It seems evident that tax credits for college expenses will benefit higher education. How they are eventually divided as between parents and institutions is indeterminable and immaterial.

c) "Tax credits would benefit well-to-do families but not help the needy ones." That families in higher income brackets would benefit relatively more from educational tax relief under the various deduction and exemption plans is true. It is not true of the flat percentage tax credit plans and the reverse of the truth in regard to the 100 per cent credit plans with dollar ceilings and of the sliding scale credits which are graduated so as to favor students in low-tuition institutions. However, Senator Wayne Morse called the Ribicoff amendment "a rich man's amendment," and Senator Long (La.), the tax bill's manager, claimed that "those who are already wealthy would be in a position to dip in Uncle Sam's Treasury to help their own folk who do not need it."[39]

The fact is that, under the Ribicoff plan, upper middle-income

[39] *Congressional Record*, February 4, 1964, p. 1749.

families who have their children in high-tuition institutions will get relatively small credits and wealthy families will get none. The table which appeared on page 205 shows that a family with an income under $25,000 p.a. with a student in an I.H.L. with tuition between $1,000 and $1,500 gets a credit which equals between 21 per cent and 27 per cent of its outlay. The credit is reduced by one per cent of the amount by which income exceeds $25,000 and reaches zero at an income level of $57,500. In contrast, a student at a low-tuition college with $200 expenses gets a credit of $150 or 75 per cent of his outlay so that his cost is reduced from $200 to $50. Under no conceivable circumstances can wealthy families get substantial benefits from any of the proposed tax credit plans.

The staff of the Joint Committee on Internal Revenue Taxation estimated that tax credits (and revenue loss) under the Ribicoff amendment would be distributed by income classes as follows:[40]

Adjusted gross income class	Amount (Million)	Per Cent
Up to $3,000	$ 10	1
3,000 to 5,000	85	11
5,000 to 10,000	375	51
10,000 to 20,000	205	28
20,000 to 50,000	65	9
50,000 and over	*	**
Total	$740	100

* Less than $2.5 million
** Less than 0.5 per cent

It is apparent that 91 per cent of the tax savings would go to families with an income under $20,000. Families in the $20,000 to $50,000 bracket would get 9 per cent of the total and those above $50,000 about one-third of one per cent. Four dollars out of every five would accrue to families with an income between $5,000 and $20,000 with about two-thirds of that concentrated in the $5,000-$10,000 brackets. So the oft-repeated claim that much of the educational tax credits would "help those who need it the least"

---

[40] *Congressional Record,* February 3, 1964, p. 1733.

is a myth.[41] Most of the savings would go to middle income and lower middle income groups. The rich would get none.

Another argument against tax credits is that they would confer "special tax privileges to one class of taxpayers":[42] they would give no benefits to parents who have no children in college. This is quite true and expresses a basic principle in our income tax system: that those with special burdens get tax relief. For example, a taxpayer who pays property taxes, state income and sales taxes, medical expenses, casualty losses, mortgage interest, etc., may deduct them from his tax base. But if he has no such expenses he obviously cannot deduct them. The purpose of the tax credit is to ease the financial burden of college attendance, and it seems obvious that those who incur no such expenses are entitled to no relief.

Some opponents assert that poor families cannot afford to send their children to college and are thus excluded from the benefits of a plan whose cost, in the end, rests on all taxpayers in the United States.[43] I discussed, in Chapters 6 and 9, the question of whether otherwise qualified young persons who wish to acquire a higher education are prevented from attending *solely* by inability to raise the necessary college expenses. The evidence suggests that though "financial reasons" are often given as a reason or excuse for not going to college, this can mean many things other than inability to obtain the necessary funds or sufficient financial aid. More often it means that the young man or woman prefers to earn a going wage, independence, marriage, or possession of a car, to four or five years of scrimping and applying his own earnings—present or future—to his education. There may be cases in which a potential student cannot obtain, earn, or borrow enough money to pay tuition, fees, and other essential costs. But I have seen no proof that they exist to any material extent, if at all. Available evidence suggests that a sufficiently gifted high school graduate can get the means of attending college if he is willing to make a sacrifice for it. That many prefer to cite "financial reasons" as the cause of their non-attendance is psychologically not hard to understand.

[41] From the title of a pamphlet by the Association of State Universities and Land Grant Colleges: *Tax Credits for Educational Expenses or How to Spend $1-1/4 Billion Annually in Tax Money to Help Those Who Need It Least.*

[42] *Congressional Record*, February 3, 1964, p. 1718.

[43] E.g., *Revenue Act of 1963*, p. 1397.

Tax credits, it has been said, may be all right for those students whose families earn enough to be liable for a sizable income tax bill. But how about families with an income too low to be taxable? They—the poorest of the poor—would be left out in the cold and be discriminated against by a system of educational tax credits. It would seem to be just as logical to say that personal exemptions (presently $600 per capita) discriminate against persons whose only income is derived from unemployment compensation, social security, or public assistance. Their income is not taxable and they get no benefit from personal exemptions—or in fact from any of the numerous types of exemptions, exclusions, deductions, credits, etc. in the Internal Revenue Code. Does this prove that all of those provisions are unfair?

In my testimony before the Senate Finance Committee on November 6, 1963, I said:[44]

> The point has been made that tax credits would be of no help to students from families with such low income that they pay no income tax. That point has little validity, if any. While no statistics are presently available on the number or percentage of families of college students which pay no federal income taxes, it may be estimated that it is quite low and certainly not higher than 10 per cent of all students. Most of those students are now recipients of scholarships and thus pay no tuition, nor would they have to pay the increased tuitions that would follow the enactment of such a plan.

For this I was taken to task in a pamphlet by the Joint Office of Institutional Research of the Association of State Universities and Land-Grant Colleges attacking educational tax relief plans:[45]

> [The tax relief plan's] leading sponsors frankly recognize that it provides no aid to students from low-income families and might increase the difficulty of their college attendance through encouragement of tuition increases, and propose to correct the situation through other forms of federal aid, such as scholarships.
> Others, such as Dr. Roger Freeman, attempt to answer the problem by saying it doesn't exist. (Dr. Freeman told the Senate Finance Committee that there were no figures on the number of students from families of such low income that tax credits would not help

44 *Revenue Act of 1963*, p. 1397.
45 *Tax Credit Plans for Education Expenses*, An analysis published by the Joint Office of Institutional Research, Washington, 1963, proc., pp. 5–6.

those now attending college, and then said he "estimated" that they were not more than 10 per cent of the college population and that "virtually all" had scholarships and would not have to pay any tuition increases. While it is difficult to evaluate an estimate made in an area in which studies are said to be non-existent, the 1961 census showed that 21 per cent of all U.S. families have incomes under $3,000; 41 per cent under $5,000; and 63 per cent under $7,000. It seems reasonable to assume that very substantial aid in other forms would be required to make it possible to continue and expand the availability of educational opportunity for young people from low-income groups, as college charges are increased under the lure of of tax-credits.)

There are so many things wrong with this statement that it takes some space to refute them. In the first place there is no need for "very substantial aid in other forms" to shield students from non-taxpaying families from tuition increases. The colleges would simply forego the increase from the small segment of students whose families are not liable for income tax. This would still leave the institutional treasuries ninety per cent of the tuition boost, if my estimate is right.

The question is: how many college students' families pay no income tax? Out of a total U.S. population of 190 million in 1962, 173 million or 90 per cent were listed on individual income tax returns as personal exemptions. In some cases, of course, exemptions and other items were sufficient to leave no tax liability. The Treasury Department said as follows in a memorandum in December 1963:[46] "The tax savings from a deduction or credit in many cases would be of negligible value to millions of low-income families who pay little or no taxes. In 1962, 40 per cent of the 47 million families had incomes of less than $5,000. Income tax data for 1960 show that of the 15.4 million joint returns with adjusted gross income of $5,000 or less, 6.6 million or 43 per cent were non-taxable." This may suggest to some that 17 per cent of the students are from families which pay no federal income tax. But that would be jumping to wrong conclusions. Let us check and analyze the statistical base of these figures.

The statement that 40 per cent of the 47 million families had an income of less than $5,000 in 1962 is apparently derived from the

---

[46] *Congressional Record,* February 3, 1964, p. 1724.

annual population survey of the Bureau of the Census, which is based on interviews in 25,000 households. The 1962 survey showed 39 per cent of all families with a *cash* income under $5,000—down from 67 per cent only ten years earlier.[47] In each of its annual bulletins the Census Bureau warned that the income data probably are underestimates, and the official in charge, Herman P. Miller, recently proved this in a paper, "New Evidence Regarding the Understatement of Income in the Current Population Survey."[48] In recent years the "missing income" has run as high as $50 billion and the difference between the 1960 Census and the 1960 annual population survey totalled nearly $30 billion, with the heaviest discrepancies at the top and bottom levels.[49] The national income division of the Department of Commerce estimated that 33.6 per cent of all families had a personal income under $5,000 in 1961 and 31.1 per cent in 1962—down from 39.7 per cent in 1958 and from 47.3 per cent in 1955.[50] The trends suggest that the percentage of families with less than $5,000 income was substantially below 30 per cent in 1964 and will, if the trends continue, be as low as 25 per cent within not too many years.

Income distribution in the general population is not at all representative of college students' families. The 47 million families include many who are just starting their earning career or who are aged and retired, etc. But six out of seven fathers of children reaching college age are in their peak earning years, between 38 and 58, and most enjoy incomes substantially above the average. In a survey at the University of Massachusetts (class of 1965) 90 per cent of all fathers reported their income above $4,000; in a 1964 survey at the University of California 95 per cent of the students reported that their parents' income equalled $4,000 or more, 88 per cent that it ran at $6,000 or more.[51] At $4,000 a couple

---

47 Bureau of the Census, *Current Population Reports,* Series P-60, No. 41.

48 In: *1962 Proceedings of the Business and Economic Statistics Section,* American Statistical Association, p. 25.

49 The cited pamphlet of the Joint Office of Institutional Research referred to a "1961 Census." There was, of course, no 1961 census. It apparently meant the annual population survey of the Bureau of the Census.

50 *Survey of Current Business,* April 1964.

51 *Congressional Record,* February 5, 1962, p. 1526. Edward Sanders and Hans Palmer, *The Financial Barrier to College Attendance in California,* California State Scholarship Commission, 1964.

with fewer than four children is taxable unless it has unusually heavy deductions.

A couple with two children and an income of $5,000 paid, under the rate scale in effect until 1963, $420 in federal income tax, and will, under the 1965 scale, pay $294. But students from families with an income of $5,000 or less are a small minority on college campuses. The College Scholarship Service reported that the median family income of students applying for scholarship was $8,436. We may assume that most students applying for scholarship come from the lower-income segment of the college population and that most students of small means did apply. Since the income level is a major consideration in the award of scholarships, it appears likely that students from families below the federally taxable income level have an excellent chance of getting a scholarship, if they meet the academic requirements, and that most of them already are recipients. In summary, we may conclude that fewer than ten per cent of all students who pay tuitions are from families with an income so low as to be federally nontaxable. The actual percentage could be determined only by a survey—which, at the present time, is not available.

If tax credits were enacted, scholarship boards and institutions would, in selecting recipients, certainly take into consideration whether the student would—or would not—be able to get a direct benefit through taxes. The availability of tax credits could free substantial scholarship funds, as Vice-President John F. Meck of Dartmouth College, representing the American Council on Education, stated when he proposed the Council's plan to the House Ways and Means Committee. "Many parents in the $8,000–$10,000 and even the $12,000 a year brackets, who now require partial scholarships in order to keep their children in college would be able to forego these scholarship funds, thus making them available for children coming from homes of less financial ability."[52]

The availability of educational tax credits could lead to a sharp increase in privately sponsored scholarships. Under the Ribicoff amendment, credits are available to anybody who pays college expenses for himself or for other persons, whether related to him

---

[52] *General Revenue Revision.* Hearings before the Committee on Ways and Means, House of Representatives, 85th Congress 2nd Session, 1958, pp. 1063-4.

or not. The tax credit plan could encourage tens of thousands of donors to sponsor scholarships which cost them only a fraction of the benefit conferred. Who would not give a few hundred dollars to aid a needy deserving college student if he could deduct much or most of it from his federal income tax?

It is of course on the whole true that students from families in the lowest income brackets—below federal income taxability—would not benefit from a tax credit plan although it is very doubtful that they could get hurt, even if the colleges raised tuitions. As mentioned before, those increases most likely would not be demanded from students who cannot recoup the increase through tax credits.

The tax credit plan offers little or nothing to the rich, little or nothing to the poor, and aims at easing the future college burden of the vast majority of students who come from families "in between."

That a tax credit plan offers little or no help to a student from a poor family is no argument against it. It may be an argument for helping him in some other form such as scholarships. But the state universities association for many years consistently and successfully opposed a federal scholarship program and has only recently relented (see page 181). It favors only the type of aid which is restricted to state and municipal institutions. Many others feel that scholarships could well supplement tax credits. But there may be a better method of helping students from families who incur little or no federal income tax liability: through a modification of the tax credit plan. Educational tax credits could be made absolute rather than conditional upon the existence of a tax liability. The student, or his parents, would prepare an income tax return and take the appropriate credit. If the final computation showed a net *credit* rather than a liability, the Internal Revenue Service would pay them the amount of the credit like any other refund claim. It could then not be said under any circumstances that the tax credit plan provides no benefits for persons at the low end of the income scale who pay no income taxes. The "absolute credit" would be tantamount to a federal scholarship and somewhat resembles Milton Friedman's plan of "negative taxation."[53]

---

[53] Milton Friedman, *Capitalism and Freedom* (University of Chicago Press, 1962), p. 192.

d. "Tax credits would break down the separation of church and state." The proponents of educational tax credits assumed that their plans would eliminate the church-and-state issue which has proven to be one of the most difficult problems in the debate over federal aid to education. No funds would flow from the government to any institution. The individual would apply part (or all) of his tuition and other college expenses to his income tax liability. Since even direct church contributions are deductible for federal income tax purposes—with no question ever having been raised about it by any responsible source—there seemed to be no possibility for a constitutional conflict. But Senator Morse shattered that illusion:

> If one thinks that, by way of a tax credit "gimmick" there is going to be eliminated the church-state issue of aid to church-related schools, he could not be more badly mistaken.
>
> The adoption of the amendment—and I sincerely hope it will not be adopted—will raise that issue in an inflamed form . . . on the ground that it is an attempted circumvention of the church-state separation principle.
>
> One of the controversies which I fear will be stirred up over the Ribicoff amendment, if it ever becomes law, is the whole question of the aid and the form of aid which can be given with propriety under the Constitution to parochial secondary and elementary schools.[54]

That the enactment of tax credits in higher education would set a precedent and pattern for parallel action at the lower levels is certain and was stressed by Senator Ribicoff and other proponents. For example, Representative Thomas B. Curtis, upon introducing a tax credit plan for higher education, concluded his speech in the House of Representatives with the following remarks: "The bill is limited to the costs of higher education. However, the principle upon which the bill rests is applicable to the costs of secondary and primary education. Once the principle has been adopted and proven to be sound in one area of education, I trust it will be extended to all areas of education."[55] It is probably for this reason that the National Education Association battles tax

---

[54] *Congressional Record*, February 3, 1964, pp. 1719 ff., 1729 ff.
[55] *Congressional Record*, January 30, 1961, p. 1374. See also Mr. Curtis' remarks in: *Congressional Record*, March 16, 1965, pp. 4972–73.

credits. In a Flash bulletin dated January 7, 1964, its Division of Federal Relations quoted the Secretary of its Legislative Commission, James L. McCaskill: *"It is my opinion that this is very dangerous legislation* in terms of possible adverse effect on public elementary and secondary education."

It is hard to conceive how a constitutional question could ever arise or be brought to court. But if it did, there can be little doubt from precedents that the U.S. Supreme Court would not rule against the type of educational tax credits which have been suggested. No public funds are involved in any transaction. Each individual would make certain deductions from his income tax liability. And each student would choose the institution he attends, as is his unquestioned right. That he or his father have more of their earnings left to pay tuition with, offers no possible objection under the establishment clause. Any institution which raised its tuition could certainly prove that the action was caused by need for additional funds and taken for essential educational purposes.

That institutions may, in an indirect way, benefit from tax credits given to individual taxpayers does not violate the First Amendment. In the Everson case the U.S. Supreme Court upheld payments by the school board to parents for bus fares to parochial schools: "It is undoubtedly true that by the New Jersey program children are helped to get to church schools. There is even the possibility that some of the children might not be sent to the church schools if the parents were compelled to pay their children's bus fares out of their own pockets when transportation to a public school would have been paid for by the state."[56] Any aid to the institution is far more indirect under a tax credit plan than under the school bus payments.

It appears certain that educational tax credits can be given "with propriety under the Constitution," to repeat Senator Morse's phrase. The issue is really not whether educational tax credits are constitutional. It would take contortion to deny that. Rather, it is a question of philosophy, whether religious education is desirable, and whether the economic penalty upon attending private educa-

---

[56] *Everson vs. Board of Education,* 330 U.S. 1 (1947).

tional institutions should be kept heavy and increased, or whether it ought to be reduced. The indirect aid which nonpublic colleges would receive would come to them not by government direction but by the choice of individuals, and the real question is: Is it desirable that students have a choice in selecting the type of school from which they want to get their education?

e) "Tax credits would discriminate against public I.H.L. in favor of private I.H.L." In a circular letter dated February 27, 1963, the secretary of the Association of State Universities and Land-Grant Colleges charged that educational tax credits would grant private higher education a "*discriminatory priority* in national support." This was echoed by the National Education Association's charge (in the earlier-cited Flash bulletin) that "the advantage of such a proposal clearly favors the private institutions." Senator Mike Mansfield declared at the conclusion of the debate on the Ribicoff amendment:

> Any deduction or credit based on tuition, regardless of its form, would give more benefits to students in the higher-priced institutions—and this discriminates against those students—including a large proportion of those students needing financial assistance—who attend public institutions where tuition is generally lower. It would also discriminate against those states with a strong tradition of providing higher education at low cost or no student tuition cost.[57]

The fact is, however, that the tax credit plans which were advanced in 1963, 1964 and 1965 would have wiped out most (or all) of the tuition and fees at the level at which the average public I.H.L. sets its charges and would have reimbursed students at high-cost institutions for only a small percentage of their cost, generally less than one-third, and in some for only one-fifth.

It may be well to study Senator Mansfield's charge in greater detail. Tuitions and fees averaged in 1962–63: in public I.H.L. $170, in private I.H.L. $690.[58] To this may be added costs of books and supplies, average $90, which are applicable expenses under some of the plans (see table page 224). It is obvious that the

---

[57] *Congressional Record,* February 4, 1964, p. 1754.
[58] *Higher Education Basic Student Charges 1962–63,* by Louis A. D'Amico and W. Robert Bokelman, Office of Education Circular 711, 1963.

student at a public I.H.L. would, on the average, be reimbursed for a greater *percentage* of his expenses but that the *amount* of his credit would be smaller. This is the inevitable result of the "tuition gap": tuitions and fees are now, on the average, four times higher at private I.H.L. than at public I.H.L. Under one plan in the table below, the student at a private I.H.L. pays 306 per cent more in fees and gets a credit which is 113 per cent higher than what the public student gets. Under another plan the "private" student's expenses are 200 per cent higher, his credit 53 per cent higher than the "public" student's. It is actually the "private" student who is on the short end of this deal, and has a right to complain under the rules which prevail throughout the rest of our tax system.

TAX CREDITS AND NET COSTS OF PLANS OFFERED 1963–65
ALL I.H.L. *(Median)*

	Tuition and Fees (100% to $300)				Tuition, Fees, and Books —Sliding Scale—					
Public I.H.L.	Howard-Bolling		Freeman		Freeman		Humphrey		Ribicoff	
Average expenses	$170	100%	$170	100%	$260	100%	$260	100%	$260	100%
Less tax credit	170	100	121	71	148	57	139	53	165	63
Net cost	—	—	49	29	112	43	121	47	95	37
Private I.H.L.										
Average expenses	$690	100%	$690	100%	$780	100%	$780	100%	$780	100%
Less tax credit	300	43	258	37	276	35	319	41	253	32
Net cost	$390	57%	$432	63%	$504	65%	$461	59%	$527	68%

If Mr. A. pays $300 in property taxes on his home and Mr. B. pays $1,200, the latter can deduct four times as much from his tax base as Mr. A. We may assume that Mr. B. is in a higher income and tax bracket than Mr. A. The latter may recoup as little as $42 on his $300 outlay. Mr. B. however (if his taxable income is $24,000 and he files a joint return), recoups $432 or ten times as much.

In that example, Mr. A. is reimbursed for 14 per cent of his expense; Mr. B. for 36 per cent. In the proposed educational tax credits the situation is exactly reversed. If A. pays $300 in tuition, etc. at a public I.H.L., he recovers (under the Ribicoff plan) 55 per cent of his cost or $175. But Mr. B. gets only 25 per cent of his expense back, or $295.

The sliding tax credit plan was conceived for the purpose of giving greater relative benefits to students in state and municipal colleges and universities. It does exactly that, and if anybody has grounds to talk about discrimination and unfair treatment, then it is the student at a private institution. At the average fee level of 1962–63, the student at a public I.H.L. would have three-fourths of his tuition wiped out by the tax credit; the student at a private institution only about one-third. Moreover, we should not forget that the student at a state or municipal I.H.L. is already the recipient of a subsidy by the taxpayer, which amounts to $1,000 a year or more for current costs, aside from the large capital investment, while the student at a private I.H.L. pays a substantial share of the cost of his education from his own or his parents' pockets.

By attending a private institution, a student saves the taxpayers of his state substantial sums. At a conference on the economic problems of higher education, sponsored by the Ford Foundation and chaired by Seymour E. Harris, it was mentioned that "It is a more economical use of public funds to spend $600 on a scholarship to a student in a private college than $1,500 on the operating costs and new university facilities required to accommodate that student" (at a public I.H.L.).[59] A tax credit can in this case serve the same purpose as a scholarship.

States with strong public higher education tradition, to which Senator Mansfield referred, would benefit most under a tax credit plan: their taxpayers have had to foot most of the bills for higher education—in contrast to taxpayers in states with a prevailing private higher education tradition. If public institutions raise tuitions—at little or no additional cost to their students under a tax credit plan—the institutional income will go up and appropriations will not need to rise as much as they otherwise might. And if

---

[59] *Higher Education in the United States: The Economic Problems*, ed. Seymour E. Harris, Harvard University Press, 1960, p. 38.

assistance to students at private I.H.L. encourages more young people to enroll there, the state's taxpayers would save even larger amounts.

Some have called educational tax credits another tax loophole which would enable students at private I.H.L. to tap the public treasury. This may be answered with a point which President Charles Cole of Amherst College made at the above-mentioned conference, namely, that "tax payments to states which finance public universities are deductible from income reported for federal taxes, but if the payment for education is made to a private institution, no tax allowance is to be had."[60]

President Kennedy recommended in 1961, and Congress subsequently enacted, tax credits to aid and stimulate industrial investment. Why should higher education not rate as much consideration and encouragement as industrial expansion? The use of tax concessions to promote desirable purposes is widespread throughout our tax system and there is no reason why education should not be considered as eligible as numerous other public purposes. One study of pension systems pointed out that "The favorable tax treatment of employer contributions to private pension plans alone has been estimated as resulting in tax savings of over $1 billion a year."[61] This has brought about a huge expansion of private pension plans.

The fact is that of the $463 billion of personal income in 1963, only $211 billion showed up as taxable income on federal individual income tax returns. More than half the total—$252 billion—was lost somewhere along the way, with personal exemptions in excess of $100 billion the biggest item.[62] A broadening of the tax base is certainly a desirable objective. But as long as less than half the personal income is subject to federal taxation, there seems to be no reason why education should be discriminated against.

To some extent the battle over tax credits is fought between

---

[60] *Ibid.*, p. 15.

[61] Philip Booth, "Public Systems for Distributing Risks to Security," *Monthly Labor Review*, June 1963.

[62] For details of the "gap" between personal and taxable income, see my testimony of November 6, 1963, before the Senate Finance Committee, *Revenue Act of 1963*, pp. 1385–86. For 1963 data see: *Survey of Current Business*, March 1964, and *Advance Data from Individual Income Tax Returns Filed During 1963*, Internal Revenue Service.

public and private I.H.L. A 1964 survey of the American Council on Education among the presidents of its member institutions showed more than four-fifths of the private favoring tax credits and almost three-fourths of the public opposing them. But size also appears to be a factor. While support for tax credits was overwhelming among the smaller private I.H.L., forty-nine private I.H.L. with an enrollment of 5,000 and over regarded them as undesirable. Eminence and prestige enable some of the great private universities to charge high tuitions, to be successful in their appeals to wealthy donors and foundations, and to attract the bulk of the huge federal research grants. They have no reason to be unhappy with their relative affluence, are loath to "rock the boat," and aim to maintain a common front, "shoulder to shoulder," with their colleagues, the state universities.

So, many of the large institutions, public and private, find themselves arraigned on this issue against the great number of private colleges and some of the smaller private universities which are fighting for survival against heavy odds. The Association of State Universities and Land-Grant Colleges is the leader of the opposition to educational tax credits. In this position, we may assume, the association expresses the attitudes of its administrators rather than of its students and their parents.

f) "Tax credits would surrender control over public tax funds to private individuals." The Joint Office of Institutional Research, an arm of the land-grant colleges, listed as the first point among the "Disadvantages of the Tax-Credit Approach": "This method of financing higher education would surrender congressional control over the amount of tax funds used for educational aid and the purposes for which it is used."[63] That Congress would surrender control over the amounts is incorrect. It would most probably first decide by how much it wishes to aid higher education and then shape the credit formula accordingly. It could revise the brackets and percentages each year if it wished to increase or lower the aggregate amount. It is, however, true that Congress would determine only the general purpose—higher education—and would not specify the curriculum subjects and specific items or projects to

---

[63] In the earlier-mentioned pamphlet, *Tax Credit Plans for Educational Expenses*, p. 7.

which institutional funds can be applied—in contrast to what has been consistent federal policy. In a memorandum on educational tax credits the Treasury Department wrote: "An important advantage of direct means, as compared with tax allowances, is that the Congress retains control of the amount of aid through the appropriation process and can distribute the aid where needed most."[64]

This seems to be a reversal of the "federal control" argument as we have known it for many years. The tenor used to be that we should—and could—have "federal aid without federal control." Now it appears that federal control through Congress and the bureaucracy which administers grant programs is sought as a desirable end, that its presence in grant programs and absence in tax credit programs is a reason—and apparently the main reason—for preferring the former over the latter. This seems to clarify the issue and the positions taken.

The head of a land-grant institution, President John A. Perkins of the University of Delaware, a former Under Secretary of H.E.W., wrote: "This approach [educational tax credits] is irresponsible governmentally. It takes money from the public purse but not by responsible government authorities appropriating on the basis of relative needs of the country."[65] The enactment of tax credits for higher education would, of course, mean that Congress *has* reached a decision "on the basis of the relative needs of the country." The benefits would clearly be earmarked for higher education and the only decision left to individuals would be the type of education they wish to acquire and the choice of the college they want to attend. Consequently, institutions which the public prefers would expand and others would be left behind. This freedom of choice is exactly the feature to which the opponents to tax credits object. They would have governmental administrators decide which institutions are to expand rather than leave this "to the vagaries of the market."

This brings the controversy down to its basic nature: a clash of

---

[64] *Congressional Record*, March 16, 1964, p. 5224.
[65] John A. Perkins, "Financing Higher Education: Perspectives and Possibilities," *The Educational Record*, April 1959; also in: *The Federal Government and Higher Education*, The American Assembly (Englewood Cliffs, N. J.: Prentice-Hall, 1960).

political philosophies between preference for governmental action or for voluntary action, between those who favor solving a problem through public appropriations and those who would rather strengthen the capacity of individuals to meet problems under their own power. The tax credit plan would not, as Mr. Perkins wrote, "take money *from* the public purse," but it would channel less money *into* the public purse. The basic decision over spending for higher education would be under public authority, but tax credits would enable students to enjoy the freedom to choose the institution in which they wish to receive their education.

If most or all of the support is allocated through public appropriations, it is government which decides which institutions are to benefit and expand. The economics of the situation then leave many students a very limited choice, if any. We have seen in recent decades that students flock to local public institutions if the economic penalty for enrolling at private colleges is raised too high, but they shift quickly whenever scholarship or similar programs reduce the additional cost of private I.H.L. to a bearable level.

The fundamental question is whether we want to expand decision-making by government or decision-making by individuals. Mr. Perkins emphasized that appropriations and control by government must go hand in hand:

> An Anglo-Saxon rubric of responsible governments reiterated in sacred documents of free government, is that along with the granting of supply ("appropriations" in today's language) goes responsibility for how the money is spent. To depart from this rubric, to give grants in aid to any function, including higher education, would in the long run defeat self-government as certainly as would the further neglect of higher education. No one responsible for higher education and believing in its importance to the preservation of self-government would demand funds on his own terms.

This clarifies the issue along ideological lines: Those who believe that decisions by government are, as a rule, more wholesome, wiser, more conducive to promoting the general welfare, will tend to prefer federal appropriations to educational tax credits. Those who would like to see the range of personal liberty and freedom of choice expanded, who believe that in the long run the ends of society are better served by letting citizens reach their own individual decisions to the greatest extent possible, are more likely to favor tax credits.

There is, to be sure, some crossing of lines. Some of those who, by inclination, prefer direct governmental action but doubt that Congress will soon approve substantial grants in aid for the general purposes of I.H.L., may support tax credits as a means of aiding higher education until a more satisfactory solution can be achieved.

What the argument over educational tax credits comes down to, in the end, is whether it is better for government to tax a man and spend the money as it deems best, or to tax him less and let him spend the money as he sees fit. It's as simple as that.

Tax Credits for Gifts to I.H.L.

The second largest nongovernmental source of general income of I.H.L. is gifts from individuals and corporations. The Internal Revenue Code now permits individuals to deduct educational donations up to 30 per cent of their adjusted gross income, corporations up to 5 per cent of their profits. The *net* cost of gifts is for most corporations 52 per cent, for individuals between 30 per cent and 86 per cent (under tax rates effective from 1965 on; rates in force until 1963 gave individuals a net cost between 9 per cent and 80 per cent).

Wealthy individuals can and do make large contributions to educational and other charitable purposes which cost them only a fraction of their value. But millions of persons in medium and lower income brackets bear somewhere between 72 per cent and 86 per cent of the amount of their gift. Thus many of them, though they feel beholden to their alma mater (or to the institution which they hope their children will some day attend), either are not regular contributors or donate only small amounts. It has been estimated that presently only one out of every five alumni makes regular donations to his college. This could be remedied and millions of additional contributors found if donors were permitted to deduct the amount of their gift (or most of it) from their income tax liability rather than merely from the tax base.

Such a plan was recommended a few years ago by the American

Association for the Advancement of Science when a study by the Surveys and Research Corporation showed its potential advantages for I.H.L.[66] The president of the A.A.A.S., Paul Klopsteg, pursued the proposal actively but with no success.[67] Chancellor Clifford C. Furnas of the University of Buffalo suggested that individuals and corporations be permitted to donate up to five per cent of their income to I.H.L. and deduct the amount from their income tax.[68] A few bills along similar lines were introduced in Congress but received no active consideration. The President's Committee on Education Beyond the High School recommended that "the Federal revenue laws be revised in ways which will even more strongly encourage larger contributions from more individuals to educational institutions. Partial credits against taxes due are a way to equalize the advantages in such giving between larger and smaller incomes."[69] This seemed to suggest that a fixed percentage of the donations be made deductible from the tax liability.

President John A. Howard of Rockford College, acting on behalf of a group of twenty college and university presidents, submitted to the Senate Labor and Public Welfare Committee on May 16, 1963, a plan which would let individuals deduct from their income tax liability up to $100 in donations to I.H.L. (but not more than 20 per cent of their tax); corporations up to $5,000 (but not more than 5 per cent of their tax).[70] The proposal is being supported by the newly formed Citizens National Committee for Higher Education and was introduced in the 88th Congress by Senator Barry Goldwater, with ceilings of $100 for individuals and $10,000 for corporations (S. 2269). Representative Thomas B. Curtis sponsored a companion bill in the House (H. R. 8981). The bill was reintroduced as S 1615 in the 89th Congress by Senator John G. Tower. A credit of this type would probably raise the size of most gifts at least close to the allowable maximum and, by enlarging the num-

---

[66] *Stimulating Voluntary Giving to Higher Education and Other Programs*, prepared for the American Association for the Advancement of Science by the Surveys and Research Corporation, Washington, D.C., 1958.

[67] Paul E. Klopsteg, "How Shall We Pay for Research and Education?" *Science*, November 16, 1956.

[68] "Direct Tax Gifts to College Urged," *The New York Times*, July 14, 1959.

[69] *Second Report to the President*, p. 90.

[70] *Education Legislation—1963*, pp.1128–29.

ber of donors, make institutions less dependent upon big contributors. It could also help to diminish the concentration of gifts and distribute them more widely among all I.H.L.

Assuming that a tax credit of that type would cause half of all alumni to contribute $100 annually to their alma mater, the aggregate amount might be estimated at from $300 to $400 million. On last count, nonalumni were contributing almost as much to colleges as alumni. If this ratio continued, the total additional income to I.H.L. could amount to $600 to $800 million. The potential of the corporate tax credit is difficult to estimate but could run up to $100 million or more. A credit on state corporate income taxes for donations to educational institutions was suggested by H. Clyde Reeves, a former Kentucky state tax commissioner and, more recently, vice president of the University of Alabama.[71]

Opponents have raised similar objections to educational gift tax credit plans as to tax credits for college expenses: it would "place the disposition of tax funds in the hands of individuals." Obviously it could be argued whether a person's pre-tax earnings can be called "tax funds." But the main counter argument is that our present tax laws give taxpayers broad discretion in the choice of the recipients of their donations. They may be given to a large number of educational, welfare, etc. organizations as well as for church and religious purposes. Individuals in high tax brackets could, until 1963, recover up to 91 per cent (and in exceptional cases, up to 100 per cent) of their gifts (reduced to 70 per cent from 1965 on) but those in low brackets could recover only 20 per cent (from 1965 on, only 14 per cent). The educational-gift tax credit would equalize the burdens of donors at various income levels and greatly expand college giving at the medium and lower income brackets.

A tax credit of this type could increase the money flow to I.H.L. very substantially while federal revenues would be reduced by an equivalent amount. Opponents would prefer to have the sums appropriated as grants to I.H.L. instead of permitting deduction from tax liability. There are, of course, some significant differences

[71] H. Clyde Reeves, "Higher Education and State Tax Policy," *National Tax Journal,* September 1962.

between the two methods: federal grants in aid have always been and are likely to remain restricted to research or selected types of construction and are earmarked for specific projects and purposes with concomitant controls. Most of the gifts which come in small amounts would be available for general purposes at the discretion of institutional boards of trustees and academic officials. Under the grant-in-aid method, decisions on the type of institution and department and the allocation among them would be made by Congress, the Office of Education, or some other governmental authority. The tax credit plan would leave it to individuals to name the institutions which they deem in need and worthy of assistance. Supporters and opponents tend to line up according to the type of control they prefer.

It has been argued that such a program would encourage other groups, acting on behalf of various charitable purposes, to demand comparable benefits for their equally worthy objectives. Congress, used to pressures though it is, might not find it easy to resist all those forces clamoring for action on their behalf and charging "discrimination." But Congress must be "discriminating" in the purposes which it decides to aid financially whether through appropriations or through tax credits and must judge the needs and merits of each case. It has long given clear indication of its desire to help higher education but has found it difficult if not impossible to do so in an effective manner through appropriations. It may thus properly give consideration to achieving through the tax system what it has found impossible to accomplish through the appropriation process.

Summary

Hundreds of legislative proposals have been advanced over the past ten years which would permit taxpayers to offset against their income tax part of the expenses occasioned by college attendance or donations to colleges and universities. The idea has been rapidly gaining popularity in and out of Congress and has reached the stage where positive action appears likely within a reasonable time.

Some regard the tax credit approach to be superior to the grant or appropriation method. They would rather see the government reduce taxes and enable individuals to take care of their own needs than have government tax and spend more. Others believe that tax credits are a good means of supplementing various direct aids to I.H.L. A third group would prefer federal appropriations but concludes from repeated defeats that they are not likely to be enacted. Most of of the federal funds so far approved for I.H.L. are earmarked for specific purposes and are not available in the areas of the most urgent need: undergraduate instruction, support for salaries and operations, general classroom construction. The third group supports tax credits because they appear at this time to be the only *practicable* method by which the national government can materially aid the finances of colleges and universities in general—rather than subsidize just *some* institutions or *some* curriculum subjects, or *some* activities, which do not include the focal and most important ones.

Educational tax credits would *directly* help students and their families. But in essence they do not aim to augment family income but to help families better to support the colleges of their choice. Claims to the contrary notwithstanding, there is no dichotomy or conflict between aiding colleges and aiding those who support colleges. In the final analysis, the purpose of the plan is not to subsidize individuals or institutions, but to promote higher education in the United States.

The weight and nature of the tax burden which the national government imposes bears no small responsibility for the financial difficulties of I.H.L. and of families trying to defray college expenses. It thus seems appropriate to meet the situation not by an increase in spending but by a selective tax reduction to ease the load of those who provide a substantial share of the college support.

Most of the objections which have been raised against educational tax credits are unsubstantiated, fictitious, and easily refuted. It is simply not true that the plans now under consideration would give aid where it is needed least. They would concentrate benefits among the middle and lower middle-income groups and for good and valid reasons: wealthy families need no help to pay for their children's college and would get none; students from the lowest income groups, if otherwise qualified, are eligible for and do get scholarships; it is the families "in between" that face the greatest obstacles.

Scholarship and loan funds, to be sure, need to be increased regardless of whether this ought to be done through federal, state or private action. But the fact that we need more scholarships offers no valid argument against tax credits.

Opposition to tax credits comes mostly from groups and persons who prefer governmental over individual or voluntary action, public over private education, secular education for all over a free choice, not unduly penalized, between secular and religious education.

The "tuition gap" between public and private I.H.L. has been consistently widening and enrollment has been rapidly shifting from private to public I.H.L. over the past fifteen years. Viewing the cost differential, it is surprising that the shift has not been even stronger. If present trends continue, in not too many years diversity in higher education will be only a sweet memory. To acquire a higher education except in a state institution will be within the reach of only a few privileged students from wealthy families. One college president made some predictions early in 1964 which could well come true. President David L. McKenna of Spring Arbor College told the Michigan Rotary Club on January 2, 1964, looking toward the close of the twentieth century,

"I predict that the colleges and universities will be organized under a national system of higher education.

"If you quote me on this prediction, I'll deny it. But the trend is clear."

"I predict that the federal government will be the major investor in higher education at every level."

"This prediction is the inevitable result of the prior prediction that there will be a national system of higher education."

"I predict that education for moral and spiritual values will become even more perplexing and difficult."

"I predict that among church related colleges only the strongest will survive to make a significant contribution to American higher education."

"With the floods of students going into public colleges, the financial pressures of rising costs, the national system of public higher education, the support of the federal government, the race to keep up with new facilities, and the shortage of faculty members, it is predicted that many of the private colleges will be taken over by public education to serve various communities."[72]

Some feel that the predicted changes would constitute a great improvement over the present "balkanization" of higher education in over 2,000 institutions. Others believe that much of value in American higher education would be lost if these changes were to come to pass.

Tax credits alone cannot maintain the diversity and freedom of choice which American higher education has traditionally represented. But they can be of great help. The events leading up to the vote in the United States Senate on February 4, 1964, show that a majority of that body favors educational tax credits, as does the American public. The fight for the credits will undoubtedly continue and, hopefully, will be won before too long.

---

[72] "A Crystal Ball for Colleges," *Vital Speeches*, February 1, 1964, p. 249.

Index

237